The Search for Public Policy

THE SEARCH FOR PUBLIC POLICY

Regional Politics and Government Finances
in Ecuador, 1830–1940

Linda Alexander Rodríguez

UNIVERSITY OF CALIFORNIA PRESS
Berkeley   Los Angeles   London

University of California Press
Berkeley and Los Angeles, California

University of California Press, Ltd.
London, England

Library of Congress Cataloging in Publication Data

Rodríguez, Linda Alexander.
    The search for public policy.

    Bibliography: p. 265
    Includes index.
    1. Finance, Public—Ecuador—History—19th century.
2. Finance, Public—Ecuador—History—20th century.
3. Ecuador—Politics and government—1830–   .
4. Fiscal policy—Ecuador—History—19th century.
5. Fiscal policy—Ecuador—History—20th century.
I. Title.
HJ953.R62   1984   336.866   84–2446
ISBN 0–520–05150–5

Printed in the United States of America

1 2 3 4 5 6 7 8 9

To
C. F. Alexander
and In Memory of
F. C. Alexander

Contents

Tables

Preface

This study is an outgrowth of my thesis, "The Liberal Crisis and the Revolution of 1925 in Ecuador." That work, which examined the July 1925 coup from the perspective of the military participants, relied on the best Ecuadorian studies to provide the context for the military's actions. I found the standard interpretations of the period unconvincing, however. Research and travel in Ecuador in 1970 and 1972 revealed to me both the country's strong regional antagonisms and the fact that most Ecuadorian history had been written by highlanders. During my travels I was impressed by the dynamism and modern attitudes of *costeños* and the more traditional values of *serranos*. These impressions, rather than any inaccuracies in the standard works, led me to question their objectivity. Historians portrayed the period I was researching (1924–1926) as one dominated by a "corrupt coastal banking oligarchy," which sought to thwart the efforts of the military and its sierra supporters to reform and modernize Ecuador's banking system and its public finances. I also was puzzled by the fact that the post-coup national regeneration required the destruction of the Banco Comercial y Agrícola, a primary agent of modernization in the years from 1895 to 1925. At that time I was unable to solve the problems that arose from placing a detailed monographic study into a broader context when the secondary sources painted a distorted picture. The solution, which involved an analysis of more than a century of Ecuadorian history and several years of research, resulted in this work.

Initially, I intended to study the Revolution of 1925 and the reforms introduced by the Kemmerer Mission that was employed by the post-coup government. I contemplated a preliminary review of government finances and public policy in the Liberal period (1895–1925) as a way of understanding the issues that engendered the coup and the subsequent reforms. It soon became clear, however, that the Liberals had not fundamentally altered government policies. Rather, they expanded tendencies already well articulated in Ecuador. They differed from earlier regimes primarily in their access to greater revenues from cacao exports. I realized that to have a clear understanding of the evolution of the Ecuadorian system, it was necessary to start in 1830, the year the nation was founded and the year it began to formulate its own financial policies.

In the absence of well-documented monographic and interpretive works, it would have been impossible to reconstruct the first century of Ecuador's national history without analyzing government budgets and other data in statistical series. I am aware of the difficulties associated with nineteenth-century statistical data, and I have taken steps to account for those problems. Although numerical data cannot be corrected with precision, I am convinced that the statistics in this volume are valuable and illustrative of trends in Ecuadorian history. My interpretation has been clarified and reinforced with nonstatistical data from Ecuadorian congressional debates, ministerial reports, laws, newspaper articles, consular and legation reports, private papers, contemporary memoirs, and interviews with participants. Because Ecuadorian economic history is in its infancy and because Ecuadorian historians have published few monographs for the period since 1910, I relied almost completely on primary sources. But my conclusion that evolutionary, not revolutionary, change characterizes Ecuadorian history derived largely from my study of Ecuadorian historical statistics. This fundamental aspect of national history has been obscured by studies that focus on a political history riddled with coups, revolts, pronouncements, and extraconstitutional governments.

Since I began research I have been fortunate in receiving the aid and support of various institutions and individuals. I am grateful for a National Defense Foreign Language Fellowship (1975–1976) that helped defray some of the cost incurred in preparing this work. I am indebted to the directors and staffs of the following institutions who facilitated my research: the United States National Archives (Washington, D.C.), the Library of Congress (Washington, D.C.), the Princeton University Libraries (Princeton), the Nettie Lee Benson Latin American Collection (Austin), the UCLA Research Library (Los Angeles), the Bancroft Collection (Berkeley), the UC Irvine Library (Irvine), the British Public Record Office (London), the British Museum (London), the Archivo Histórico del Guayas (Guayaquil), the Biblioteca Municipal (Guayaquil), the Archivo Histórico de la Biblioteca Municipal (Guayaquil), the Biblioteca de la Casa de la Cultura Ecuatoriana: Nucleo del Guayas (Guayaquil), the Archivo Nacional de Historia (Quito), the Biblioteca de la Casa de la Cultura Ecuatoriana (Quito), the Biblioteca Municipal (Quito), the Biblioteca del Poder Legislativo (Quito), the Biblioteca del Banco Central (Quito), and the Biblioteca Ecuatoriana, Aurelio Espinosa Pólit (Cotocollao).

I am indebted to many scholars for assistance, advice, and encouragement during the research and writing of this work. While in Ecuador I benefited from long talks with Juan Freile Granizo, a friend and scholar, who has unparalleled command of Ecuadorian history and sources. Julio Estrada Ycaza, the director of the Archivo Histórico del Guayas and the most distinguished historian of the coast, not only discussed Ecuadorian history, politics, and the nature of regionalism with me but also granted access to his private library that contains unpublished manuscripts by Víctor Emilio Estrada. Luis A. Rodríguez S., a participant in the 1925 coup and an important actor in Ecuadorian politics thereafter, allowed me to interview him extensively in 1972 and 1976 and gave me free access to his unpublished memoirs. He also introduced me to a number of men who were active in civilian politics or the military in the period from 1920 to 1940. These men spent long hours discussing with me their recollections of Ecuadorian events. None of these generous Ecuadorians is responsible for the interpretations found in this work; most would oppose some of my conclusions. Rosemary D. F. Bromley and R. J. Bromley, British historical geographers researching in Ecuador, discussed with me their views of Ecuadorian history.

Mark van Aken kindly allowed me to read portions of his manuscript on Juan José Flores and directed me to valuable nineteenth-century sources. I am grateful to Donald Kemmerer for permission to use the Kemmerer Papers and photographs at Princeton University. Conversations about Ecuadorian, Mexican and Latin American history with María Beatriz Ordoñez, Roberto Moreno, María del Refugio González, and Robert N. Burr helped to clarify and enrich my analysis of Ecuador's past. Nettie Lee Benson, Colin M. MacLachlan, John Tepaske, and James W. Wilkie read the study in whole or in part and provided helpful criticism. Marvin Bernstein and William F. Sater read the manuscript with great care and provided detailed suggestions for its improvement. I am grateful to Leon Campbell, Vicente González Losartales, William Glade, Carol and Keith Polakoff, Patricia O'Brien, Miguel León Portilla, Robert Rosenfield, and Sandra Kunsberg for much needed support and encouragement. Finally, I am grateful to Jaime E. Rodríguez O., friend, companion, and colleague, for his constant help and support in this seemingly interminable venture.

Los Angeles   Linda Alexander Rodríguez
August 1984

Introduction

Throughout its history Ecuador has faced two fundamental obstacles to development: geographic fragmentation and limited natural resources. Geography, which has been a major barrier to national integration, fostered political, social, and economic division. Since the country possessed no precious minerals or other valuable resources that could attract sufficient capital investment to overcome the area's geographic barriers, for most of its history Ecuador has remained a poor country, deeply divided by sectionalism. Regionalism, the political expression of the division and isolation imposed by geography, has been a significant and enduring factor in Ecuadorian politics. The country's chronic political instability becomes intelligible when one realizes that control of the state and its resources was not only important for individual economic advancement in a land with limited opportunities but also was critical to the well-being and development of the nation's regions. Although the country's history is characterized by violent political change, that turmoil is misleading because it masks fundamental continuities in political and fiscal practices. The study of Ecuadorian historical statistics demonstrates that evolutionary, not revolutionary, change typifies the nation's history.

Ecuadorians believe that their contemporary history began in 1895 when the Liberal party gained power and used the growing revenues from cacao exports to consolidate its position. According to the standard interpretation, the Liberal governments (1895–1925) wasted an opportunity for development. Although revenues from cacao exports reached an all-time high, the country's leaders failed to build the infrastructure necessary to modernize Ecuador. Instead, they deferred to regional demands at the expense of national needs. The Liberal era has been called the age of "railroad politics," a pejorative phrase that refers to the custom of approving, with insufficient funding, a wide variety of local projects from railroads and sanitation systems to statues and parks. Critics argue that the Liberals dissipated Ecuador's scarce resources on a large number of uncoordinated and uncontrolled public works projects that were not only economically unproductive and seldom completed but prevented the formation and implementation of a rational, coordinated national development program. Proponents of this interpretation claim that the military coup of July 9, 1925, repudiated the railroad politics of the Liberals and replaced it with a program calling for a planned and centralized approach to modernization. To Ecuadorians modernization signified not only the creation of an infrastructure necessary for economic growth but also the establishment of a strong and effective government to promote national integration and development. The new regime supposedly "ended" regionalist politics, freeing the nation from the domination of the "corrupt coastal banking oligarchy."

Initially, the military entrusted national renovation to a plural executive and when that proved cumbersome, the armed forces installed a "progressive dictator," Isidro Ayora. According to the standard interpretation, President Ayora commissioned Princeton economist Edwin Kemmerer to assemble a team of foreign experts to study the Ecuadorian situation and to recommend reforms designed to modernize the nation. Acting on the advice of the Kemmerer Mission, the Ayora administration subsequently established new national institutions such as the Central Bank and the Comptroller's Office. In addition, fiscal, judicial, and administrative legislation created an effective national government structure. Contemporary observers believed Ecuador finally was prepared to progress, that regionalism would soon cease to be a factor in national life, and that prosperity was within reach. They were wrong. Within a short time the new institutions and procedures were modified to conform to Ecuadorian reality and hopes for rapid economic development faded in the face of world depression. A coup overthrew the Ayora regime in 1931 and since then Ecuador has enjoyed little political stability.

This study challenges the negative interpretation of the Liberal period and its corollary that the 1925 coup represented a disinterested nationalist movement. It demonstrates that both the Liberal era and the post-1925 reforms constituted integral parts of an evolving Ecuadorian system whose main characteristics were established early in the national period. They were not, as many Ecuadorians maintain, a break with the country's past.

The first three chapters of this study provide a framework for an analysis of the Liberal era, its finances, and the subsequent role of foreign advisers in reforming that system. The volume begins in 1830 when Ecuador became independent. The first chapter examines the factors contributing to the country's disunity, particularly geography, which has

handicapped the nation's economic and political development. Chapter
two explores Ecuadorian politics from 1830 to 1925, emphasizing the
characteristic features of Ecuadorian politics: regionalism, authoritarianism, militarism, and personalism. A third chapter examines government
finances and public policy during the period from 1830 to 1895, demonstrating that public finances in those years were characterized by
inadequate revenues, poor administration, and bad external credit—the
latter the result of the government's failure to service the nation's foreign
debt. Nineteenth-century governments, therefore, resorted to internal
loans, particularly from banks, to pay for national development and,
especially, to defray the cost of subduing internal upheavals. Despite such
problems, during the nineteenth century there was a slow but continuous
expansion of the role of the state, particularly in the areas of welfare,
education, and public works.

Chapter four analyzes government finances and public policy from
1895 to 1925, demonstrating that government finances in the Liberal
period were anchored firmly in nineteenth-century traditions and that
Liberals differed from their predecessors primarily because they enjoyed
greater revenues. Although the Liberals instituted beneficial changes in
education, communications, sanitation, and other social services, Liberal
regimes failed to introduce effective systems of taxation and fiscal administration. Instead, they continued the symbiotic relationship between
coastal banks, the nation's strongest private institutions, and the government thus exacerbating the regionalist fears of the highlanders. When an
international economic crisis in the mid-1920s combined with declining
productivity to cripple the export economy, highlanders used the opportunity to wrest political and economic power from their coastal rivals.
Chapter five examines the complex relationships existing among local
interest groups, the national government, and foreign advisers. An analysis
of the Kemmerer Mission and the fate of its proposals provides insights
into the varied functions of foreign experts in the modernization process
and the way in which existing structures co-opt new institutions and
procedures.

This study concludes with a brief analysis of the impact of the Great
Depression on the Kemmerer reforms and institutions. The unparalleled
economic and political crises of the 1930s sparked a widespread debate
about the appropriate role of government in the national economy. Faced
with a drastically altered national and international economic situation,
Ecuadorians opted for a direct role by government in stimulating recovery
and economic development. In keeping with tradition, they invited the

Mexican economist Manuel Gómez Morín to recommend reforms to bring national structures into agreement with their new vision of an active state.

The conclusion of this work coincides with the beginning of a new era in Ecuadorian history. The period differs from the preceding years because the nation possessed new and expanding resources with which to confront traditional obstacles to development and national integration, not because geography, regionalism, and political instability had been overcome. After World War II Ecuador obtained, for the first time, relatively unrestricted access to foreign development capital. New technologies also appeared to overcome the age-old fragmentation, and new exports, particularly bananas and petroleum, put those technologies within reach.

1. The Setting

The founding of the Republic of Ecuador in 1830 only initiated the process of national building.[1] Tendencies toward unification had existed earlier, but they operated on a superficial level. The Inca Empire had just subjugated various Indian groups residing in the Ecuadorian highlands when the Spaniards arrived in 1532. The new conquerors created the Audiencia (or Kingdom) of Quito as one of the subdivisions of the Spanish Empire. But the area did not become a clearly defined political entity. The Spanish economic, social, and political structure was little more than a thin patina. Neither the Incas nor the Spaniards could integrate the economy of the area or forge a sense of nationality in the territory that became Ecuador.[2] Efforts to create an integrated nation-state continue today.

Isolation and division rather than integration and cohesion have been among the most powerful forces in the history of Ecuador. Political, racial, economic, and social diversity have persisted from pre-Columbian times to the present. Geography has hindered national integration and development by complicating transportation and commerce. The country's failure to build an adequate transportation network produced an economy characterized by a series of isolated markets. By restricting the flow of goods, people, and ideas, geography also exacerbated social and political factionalism.[3] Viewed from this perspective, the regionalism that has characterized Ecuador's politics merely reflects a rational expression of the segregation and division imposed by geography.[4]

Political Geography

Ecuador's borders have been in doubt during most of the nation's life. When it seceded from Gran Colombia in 1830, the new nation claimed 707,430 square kilometers. Two years later with the incorporation of the

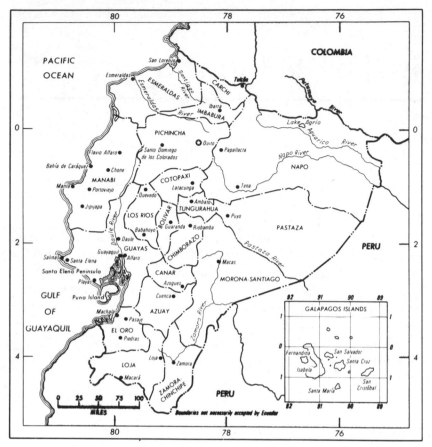

Map 1. Ecuador: Political Divisions. Source: Area Handbook for Ecuador (Washington, 1973).

Galápagos Islands the figure increased to 714,860 square kilometers.[5] Colombia and Peru disputed Ecuador's claim to much of this territory, however. Border incidents became a frequent source of friction among the three nations. Ecuador and Colombia finally settled their boundary conflict in 1916; an agreement with Peru has proved more difficult to achieve.[6]

Most of the area claimed by both Ecuador and Peru was in the *Oriente*, the lands east of the Andes. Ecuador failed to occupy the region effectively. In contrast, Peru advanced steadily into the disputed territory. By 1892 the southern republic had occupied 116,930 square kilometers of the contested area and claimed another 386,500 square kilometers.[7]

After two wars and decades of conflict, Ecuador and Peru seemingly agreed to a firm border in 1942 by signing the Protocol of Rio de Janeiro. The agreement reduced Ecuador to approximately 264,500 square kilometers. The settlement proved unsatisfactory to many Ecuadorians. President José M. Velasco Ibarra repudiated the accord in 1960 claiming that it had been imposed by force of arms. The issue remains unsettled and border clashes continue in the region.[8]

Although the actual size of Ecuador is not definitely established, this study will focus on the 135,391 square kilometers that comprise the nation's highland and coastal regions. The thinly settled Oriente and the Galápagos Islands, comprising about half the country's territory, have had little political or economic importance until recently (see table 1).

The present political subdivisions did not exist when Ecuador became independent. Initially the country consisted of three departments: Quito, Guayas, and Azuay. The Constitution of 1835 organized seven provinces: Manabí, Guayas, Loja, Azuay, Chimborazo, Imbabura, and Quito—subsequently called Pichincha. During the next forty-nine years, the government created eight new provinces. No new provinces have been created in the highlands or on the coast since 1884 (see table 2).[9] Presently, there are ten highland provinces: Carchi, Imbabura, Pichincha, Cotopaxi, Tunguragua, Chimborazo, Bolívar, Cañar, Azuay, and Loja; and five coastal provinces: Esmeraldas, Manabí, Los Ríos, Guayas, and El Oro.

Physical Geography

The twin cordilleras of the Andes, which traverse the country from north to south, divide mainland Ecuador into three distinct geographic zones. These great mountain ranges include among their high peaks, Mount Chimborazo (6,267 m above sea level), Cotopaxi (5,897 m), Cayambe (5,790 m), and Antisana (5,705 m). They partition the country into the Oriente or eastern region, the *Sierra* or highland region, and the *Costa* or coastal region.[10]

The Oriente contains approximately 46 percent of the national territory. It extends from the foothills of the eastern cordillera to the lower regions of the Amazon basin. Most of the area is a single floodplain covered with tropical woodlands and rain forest. This hot and humid region has a heavy annual rainfall that ranges from 2,100 mm in the south to 4,900 mm in the north. Median temperatures range from 23° to 27° C. The Oriente has an excellent system of navigable rivers, but they

TABLE 1

AREA OF ECUADOR BY PROVINCES

Province	Area km²	% National territory
Coast	66,049	25.0
Esmeraldas	14,978	5.7
Manabí	18,255	6.9
Los Ríos	5,913	2.2
Guayas	21,077	8.0
El Oro	5,826	2.2
Sierra	69,342	26.2
Carchi	3,701	1.4
Imbabura	4,817	1.8
Pichincha	19,543	7.4
Cotopoxi	5,028	1.9
Tungurahua	3,212	1.2
Chimborazo	5,555	2.1
Bolívar	4,271	1.6
Cañar	3,378	1.3
Azuay	7,804	3.0
Loja	12,033	4.5
Oriente	121,263	45.8
Galápagos Islands	7,812	3.0
Total	264,466	100.0

Source: Ecuador, Junta Nacional de Planificación y Coordinación, *División Territorial de la República del Ecuador* (Quito, 1969), p. 14.

unfortunately flow southeastward, away from the heavily settled parts of Ecuador into Brazil and the Atlantic.

The Oriente is sparsely populated and, until recently, produced nothing of sufficient value to attract large scale settlement or investment. Only since the 1960s with the discovery of petroleum has the region begun to enter the mainstream of national political and economic life. Previously the area did not command national attention unless a border dispute became the subject of intense diplomatic activity or exploded into open conflict. Generally, however, the government made only desultory efforts to explore or colonize the Oriente. On various occasions nationals and

TABLE 2

SIERRA AND COASTAL PROVINCES

Province	Provincial capital	Date established[1]
Sierra		
Carchi[2]	Tulcán	1860
Imbabura	Ibarra	1835
Pichincha[3]	Quito	1830
Cotopoxi[4]	Latacunga	1850
Tungurahua[5]	Ambato	1859
Chimborazo	Riobamba	1835
Bolívar[6]	Guaranda	1884
Cañar[7]	Azogues	1880
Azuay	Cuenca	1830
Loja	Loja	1835
Coast		
Esmeraldas[8]	Esmeraldas	1846
Manabí	Portoviejo	1835
Los Ríos	Babahoyo	1860
Guayas	Guayaquil	1830
El Oro[9]	Machala	1884

Sources: "Constitución de 1830," in Ramiro Borja y Borja, *Derecho constitucional ecuatoriano*, 3 vols. (Madrid 1950), III, 105–123; "Constitución de 1835," in ibid., III, 125–152; Juan Morales y Eloy, *Ecuador: atlas histórico-geográfico* (Quito, 1942), Tab, 75–76.

[1]The 1830 constitution divided the country into three departments: Quito, Guayas, and Azuay. The constitution of 1835 is the first to use provinces as the principal political divisions of the country.

[2]Part of Imbabura prior to 1860.

[3]Formerly Quito.

[4]Established as León but name changed to Cotopoxi in 1938. Prior to 1850 part of Pichincha.

[5]Part of León prior to 1859.

[6]Part of Chimborazo from 1830 to 1860 and of Los Ríos from 1860 to 1884.

[7]Part of Azuay prior to 1880. Established as Province of Azogues but took current name in 1884.

[8]Part of Pichincha prior to 1846.

[9]Formed from territory formerly included in Guayas and Loja.

foreigners, convinced that the jungle hid rich resources, sought government support to explore and develop the area, but the authorities generally ignored their pleas.[11] Since most of the Oriente's tiny population consisted of Indians with no political power, the national government could avoid

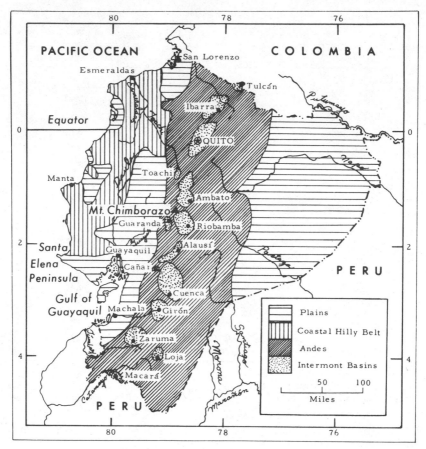

Map 2. Topography of Ecuador. Source: Area Handbook for
Ecuador (Washington, 1966).

committing its scarce development capital to the area. This proved to be
sound policy. Ecuador's densely populated areas still lacked basic infrastructure.[12] Furthermore, large sections of the coastal region, which were
more accessible than the Oriente, also remained unsettled. Thus a decision
to commit the country's limited resources to the Oriente would have
been politically, socially, and economically indefensible.

Even if sufficient capital existed, the contemporary level of technology could not develop the area efficiently. The cost of exploiting the
Oriente remained prohibitive, even after World War II when scientific
advances removed many barriers. Circumstances changed in the late 1960s
because of the growing world demand for energy, dwindling petroleum
reserves, and the rise of OPEC. At that time significant petroleum deposits

were confirmed in the Oriente's Aguarico basin.[13] The increase in the world market price of oil made the cost of developing the area acceptable. The Oriente is currently an important focus of national concern and government development policy.

The highlands, sandwiched between the Cordillera Occidental and the Cordillera Oriental, comprise about a quarter of the nation's territory. This central zone is divided into a series of narrow basins formed when lava flows linked the Andean ranges. The eleven basins between 2,130 meters and 2,750 meters—Tulcán, Ibarra, Quito, Ambato, Riobamba, Alausí, Cañar, Cuenca, Jubones, Loja, and Macará—are as isolated from each other as the sierra is from the Oriente or from the coast. Each basin varies from mountainous to slightly rolling terrain and, in most, there are deep valleys cut by streams. The rivers that drain the region are not navigable in the highlands. All the basins are densely populated with most of the land exploited either for subsistence agriculture or for livestock.

Temperatures range from below freezing above the permanent snow-line (about 4,875 m) to a pleasant 22° C in the subtropical valleys. Sierra agriculture varies with altitude. Most basins contain four climatic zones. The *paramos*, above 3,050 meters, are used for pasture and to grow potatoes and other native tubers. In this barren windswept region, temperatures frequently drop to −18° C at night, but can rise to 21° C for short periods during the day. The *altiplano*, which lies between 2,440 meters and 3,050 meters, is suitable for grain cultivation and pasture. The growing season, however, is short and frequent frosts endanger even hearty crops. The region is also subject to wide daily and seasonal temperature fluctuations. Daily variations between −2° C and 18° C are not uncommon. Annual rainfall in the paramos and the altiplano is about 1,020 mm. The temperate valleys, at elevations from 1,830 meters to 2,440 meters, are devoted to a variety of temperate crops. The average yearly rainfall of 510 mm is supplemented by the runoff from higher altitudes. Located at elevations between 915 meters and 1,830 meters are the tropical valleys that produce vegetables, cotton, sugarcane, citrus fruits, as well as the highland staples: potatoes and grains. The annual rainfall in these lower valleys is also supplemented by drainage from higher elevations.

The productivity of the sierra varies. Centuries of continuous cultivation by primitive methods have eroded and depleted soils. The fertility of the Ambato and Riobamba basins suffers because the soil is of recent volcanic origin and does not retain moisture. In contrast, the Cuenca basin, with ample rainfall and one of the least porous soils in the highlands, enjoys much greater agricultural potential. Slightly less favorable conditions exist in Quito; the rolling hills in the southern part of the basin are the site of extensive grain cultivation and livestock raising.

The coast or littoral region of Ecuador encompasses approximately 69,300 square kilometers of plain, hills, and Andean piedmont. It is bounded by the Pacific Ocean on the west and by the Andes on the east. About half of the region is a low alluvial plain known as the Guayas lowlands; it lies below 300 meters and varies in width from 32 to 185 kilometers. The littoral also contains two hilly areas; the foothills of the Andes that rise to an altitude of 490 meters and the hilly region that extends west of Guayaquil to the coast and then northward. Altitudes in the latter increase as one moves north, but seldom exceed 600 meters.

The natural vegetation of the coast reflects the decrease in rainfall from north to south. While there are two rainy seasons at the Colombian border, most of the littoral has a single rainy season that becomes shorter as it moves south. Annual precipitation ranges from 2,000 mm to 400 mm. The rain forests of the north give way to semideciduous forests and tropical woodlands in the south. Along the Santa Elena peninsula and in the extreme south only zerophytic shrubs can survive without irrigation. In the east, however, the foothills of the Andes receive enough precipitation to support rain forests.

The littoral is a very productive region. Coastal soils are generally fertile, well watered, with a temperature that averages between 23° C and 25° C. While a wide variety of fruits and vegetables are grown for local consumption, coastal agriculture is oriented primarily toward an export market. The Guayas lowlands, which extend north and southwest of Guayaquil, possess ideal conditions for tropical agriculture. Navigable rivers provide the region with access to the sea. As a result, the Guayas basin became the country's primary producer of agricultural exports including cacao, bananas, and coffee. Since these products constitute Ecuador's most important exports, the coast and its major port, Guayaquil, dominated the country's economy (see Appendix A).

The Galápagos Islands, or the Archipielago de Colón, are also a part of Ecuador. This group of volcanic islands, about 1,200 kilometers due west of the mainland, suffers from a scarcity of water, and consequently the islands are thinly populated and of little economic value. However, the wide variety of exotic fauna and flora that survives makes the Galápagos interesting to scientists and to tourists. The waters surrounding the archipelago are excellent fishing grounds that Ecuadorians have only recently begun to exploit. The economic importance of this national resource can be expected to increase in the future.

Since colonial times, both residents and travelers have described Ecuador as a potentially wealthy country. Many have argued that the nation's poverty results from indolence, or lack of initiative on the part of the government and the people, particularly the elite. At one level, this analysis appears correct. Large sectors of the country have not been developed or have been poorly utilized. Even today, the government has not properly surveyed extensive areas of the nation to determine the location and extent of national resources. The nature and quantity of these resources often remains unknown. A casual observer might well conclude that a lack of initiative caused the nation's failure to develop. Such an explanation, however, ignores the complexity and the cost of the development process. In Ecuador, geography and climate—torrid rain forests, massive jagged mountains, glaciers, earthquakes, floods, and volcanic eruptions—have retarded national development, hindering the construction of communication networks.[14]

Transportation Systems

Scholars disagree about the exact relationship between transportation and other factors in the development process.[15] They admit that transportation plays an important role but dispute the optimum levels of investment in this area. Current research emphasizes the permissive role of transportation. It is a necessary, but not a sufficient, precondition to political, social, and economic development. Effective networks of communication facilitate commerce, strengthen national governments, and promote national integration. Where they do not exist national markets cannot develop, national governments remain ineffective, and regional loyalties and identity prevail. Ecuador provides a good example of such a country.

Ecuador's climatic and geographic diversity impeded the development of an adequate national transportation network. During much of the country's history, existing technology could not provide economical solutions to these problems. The present modern complex of road, rail, air, and water transportation has greater potential for integrating the varied regions of Ecuador than the more limited technology of the pre-World War II period.[16]

Water has both hindered and aided communications in the coastal region. Great swamps and meandering rivers have impeded road and railway construction; heavy precipitation during the wet season destroyed roads, trails, and paths. In the north, especially in Esmeraldas, lush tropical vegetation immediately reclaimed all land communication networks. The tropical rain forest easily defeated man's efforts to keep roads open during the colonial period and the nineteenth century. Most of the time travelers had to cut their way through the dense vegetation. As late as 1920 the situation remained largely unchanged. To the south, the more populated areas of southern Manabí, Guayas, and Los Ríos managed to keep primitive roads and bridle paths open despite yearly floods that covered large sections of the lowland plain. Toward the end of the nineteenth century, improved maintenance made travel on horseback between towns and plantations of the south relatively easy during the dry season. These bridle paths formed an important communications network but were less significant for commerce.[17]

Coastal shipping and river navigation provide the most efficient transportation system in the littoral. While the Guayas, Esmeraldas, and Santiago river systems constitute the most important fluvial networks, many other smaller rivers like the Chone, Charapoto, El Cayapas, and Palenque are navigable with small craft. These water routes allowed the products of coastal provinces to reach the port cities of Guayaquil, Esmeraldas, Manta, Bahía, and Puerto Bolivar.[18] Without this natural transport system it is doubtful if the littoral could have expanded its production to take advantage of the growing world demand for tropical agriculture in the nineteenth and twentieth centuries. The expansion brought increasing numbers of people into the market economy, stimulating internal commerce. The coastal transportation network also had political and social consequences: by facilitating travel, it created a degree of social integration and political awareness in that region that did not exist in the highlands.

Unlike the coast, the sierra had to rely on land transportation.[19] No navigable rivers link the highland provinces or the sierra and the littoral. Topography and climate hampered the development of the land transportation networks necessary for highland travel and commerce. The cordilleras of the Andes that traverse Ecuador are extremely high and rugged. Several peaks approach 6,100 meters and extensive regions are covered by glaciers. In addition, the area is subject to volcanic eruptions and to landslides. These factors make highland roads expensive and difficult to build and maintain. The deep gorges that scar most highland basins forced builders to cut roads and trails directly into the face of sheer cliffs. Costly

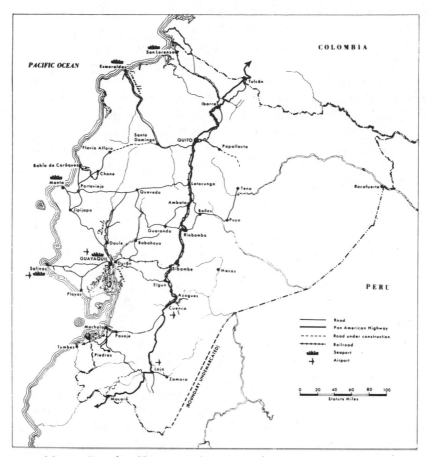

Map 3. Ecuador: Transportation Network, 1965. Source: Area Handbook for Ecuador (Washington, 1966).

bridges had to be constructed over great ravines. Unstable soil conditions in the mountains hampered building and constantly threatened completed roads and trails. Landslides triggered by earthquakes or by excessive precipitation often destroyed years of construction in a few seconds. Although modern tools and building techniques are beginning to overcome these problems, road construction in the sierra in the 1980s still remains a costly and difficult process.[20]

In the colonial period, the best and most traveled road in the highlands ran from Quito to Riobamba, the capital of the province of Chimborazo. It linked the provinces of Pichincha, Cotopaxí, Tunguragua, and Chimborazo. After independence the route deteriorated and became virtually impassable. President Gabriel García Moreno rebuilt it as a carriage road in the 1860s. Until the completion of the Guayaquil-Quito Railway, the García Moreno Highway remained the most important link connecting the highlands. In the 1920s the road was improved for the use of motor vehicles. Other roads in the sierra remained no more than bridle paths until well into the twentieth century. A traveler who ventured on to those arteries was fortunate if he encountered bridges over the ravines. As late as the 1920s, the 223-kilometer trip north from Quito to Tulcán required a five-day journey. Travelers from the capital to Cuenca and Loja, situated respectively, 306 kilometers and 510 kilometers south of Quito, preferred a route that took them from the capital to Guayaquil and then southeast to Cuenca or Loja.[21] Although the itinerary involved a much greater distance than a direct highland route, it was easier and faster.

Travel between the sierra and the coast was also difficult. Throughout the nineteenth century, the road from Guayaquil to Quito remained practically impassable during the six-month rainy season. Even during the dry period, when most travel and commerce took place, the trip could take fourteen days. At mid-century the journey involved an 80-kilometer voyage by water from Guayaquil to Babahoyo. For the remaining 340 kilometers the traveler proceeded on horseback or on mule. The route from Babahoyo to the base of the Andes was dangerous because it crossed swampy tropical lowlands. The most arduous part of the journey, however, began after leaving the Guaranda valley situated at 2,668 meters above sea level. This part of the trip could only be made on foot or by mule. As it entered the rugged Andes, the route climbed to an altitude of 3,660 meters. At that height travelers fell prey to *soroche*, an altitude sickness. After entering the sierra, the traveler passed through two provincial capitals, Ambato and Latacunga, before reaching Quito. In 1891, President Antonio Flores inaugurated the Via Flores that ran from Babahoyo to Guaranda. The new road, and improvements in the García Moreno Highway, reduced travel time and discomfort. In spite of these and other efforts to improve and maintain roads, however, travel in the highlands and between the coast and the sierra remained almost as difficult in 1899 as it had been before independence.[22]

Since the colonial epoch, the northern highland provinces have sought an alternate route to the sea that would free them from what they considered to be Guayaquil's domination. The numerous attempts to link Quito and Ibarra to Esmeraldas failed because roads that were built quickly fell into disrepair and were reclaimed by the tropical forest. Maintenance was prohibitively expensive because the roads passed through sparsely populated, undeveloped areas. In 1940 the government finally constructed an all-weather road between Quito and Santo Domingo de los Colorados, southwest of the capital. Not until 1954 did it complete soft surface branches between Santo Domingo and the coastal towns of Esmeraldas and Bahía de Caraquez.[23]

The southern highland provinces also sought access to coastal ports. Historically, four major routes connected these provinces and the coast. Two led from Cuenca to Guayas province; the others connected Puerto Bolívar in El Oro with the provinces of Azuay and Loja. All four routes were both arduous and dangerous, and throughout the nineteenth century all attempts to improve them failed. Following the completion of the Guayaquil-Quito Railway in 1908, the most traveled route between the coast and Cuenca consisted of a rail trip from Guayaquil to Huigra, followed by a three-day ride by horse or mule to Cuenca. Although the government continuously improved sections of the four roads, land communications between the southern highlands and the coast remained primitive until 1950. As late as 1980 a trip by car or bus from Cuenca to Guayaquil was an exciting experience; large sections of the road were not hard surface and frequent detours were necessary because of landslides and washouts.[24]

In the middle of the nineteenth century, Ecuadorians turned to the use of railroads as a means of improving transportation. In 1865 President García Moreno authorized the construction of a rail line between Guayaquil and Quito. The first section would run from Yahuachi, a town accessible by river steamer from Guayaquil, to Sibambe in the sierra, a terminus of the García Moreno Highway. By 1875 the year of García Moreno's death, the railroad consisted of 45 kilometers of track. Work continued sporadically during the next twelve years. By 1887 the line connected Durán, a town across the Guayas river from Guayaquil, to Chimbo in the foothills of the Andes. The train, however, carried few passengers and even less freight. Chimbo was not on the favored route from Guayaquil to Quito, because individuals utilizing the railroad had difficulty obtaining pack animals at Chimbo to continue their trip into the highlands. Thus, the line did not become an important interregional carrier.

Although the public periodically demanded that the government complete the railroad, the line remained unfinished until the Liberals came to power in 1895. New construction under the direction of the American John Harmer began in 1899. He altered the original route in 1900 to utilize the gorge of the Chanchan River. The new route crossed the

Chanchan River twenty-six times, climbing almost 3,050 meters in 80 kilometers. Frequent landslides nearly halted construction on various occasions. After completion in 1908 landslides still interrupted traffic between the coast and the sierra. Nonetheless, the completed railroad was hailed as a marvel of engineering by Ecuadorians and foreign visitors.[25]

Ecuadorians expected much from the completion of the railroad that linked the sierra with the country's most important port. Highland newspapers confidently predicted an economic renaissance for their region. The predictions were overly optimistic. Commerce did increase between the two areas; some highland products replaced items formerly imported by the coast. But the sierra could not raise foodstuffs inexpensively. In addition, high operating and maintenance costs, the result of unstable conditions in the mountains, prompted the line's management to impose high rates which in turn discouraged rail shipments. From the inauguration of the Guayaquil-Quito Railroad, highland shippers complained about exorbitant rates that handicapped the region's development. In reality, until 1927 shipping rates were based solely on distance traveled and failed to cover the costs of handling agricultural products. When the line received a rate increase in 1927, many sierra agriculturalists stopped shipping their products to the coast, claiming that the increase eliminated their small margin of profit. While food shipments eventually resumed, many interregional shippers continued to utilize mule trains and, after 1930, motor vehicles. The railroad operated at a profit only for a few years in the 1920s and in the 1940s.[26]

Despite the problems of the Guayaquil-Quito Railway, highlanders did not lose their faith in railroads. They made several abortive attempts at the turn of the century to build a line from Quito to Esmeraldas. In the mid-1920s these difficulties led some serranos to question the efficacy of rail transport. But when coastal newspapers also opposed additional railroad construction, the highlanders reversed their position. They charged the coastal press with parochialism and accused them of trying to stifle sierra development. In reality, most critics of an expanded rail network believed that the economic development of the highlands would be enhanced by highway construction. Roads possessed the advantage of being cheaper than trains to construct and to maintain. They could be completed more quickly and were particularly suited to serve the dispersed population of the sierra. Recent studies, which have analyzed the economic benefits of rail versus road construction, indicate that the Ecuadorian critics of an expanded railroad construction program were correct; the country would have derived maximum benefits by investing its scarce resources in highways.[27] But short-term political considerations triumphed: the government renewed railroad construction, completing the line from Quito to Ibarra in 1929. The highland's dream of a railway to Esmeraldas did not become a reality, however, until 1957 with the completion of the line from Ibarra to San Lorenzo. The project was undertaken even though the section in operation between Quito and Ibarra generally operated at a loss.[28] The completed line has been no more successful.

Like their northern neighbors, the southern highlands considered railroads a means of ending their historic isolation and gaining access to larger markets. There were numerous schemes for linking the southern provinces directly to the coast by rail. Instead of uniting to obtain railways, the provinces of Azuay and Loja competed for the nation's scarce resources. Despite the intense and sustained political activity, neither province succeeded in obtaining direct access to the coast via Puerto Bolívar. Azuay finally managed to get a rail connection to the coast when a spur of the Guayaquil-Quito Railroad was completed from Sibambe to Cuenca. The work, begun in 1913, required thirty years to complete.[29]

Ecuador failed to develop an integrated transportation network for a variety of reasons. It attempted to introduce railroads, a mode inappropriate for the country's geographic and climatic conditions. Although railroads represented an advanced technological system of land transportation, they could not meet the needs of Ecuador. Their construction wasted effort and money and the government could have more productively invested its capital in road building.[30] Inadequate funding and intense regional competition for the nation's limited developmental resources severely retarded many projects.[31]

Commerce

Ecuador's rugged topography and its poor transportation network hindered trade and commerce in the sierra. Highlanders consumed their own products. Indeed, each basin developed as a self-contained production and consumption unit. In the highlands, most interprovincial exchange took place among the towns located along the Carretera García Moreno. This trade grew as urbanization intensified and it was given added impetus by the Guayaquil-Quito Railroad. Quito and the provincial capitals of Latacunga, Ambato, and Riobamba could exchange goods with relative ease. Even this commerce was limited, however, because each intermont basin tended to produce similar goods and to meet its own needs. Other provincial cities and towns in the sierra bore the added burden of depending principally on mules or Indian bearers to transport their products to market. Since many roads were impassable during the rainy season, most highland provinces developed important commercial ties only with contiguous provinces and possibly with the coast.[32]

Loja provides an extreme example of sierra isolation. As late as the 1940s only rough trails linked the province of Loja with the rest of Ecuador. Loja's principal trading partner was the neighboring province of Azuay. Because of the difficulty in communicating with the Ecuadorian coast, Loja developed important commercial relationships with the Peruvian department of Piura to which the Ecuadorian province exported livestock, coffee, loaf sugar, and hides, and from which it imported flour, cloth, wine, alcohol, salt, metal tools, and other manufactured items. In 1909 the balance of trade between Loja and Piura favored the Peruvian department by an estimated 100,000 sucres. Lojan officials noted that without roads to the Ecuadorian coast, the adverse balance of trade would not only continue but increase as population grew. The situation did not change appreciably for nearly half a century.[33] Loja still trades extensively with Peru even though an all-weather road and air connections presently link the province to the rest of the nation.

The sierra traded principally agricultural products with the coast. By the mid-nineteenth century the central highland provinces of Chimborazo and Tunguragua had increased production and supplied food to Guayaquil. The completion of the Guayaquil-Quito Railroad facilitated the exchange. As a result, highland products began to replace some imported agricultural items. Guayaquil's growing dependence on sierra foods is evident from the economic and political dislocations that accompanied any disruption of traffic on the railroad. Since some highland products such as flour and lard could not compete either in price or quality with foreign counterparts, foodstuffs still comprised a big segment of Ecuador's imports.[34]

The principal manufactures of the highlands were straw hats, *aguardiente*, and textiles. The weaving of hats was a widespread cottage industry in Azuay and Cañar and to a lesser extent was practiced in most sierra provinces. While some hats were sold locally, the majority were shipped to Guayaquil where they were exported along with the hats made in the coastal province of Manabí. Ecuadorian straw hats, inaccurately dubbed Panama hats, enjoyed several periods of popularity in foreign markets (see Appendix A). Aguardiente, the local liquor generally produced under license from a government monopoly, was usually consumed locally. Some highland distillers, however, sold their production in the intraregional market either as government controlled trade or as contraband.

Textile manufacturing had been an important highland industry since colonial times and cloth became the sierra's major export. But the *obrajes*, the colonial textile sweatshops, declined in the late eighteenth century. After independence there were various attempts to introduce modern machinery and practices, and by the end of the century cloth had again become an important highland product. In 1905, Ecuador concluded a commercial treaty with Colombia allowing both nations duty-free import and export of products. The accord greatly benefited the Ecuadorian textile manufacturers who sold substantial amounts of their cloth to Colombia. This trade spurred expansion in the industry; plants in Otavalo, Quito, Riobamba, and Ambato increased production. Some factories acquired modern equipment and employed foreign technicians, mostly British and North American. Ecuadorian textiles flooded Colombian markets, retarding the industrial development of that country's southern provinces. As a result, in 1930 Colombia repudiated the part of the treaty that permitted traffic in that commodity.

Although the textile trade with Colombia helped the sierra economy and many highlanders considered it significant in the country's international commerce, the exchange comprised only a small part of total Ecuadorian exports. In 1925 the goods passing through the customs at Tulcán, the entrepot for Ecuadorian products to Colombia, amounted to only 1.3 percent of Ecuador's total exports. Highland foreign trade was always minuscule compared with the exports of the coast. It also did little to expand national government revenues since the 1905 treaty exempted that commerce from taxes or duties.[35]

In contrast to the sierra, the coast concentrated on agricultural production for the export market (see table 3 and Appendixes A and B). The world demand for tropical agriculture increased rapidly after the middle of the nineteenth century and the Ecuadorian littoral shared this boom. Although the region produced a substantial part of its own food, the expansion of production for export made the coast an important market for both sierra and foreign foodstuffs. As international trade developed, increasingly larger percentages of the coastal population entered the money economy, in sharp contrast to the highlands where most people remained at the subsistence level. Foreign trade has always been the most dynamic

TABLE 3

COMPARISON OF COAST AND SIERRA EXPORTS

Year	Sierra exports		Coastal exports	
	1000s of sucres	% of total exports	1000s of sucres	% of total exports
1900	531	3.4	14,888	96.6
1901	524	3.2	15,869	96.8
1902	721	4.0	17,385	96.0
1903	784	4.2	17,842	95.8
1904	743	4.0	17,667	96.0
1905	1,270	6.8	17,296	93.2
1906	1,869	8.5	20,096	91.5
1907	1,984	8.6	21,102	91.4
1908	1,133	4.3	25,426	95.7
1909	1,610	6.5	23,269	93.5
1910	1,862	6.6	26,200	93.4
1911	1,565	6.0	24,550	94.0
1912	1,200	4.3	26,968	95.7
1913	1,977	6.3	29,461	93.7
1914	1,356	5.0	25,520	95.0
1915	1,608	6.1	24,925	93.9
1916	2,467	6.8	33,684	93.2
1917	3,626	10.8	29,840	89.2
1918	2,835	10.3	24,664	89.7
1919	2,784	6.4	40,436	93.6
1920	2,690	5.4	47,127	94.6

Source: Calculated from data in Víctor Emilio Estrada, *Ensayo sobre la balanza económica del Ecuador* (Guayaquil, 1922), p. 74.

sector of Ecuador's economy. The performance of the tropical agricultural products, the country's principal exports, set the limits of Ecuador's economic development. Since taxes on foreign trade, particularly imports, provided a major source of government revenue, changes in the amount or value of Ecuador's exports profoundly affected national politics (see Appendixes B and C).

Cacao was Ecuador's most important export until 1952 (see Appendixes A and D). Grown principally in the provinces of Guayas, Manabí, Los Ríos, and El Oro, cacao production became well established in the colonial period and continued to expand in the early nineteenth century.

Although suffering occasional reverses, the secular trend of output was upward during the rest of the century. This situation changed after 1920 when the industry suffered severe setbacks. Brazil and the Gold Coast became serious competitors for markets formerly dominated by Ecuador. In 1920 the price of cacao commanded fifty-nine cents in the New York market; the following year it dropped to nineteen cents. As Ecuador's income from cacao plummeted, crop diseases further damaged Ecuador's cacao industry. Thereafter fluctuations in world prices and production made cacao a volatile factor in Ecuador's exports. Although it never regained its former preeminence among national exports, cacao still remained important.[36]

The coast also exported a variety of other tropical products such as coffee, tobacco, tagua nuts, and rubber (see Appendixes A, E, and F). Coffee, which had been exported intermittently in the nineteenth and early twentieth century, increased in importance as cacao declined. Planters in the provinces of Manabí and Guayas led the movement to substitute coffee for cacao. By 1921, coffee became Ecuador's second most important export, and although exports continued to grow, its performance was erratic because annual production and the world market price fluctuated dramatically. Coffee surpassed cacao only after 1952.[37] Another coastal export, bananas, developed at a spectacular rate in the 1950s. The fruit had been exported in small quantities for many years, but its importance increased dramatically after World War II. In 1950 bananas accounted for 12.8 percent of exports; two years later the fruit had become the country's most important export product. By 1959 it constituted 63 percent of Ecuador's total exports. During the years 1955 through 1959, bananas accounted for approximately 40 to 60 percent of the nation's export earnings (see Appendixes A and G).[38] Only cacao before 1922 had so dominated the Ecuadorian economy.

The coast's virtual monopoly of exports gave the region and its principal seaport, Guayaquil, great economic and political power. Costeños became Ecuador's most active and innovative businessmen. Increased foreign trade prompted the development of sophisticated banking and financial institutions. Coastal financiers always had aided the national government with loans, but in the last quarter of the nineteenth century, loans from new and more powerful coastal banking houses became a vital part of government fiscal policy. The growing financial power of the coast coincided with the region's population growth. These factors allowed the littoral to challenge political domination by the sierra.[39]

Human Geography

Climate and physical geography also have influenced the patterns of population settlement and growth in Ecuador. Coastal and highland patterns that are significantly different have influenced greatly the political, economic, and social development of the two regions.

Since the government conducted its first national census in 1952, any discussion of population size, composition, and distribution before that date must be based on estimates, fragmentary municipal or provincial census data, and the civil registry data on births and deaths. The bulk of this material has yet to be collected or analyzed by demographers or historians. The few specialists currently studying Ecuador's population history have concentrated on the colonial period and the nineteenth century.[40] Therefore, any discussion of Ecuadorian population trends must be tentative.

One of the thorniest problems encountered in analyzing Ecuador's population is defining race and ethnicity. In general, Ecuadorians classify persons as white if they possess European ancestry, are literate, and relatively light skinned. Many of these same individuals if they were poor or illiterate would be classified as mestizos. One encounters similar difficulties with other ethnic categories. In the absence of accepted definitions concerning race and ethnicity, estimates of the size of various groups are more likely to reveal the cultural biases of the person making the estimate rather than any objective reality. For example, Leslie Rout has recently called Eugenio Espejo, Ecuador's most "celebrated Afro-Ecuadorean."[41] Yet Ecuadorians consider Espejo, whose father was an Indian and whose mother was a *mulata*, one of the country's outstanding "Indians." They would be surprised and perhaps disturbed to have such a national hero labeled black. Ecuadorian intellectuals and politicians have discovered the virtues of indigenismo; they have yet to understand black pride. Such factors help to explain the widely varying statements made about the size of racial and ethnic groups in Ecuador.

The size, as well as the racial and ethnic composition of the country's population remains in dispute. Michael Hamerly calculated that the 1778/1781 population of Ecuador numbered approximately 428,693. It was composed of 66.1 percent Indians, 25.4 percent whites and mestizos, 1 percent black slaves, and 6.5 percent mulattoes—the progeny of blacks and whites—and free blacks.[42] Although he subsequently calculated the population for 1825 as 488,473, for 1838/1840 as 617,192, and for 1857/1858 as 748,287, Hamerly did not provide estimates of the racial breakdown.[43] Since Hamerly based his calculation on an analysis of various partial censuses taken during those years, they seem reasonably reliable. Unfortunately, other estimates are not as accurate.

The Ecuadorian geographer Manuel Villavicencio calculated that the country contained 1,108,042 persons in 1856. Although this figure is clearly incorrect, it is important because it highlights some of the problems connected with many population estimates.[44] Since population of size has been generally associated with national wealth or potential wealth, there is a tendency to overestimate, particularly for underdeveloped countries. Villavicencio's calculations also overrepresented the white segment of the population. This is consistent with the racial and cultural stereotypes of the time that equated a nation's potential and acceptability in the world community in terms of the "whiteness" of the population. Ecuadorian elites, like their European and North American counterparts, had yet to achieve an appreciation for racial and ethnic diversity. This explains Villavicencio's tendency to underestimate the size of the nonwhite population. He divided Ecuador's population into 601,219 whites (54.3%), 462,500 Indians (41.7%), 7,831 blacks (0.7%), and 36,592 people of mixed racial background (3.3%). The disdain for miscegenation then popular in the Western world clearly accounts for the last figure.[45]

White foreigners, convinced of their own racial superiority, seemed more impressed by the size of Ecuador's nonwhite and racially mixed population. Thus George Earl Church, in a report published by the United States Senate in 1881, estimated Ecuador's population to be 1,000,000, of whom 10 percent were white, 60 percent Indian, and 30 percent racially mixed. He also noted that the few blacks in the country had almost disappeared because of miscegenation.[46]

In 1887 the Ecuadorian scholar Pedro Fermín Cevallos calculated that Ecuador had a population of 1,271,761 people, which he maintained was broken into two groups: Indians and racially mixed persons.[47] He exaggerated; small but recognizable groups of whites and blacks still existed in Ecuador.

In 1892 Theodore Wolf reinterpreted Cevallos's figures. The German scholar, who had lived and researched in Ecuador for more than twenty years, could make informed judgments about the nation's population. Wolf accepted Cevallos's numerical estimate but rounded the figure to 1,272,000 inhabitants to indicate that it was only an approximation. But he revised the Ecuadorian's ethnic analysis. The German calculated that about 50 percent of the population were Indians and that the rest consisted principally of mestizos, mulattoes, and zambos, the offspring of Indians and blacks. His travels, however, also left him with the impression that whites were a measurable, although small, segment of the population. In the countryside and in small towns, whites comprised no more than 1 percent of the inhabitants. But in the larger cities such as Quito, Guayaquil, and Cuenca, he believed that whites comprised possibly an eighth of the population. Since only a small fraction of the population lived in cities and towns of any size in 1892, Wolf's observations suggest that the white population of Ecuador numbered less than 2 percent of the total. The German agreed with Church and Cevallos that the black population was small and dwindling.[48]

Disagreements about the relative size of racial groups in Ecuador continue. An analysis based on 1930 civil registry data divided the nation's population as follows: 10 percent white, 41 percent mestizo, 39 percent Indian, 5 percent black and mulatto, and 5 percent other,[49] while a recent U.S. government publication estimates whites to be from 10 percent to 15 percent of the population, mestizos 22 percent to 50 percent, Indians 39 percent to 60 percent, and blacks and mulattoes from 3 percent to 10 percent.[50] The 1950 national census, which recorded a population of 3,202,757, failed to resolve the question of race. The census did not identify people by race. But, since a question was included concerning language preference, some analysts have used linguistic data to isolate Ecuador's Indian population. John Saunders, however, has demonstrated that such calculations might be flawed.[51] An analysis of language patterns also fails to provide information about the various non-Indian groups. Unfortunately, the 1962 census also failed to identify racial groups.

Although disagreements about race remain unresolved, observers generally agree concerning the geographic distribution of ethnic groups in Ecuador. Most Indians reside in the sierra, where, according to Rosemary Bromley, they are overwhelmingly rural.[52] Hamerly's data shows that in 1780 only 2 percent of Ecuador's Indian population lived in the region that includes the modern provinces of Guayas, Manabí, Los Ríos, and part of El Oro. If one allows for a few Indians living in Esmeraldas and the Oriente, one must conclude that at the end of the eighteenth century 95 percent of the Indians lived in the highlands.[53] Travelers and scholars agree that this pattern did not alter in the nineteenth and twentieth centuries. In 1961 the Instituto Ecuatoriano de Antropología y Geografía calculated that 93.1 percent of all Indians lived in the sierra, 6.7 percent on the coast and .2 percent in the Oriente.[54]

Like the Indians, blacks and mulattoes tend to live in specific regions, generally on the coast. Luis T. Paz y Miño calculated that in 1781, blacks constituted 6.85 percent of the coastal population but only .83 percent of the highland population.[55] My calculations indicate that in 1780, 61.5 percent of the country's approximately 33,500 blacks, mulattoes, and zambos lived in the southern coastal province of Esmeraldas.[56] In 1892 Wolf argued that most blacks were living in isolated districts of the province of Esmeraldas.[57] Post-1950 investigations by the Instituto Ecuatoriano de Antropología y Geografía demonstrate that the majority of Ecuador's blacks, mulattoes, and zambos currently reside in the coastal provinces of Esmeraldas, Manabí, Guayas, and El Oro.[58]

Since independence, the sierra has retained its position as the nation's most populous region. Throughout Ecuador's history, however, the population has moved steadily from the highlands to the coast (see Appendix H). In 1830 about 85 percent of the population lived in the sierra. The century that followed witnessed extensive migrations to the coast.[59] After 1918 when health authorities managed to control malaria and yellow fever, the death rate on the coast declined. This factor, and the littoral's high birth rate, explained Ecuador's population growth. Estimates indicate that there was a large increase in the population of the province of Guayas from 1889 to 1909. By 1909 Guayas had become the most populous province in the country, a status it retained in 1950 with 18.2 percent of Ecuador's population. In that same year, 58 percent of the country's population still lived in the highlands, while 40.5 percent resided in the coastal provinces. The 1962 census indicated that coastal population continued to grow at a faster rate than sierra population.[60]

Since Ecuador is predominately agricultural, most of the population lives in rural areas. While cities and towns emerged as important political and commercial centers early in the country's history, only a minority of the population is urban. Indeed, during the first years of the republic there was an urban recession; urban growth resumed in the 1860s and 1870s.[61] Although the historic trend toward urbanization continued, only the provinces of Guayas and Pichincha contained a predominantly urban population by 1950. The capitals of these provinces, Guayaquil and Quito, accounted for 51.3 percent of the urban population of Ecuador.

The population is not distributed equally among the provinces of the coast or the sierra (see Appendix I). The 1950 census indicated that the population density of the littoral averaged 19.7 persons per square kilometer. Guayas, the most densely populated coastal province, had 27.6 persons per square kilometer while Esmeraldas, the least densely populated, averaged 5 people per square kilometer. The range in the sierra, however, was from 58.5 in the province of Tunguragua to 18 in

Loja.[62] Since these figures are based on the total area of the two regions or of the provinces, they do not reflect the true severity of population pressure in the highlands. The sierra has been intensely cultivated since pre-Columbian times. It is a region of poor and badly eroded soils. Yield per hectare is low and declining. The coast, in contrast, did not come under intense cultivation until recently. It is a region of rich tropical soils with high yields.[63] Consequently, population pressure in the highlands is even greater than the figures suggest.

Sierra landholding patterns aggravated the social and economic consequences of the maldistribution of population. The highlands contained large estates (*latifundia*) and semifeudal tenancy arrangements such as *concertage* (1816–1918) and *huasipungo* (1918–1964). As late as 1954, .2 percent of landowners in the highlands controlled 48.7 percent of the agricultural lands, conversely 81.7 percent of all holdings contained less than five hectares and occupied only 11.4 percent of the farm lands of the sierra.[64] Most of these small plots could not meet the subsistence needs of a single family. The coast, unlike the highlands, does not suffer a significant *minifundia* problem; the average littoral holding is twice as large as a sierra property.

The different economic opportunities of the two regions had important political consequences. The Indians, concentrated in the rural highlands, had limited opportunities.[65] Since they subsisted outside the money economy, they enjoyed little mobility and failed to develop a sense of political consciousness. They were effectively excluded from political participation. As a subjugated group, their defense against the oppressive acts of whites and mestizos has been psychological withdrawal. Thus by default highland elites have dominated the countryside, despite sporadic acts of individual or collective violence and rebellion by Indians. In the cities of the sierra, the traditional elite have made only minor concessions to a middle class that also engages in politics.

The situation of the coast contrasts sharply with the sierra.[66] The subsistence sector was much smaller on the coast, consisting principally of blacks living in isolated parts of Esmeraldas. Although the upper classes continued to dominate politics, other groups increasingly challenged their position. Commercial growth fostered the expansion of the middle class that insisted on political participation. The workers of the littoral began to organize late in the nineteenth century. By the 1920s some unions started making political demands. These differences had a profound effect in Ecuador's history. The coast assumed the role of a market-oriented, modernizing society, whereas the sierra became increasingly identified with traditional values.

Regionalism

Isolation caused by geography and a poor communication network accentuated regional and provincial differences. In politics, these factors found their expression in regionalism. Most authors who have written about Ecuador describe regionalism as a conflict between the sierra and the coast. They have seen the competition between Quito and Guayaquil as the fundamental expression of that rivalry. Indeed, Arthur P. Whitaker described the history of Ecuador as "A Tale of Two Cities."[67] While true, this rivalry provides only the best chronicled example of a much wider phenomenon.

Geographic isolation encouraged the development of a series of largely self-sufficient communities. Although a few settlements of this sort existed on the coast, they were typical of the sierra. Until communications improved substantially in the twentieth century, most highlanders seldom left their communities. In the nineteenth century, only a tiny minority of politicians, military men, clerics, and merchants traveled beyond their provinces. For the vast majority of Ecuadorians the concept of a *nation* was meaningless. A person owed loyalty first and foremost to his own household and extended family. Ties weakened as one moved from the family to the neighborhood, town, province, and region. At each level, fewer people recognized the advantages of cooperating or making sacrifices for the common good. Feelings of suspicion and hostility increased as one left the sanctuary of the family, a phenomenon observed and commented upon both by foreigners and Ecuadorians.[68]

Indians, the powerless majority, were the most alienated sector of the population. Recent anthropological studies indicate that familial isolation was common among the Indians of Ecuador. Even within their own communities, close cooperation seems to be limited to relatives. The concept "Indian" is alien to the indigenous people of Ecuador. Rather than a homogeneous "Indian" group, as perceived by the government and the hispanized society, the Indians belong to one of hundreds of communities. They identified with individual groups, not with a larger "Indian" society.[69]

Patterns of social interaction among all sectors of Ecuadorian society have tended to reinforce the barriers that climate and geography imposed on political and economic integration. Intraregional sierra rivalries proved as bitter and divisive as the better known conflict between the highlands and the coast. As a result, provinces such as Azuay and Loja often joined Guayas in opposing Quito. At other times, Loja and Azuay themselves became embroiled in acrimonious debates. Although such intraregional rivalries existed on the coast, they were partially mitigated by a better transportation network and an expanding economy.

Ecuadorian society historically has been characterized by a low level of civic consciousness and civic culture. But in every generation a few individuals, surmounting their cultural limitations, have sought to strengthen the national state and overcome the centrifugal forces described in this chapter. Such men were always in a minority; others often advanced their careers by exacerbating the regional divisions of the country. Nonetheless, the national government slowly has extended its authority throughout Ecuador.

2. Ecuadorian Politics

The Structure of Politics

There is no simple explanation for the political turmoil that has characterized Ecuador since independence. Several factors are significant. Geography has been a formidable obstacle to the creation of national transportation and communications networks. The unequal distribution of national resources and of population has led to regional conflicts. The development of divergent economic and social systems in the coast and the highlands resulted in antagonistic political attitudes and interests. As the nineteenth century progressed, ideologies grew in importance in national and regional politics. The coast became the home of liberalism while the highlands became the stronghold of conservatism. These competing philosophies were rooted in the economic and social realities of the areas. The development of ideologies and political parties dedicated to implementing them, however, had little effect on the manner in which national leaders governed. Both liberals and conservatives responded in similar ways to the challenges of ruling a divided country. The characteristic features of Ecuadorian politics—regionalism, authoritarianism, militarism, and personalism—provide coherence and continuity to the nation's chaotic political history.

The demise of Spanish authority plunged the country into a crisis of legitimacy. None of the subsequent regimes could restore either authority or legitimacy to the nation.[1] The ruling elite failed to reach a consensus that would have allowed them to resolve their conflicts amicably. The chief executive immediately became the target for all ambitious politicians. To curb the tendencies toward fragmentation, strong national leaders resorted to force. The "presidents" of Ecuador utilized authoritarian measures to sustain national existence and maintain themselves in power. In some instances, they could temporarily force individuals and regions to comply with their view of national interest. But few dissenters were actually persuaded. At the first opportunity, they resorted to armed struggle to attain power for themselves and their regions. From 1830 to 1983 only fourteen presidents completed their constitutional terms of office (see Appendix J). Before Camilo Ponce Enríquez (1952–1956), no chief executive completed his term of office without having to overcome armed challenges to his incumbency. There have been only two periods, from 1912 to 1925 and from 1948 to 1961, when several presidents were elected, completed their terms, and transferred power to other elected chief executives. Since 1960 no president has completed a four-year term.

The Ecuadorian case is an extreme example of the crisis that engulfed most of Spanish America in the postindependence period. As shown in the preceding chapter, geography, social structure, and the economy combined to strengthen localism and hinder the formation of an integrated nation. Politically this disunity was expressed in the repeated challenges of local leaders to national authority whenever the country was governed by a weak administration or the economy faltered. It would be incorrect and simplistic to explain the country's political turmoil in terms of struggles among *caudillos,* as has been the practice in previous analyses of nineteenth-century Ecuadorian politics. While it is true that the country had an abundant supply of personally ambitious men, most derived what authority they possessed, not from personal magnetism but from their understanding of regional interests and their willingness to champion the causes of particular areas. Followers, as well as their leaders, understood clearly their self-interests, arising from the economic and social realities of their "world." In Ecuador that "world" was the region, not the nation.

The seemingly endless coups, pronouncements, and insurrections that punctuated and enlivened Ecuador's political history were rooted in the regions' conflicting economic and social interests. The elite who governed Ecuador were not a homogeneous group whose interest would be served by any of the members. Regional antagonism was not limited to conflict between the coast and the sierra. Although serranos sometimes united to oppose the coast, such alliances lasted only a short time. Divergent economic interests also splintered highland unity. Production and marketing systems in the sierra provinces tended to isolate rather than integrate the area. For example, Loja in the south had its closest economic ties with Peru and Tulcán in the north with Colombia. As a result, these provinces were frequently in opposition to policies emanating from Quito. The coast was similarly divided.

Historically a small "white" elite has dominated effective political participation in Ecuador. Large landowners, wealthy businessmen, professionals, and high-ranking military men were the principal power contenders in the nineteenth century. Politicians were usually urban, literate, and male. Although upper-class Ecuadorian women have a reputation for political involvement, none held public office in the nineteenth century. Women exercised their influence behind the scenes.[2]

The masses, until recently, only participated sporadically and ineffectively in politics. The nineteenth century was punctuated by Indian revolts that had no enduring effect on the political system. At best, local rebellions succeeded in obtaining redress of specific grievances. More frequently, the government crushed Indian revolts with great severity.[3] Although the urban masses also were excluded from the political process, they obtained their ends more often than did the Indians. As cities grew and government institutions developed, artisans, workers, and petty bureaucrats occasionally influenced politics. Early in the nineteenth century, these urban groups relied on traditional forms of mass protest such as the *tumulto*. Toward the latter part of the century, they organized syndicates and trade unions to defend their interests. Since literacy qualifications denied the vote to the urban lower class, they attempted to influence political decision by taking to the streets. Although strikes and riots usually failed to improve working or living conditions, some elites encouraged these actions to enhance their political fortunes. Ambitious politicians often utilized urban lower-class discontent to launch attacks upon the government. While these movements threatened individual regimes, they posed no challenge to the political structure that excluded the overwhelming majority of Ecuadorians.[4]

Middle-class individuals usually participated in politics to obtain employment. The government was an important, if unreliable, source of white-collar jobs. Each new administration dismissed the employees of the previous regime. Former government workers immediately threw their support to a politician who would offer them employment once again.[5] The spoils system was a manifestation of the highly structured patron-client relationship that dominated all aspects of Ecuadorian life. Political patronage was vital to the small middle class that could find no other source of livelihood in a backward rural economy. The scarcity of white-collar jobs existed in all parts of the country, but was particularly acute in the isolated highlands. The problem remains unresolved. Several attempts to create a civil service with security of employment and promotion based on merit have failed.[6]

The spoils system has had far-reaching negative effects. Administrative discontinuity meant that few programs could be completed. With rapid turnover, lines of authority were blurred and systems of account-ability were difficult to establish and enforce. In such circumstances, sloth, incompetence, and fraud were seldom punished and initiative, effi-ciency, and honesty rarely rewarded. The system strengthened the public view that government employment was a temporary stroke of good luck. As a result, bureaucrats seemed principally concerned with improving their lot and that of their family and friends. They expected to "profit" from government employment. A tradition of public service devoted to promoting national welfare, therefore, did not develop.[7]

Despite the trend toward greater political participation that emerged during the nineteenth and twentieth centuries, the elite continued to dominate Ecuadorian politics. Since the 1930s, the growth of the electorate has accelerated but the number of voters remains small. In the national elections of 1960, only 22.4 percent of the population of Ecuador was registered to vote and only 17 percent of the population actually voted.[8]

Ecuador's political process has not remained static. Political institu-tions and parties have evolved. New groups and ideas have brought change to the Ecuadorian political scene. Since World War II the rate of change has accelerated. Nonetheless, traditional social and economic structures have remained highly resilient, molding men and movements to conform to the requirements of these structures. The facade of change is greater than the reality.[9] The ability of national leaders to act—that aspect which political scientists call policy space—remains limited. The remainder of this chapter will examine the impact of regionalism, authoritarianism, militarism, and personalism on Ecuadorian politics in the first century of national life.

Regionalism

Regionalism has been a significant and enduring factor in Ecuadorian politics. As chapter 1 indicated, regionalism may be viewed as the political expression of the division and isolation imposed by geography. Since independence, regionalists have struggled to receive adequate representa-tion in national government, to obtain a significant share of national revenues for their areas, and to maintain local autonomy. At times, they sought to gain their ends by pressing for constitutional changes, passing laws favorable to their provinces, or by electing candidates sympathetic to their interests. But they were also willing to employ extralegal means to obtain their goals. Thus, regionalism has become an important element in Ecuador's political instability.

In 1830 the framers of Ecuador's first constitution designed a government structure to avoid regional conflict by dividing congressional representation equally among the departments of Quito, Azuay, and Guayas, regardless of their population.[10] They also concentrated power in the three departmental capitals: Quito, Cuenca, and Guayaquil. However, since each department included more than one historic province, the constitutional accommodation merely shifted the focus of regionalist antagonism. For example, Quito, the capital of Pichincha, also governed Imbabura and Chimborazo provinces; Guayaquil, the capital of Guayas, had jurisdiction over Manabí; and Cuenca, the capital of Azuay, ruled Loja. The arrangement led to intradepartmental feuding about real or imagined inequities. As a result, the outlying provinces attempted to change the departmental system.

Provincial representation became a major issue in the constituent congress of 1835. The representatives of Quito, Cuenca, and Guayaquil defended the departmental system, while their counterparts from Imbabura, Chimborazo, Manabí, and Loja demanded that a provincial system be established. Ultimately, the issue was settled through compromise. Departmental governments were abolished and replaced by provincial governments; the three departments were broken into seven provinces (see table 2). This permitted greater local control. The question of equitable national representation proved more difficult to resolve, since provinces differed greatly in size, population, and wealth. An agreement was finally reached that maintained the political balance among the three principal regions: the northern highlands, the southern highlands, and the coast. The constitution of 1835 retained the department structure for electoral purposes.[11]

The question of provincial representation, however, continued to divide the country, becoming an important factor in the 1859 civil war when three competing governments attempted to impose their will on the nation. A three-man junta, headed by Gabriel García Moreno, controlled Quito and the northern highlands. General Guillermo Franco formed a government in Guayaquil that ruled the coast. The people of Loja established a separate government under Manuel Carrión Pinzano. But the southern province did not possess the population or the wealth to remain separate indefinitely. Therefore it called itself a federal state and urged the adoption of a federal system hoping to free itself from

Cuenca's domination.[12] Since no strong leader emerged in Cuenca to establish a fourth regional government, that province initially sided with Guayaquil against Quito because it wished to retain its prerogative as a department capital. But García Moreno ultimately forced Cuenca to submit to his government. Eventually Loja also sided with the northern highlands, in part because García Moreno agreed to support Loja's desire for greater autonomy.[13] In addition, the Quito government formed new provinces to secure backing and to weaken its principal antagonist, Guayaquil. The clearest instance of this kind of regional politics can be found in the creation of Los Ríos province. The region, which lies astride the main road from Guayaquil to Quito, had long desired home rule. During the civil war it sided with Quito and received provincial status as its reward in 1860 (see table 2).[14]

After García Moreno's victory in the civil war, a constituent assembly met in 1861. Although the assembly retained centralism, changes in the electoral system vindicated the politics of the rebellious outlying provinces. The congress established provincial representation on the basis of population, thus ending the legal justification for the dominance of the departmental capitals in the electoral process.

The problem of equitable representation has found no permanent solution in Ecuador. The formation of new provinces provided only temporary relief because internal migration eventually produced new inequalities. The constitution of 1967 provides representation in the chamber of deputies on the basis of population; each province must have a minimum of two deputies. In the senate, each province has two senators. In view of the population differences, some areas enjoy greater representation than others. The Oriente's four provinces contain a combined population of 103,800, making it one of the least populated regions in the country. Nevertheless, the Oriente can send sixteen legislators to congress. That is more representation than Manabí province with a population seven times larger. The highland provinces favor the arrangement because the eastern region tends to side with them against the coast. The coastal provinces complain that they are underrepresented. That area has a larger population than the sierra and demographic trends indicate that the coast will continue to grow rapidly. But the coast has less representation than the highlands because there are only five coastal provinces while the sierra has ten. A solution currently favored by costeños is the creation of new coastal provinces, to provide the region's growing population with more equitable representation.[15]

Regionalist politics have not always been settled through the legislative process. During the nineteenth century, Ecuador endured five civil wars that threatened to dismember the country. The first war occurred even before independence was achieved. When Quito formed a local government in 1809, Guayaquil and Cuenca joined the royalist forces in crushing it.[16] The second erupted in 1834 when opposition to President Juan José Flores ended in a regionalist civil war. Vicente Rocafuerte formed a government on the coast while José Félix Valdivieso claimed to rule from Quito. Cuenca and the south wavered between the two areas. Ultimately, Rocafuerte allied himself with his former enemy, Flores, and unified the nation by force. Rocafuerte and Flores achieved victory in the battle of Miñarica, one of the bloodiest in Ecuadorian history.[17] The nation suffered another civil war from 1854 to 1861 that coincided with a Peruvian attack on Ecuador. The foreign threat did not prevent regionalists from fighting against one another. The internal conflict ended when García Moreno obtained power; only then could the foreign struggle be resolved.[18] The country again disintegrated in 1883 when attempts to remove General Ignacio Veintimilla from the presidency resulted in a civil war. Eloy Alfaro became the leader of a faction that controlled Manabí and Esmeraldas; Guayaquil formed a government under the auspices of Pedro Carbo, a distinguished liberal; and a five-man junta seized control of the government in Quito. Various movements developed in other provinces. They eventually ousted and exiled Veintimilla, but the nation remained bitterly divided. The representatives of Guayaquil called for the establishment of a federal system to end the conflict. Ultimately, a coalition of highlanders restored order under the presidency of José María Plácido Caamaño, driving Alfaro and various other coastal leaders into exile.[19] These men eventually returned to lead the liberals to victory in 1895, but their triumph did not end regional conflict. The period from 1895 to 1916 was one of intermittent civil war. At times the government lost control of entire regions to local leaders. Eventually, the newly institutionalized and modernized army concluded the Esmeraldas civil war in 1916. Thereafter, the national armed forces crushed the guerrillas that threatened the unity of the country.[20]

The supremacy of the national armed forces, however, did not mean that regional conflicts could not lead to civil war. In 1932 conservatives managed to elect Neptalí Bonifaz president. When congressional liberals disqualified him on the grounds that he was technically a Peruvian citizen, the highland conservatives rebelled with the support of the noncommissioned officers and the soldiers of the Quito garrison. Congress fled the capital, but returned later with the provincial garrisons. In the "War of the Four Days" provincial troops crushed the Quito regiments, restoring the liberals to power.[21]

Authoritarianism and Militarism

Although nineteenth-century Ecuador was, in theory, a constitutional republic, force became the accepted method of transferring or retaining power (see Appendix J). All eleven constitutions promulgated in that period provided for elected officials. They also generally prohibited the reelection of a president. Political reality, however, was quite different. Ecuador has enjoyed few free elections. Indeed, elections often were held not to select a president but to ratify or legalize the power of a person who gained office through force. In such cases, elections were usually preceded by the writing of a new constitution.[22] In other instances, the government controlled elections to insure the victory of its official candidate. In either situation, disappointed presidential contenders often violently challenged the outcome. The issue was settled temporarily when one side was defeated in battle. Such settlements, however, were always tenuous and the incumbent could expect repeated insurrections during his term of office. The use of force was not limited to military politicians: Generals Juan José Flores (1830–1834, 1839–1845), José María Urvina (1851–1856), Francisco Robles (1856–1859), and Ignacio Veintimilla (1876–1883) relied on armed might either to bring them to power or to help them retain it. But so did the leading civilian politicians. The two great nineteenth-century statesmen, Vicente Rocafuerte (1835–1839) and Gabriel García Moreno (1861–1865, 1869–1876), achieved power through armed conflict and then relied on force to remain in office.

A pattern of authoritarian politics developed in nineteenth-century Ecuador. Once in power, chief executives rapidly concluded that only a strong and unyielding authoritarian ruler could govern the country. Nothing could be accomplished if the government was preoccupied with combatting subversion. Regimes abandoned the civil guarantees enumerated by the various constitutions in an effort to secure the order and stability considered necessary prerequisites for development. Liberals, conservatives, and opportunists all relied on controlled elections, press censorship, and extralegal coercion to limit the opposition. Strong leaders, whether civilian or military, reacted alike. Indeed, Rocafuerte and García Moreno proved harsher and more violent than their military counterparts.[23]

A close relationship emerged between authoritarianism and militarism during the immediate postindependence period. The struggle for independence resulted in the formation of a large military caste that considered itself above the law.[24] In Ecuador the problem was exacerbated because the country was under martial law for several years to facilitate the liberation of Peru. Following Spain's defeat, many Gran Colombian military men returned to Ecuador. These uprooted men, who had no economic or social ties to the region, destabilized the political system. They were always ready to support a "revolution" or to back a politician who promised them rewards. After being accorded military honors, they considered themselves "liberators" entitled to privilege and rank. As such, they were unwilling to return to their former peaceful pursuits, which in most instances would have reduced them to the role of artisan or farmer. Even had they desired to abandon their military "careers," the Ecuadorian economy could not absorb them since after independence, the country underwent a period of severe economic depression. Thus the Venezuelans and Colombians who found themselves in Ecuador in the postindependence period had few opportunities open to them. They found it easier to prosper through intrigue, plunder, or extortion.[25]

Not all foreign military men became predators. The ablest, those who distinguished themselves in combat or in administration, allied themselves with the Ecuadorian elite. They married into wealthy families and acquired property or became high-ranking officials in the national army.[26] Indeed, Ecuador's first president, General Juan José Flores, was a Venezuelan who had married into the Quito aristocracy. The limited peace and stability which Ecuador enjoyed in the period 1830 to 1845 was owing in part to Flores's ability to retain the support of the foreign element that dominated the armed forces. His relationship with that group, however, ultimately provoked an anti-Flores reaction. Local politicians and national military chieftains relied on a growing xenophobia to oust Flores and exile him in 1845.[27]

Two types of armed forces—the national military and the armed guerrillas or *montoneras*—dominated national politics until 1916, when the national army defeated the last montonera band. During the nineteenth century it was often difficult to differentiate between the two armed groups. The national armed forces usually gave their loyalty to the government; the guerrilla bands generally served individual strong men, usually large landowners or former military men. If the insurgents succeeded in overthrowing the government and bringing their leader to power, they were usually rewarded with employment in the national armed forces. The defenders of the fallen government would often find themselves dismissed from the service and exiled by the victors. The cashiered officers were then available to support another political contender who might restore them to their former position and, perhaps, promote them. The cycle of rebellion became the norm because every new revolution created more "outs" who wanted to get back "in."

The history of nineteenth-century Ecuador is filled with instances of the process described above. For example, the Flores defeat in 1845 led to the dismissal of loyal officers. Many were forced into exile with Flores while others were simply cashiered. The ousted military men seized every opportunity to overthrow the new government. As a result, President Vicente Ramón Roca (1845–1849) faced more than twenty armed insurrections during his term.[28] Although the pro-Flores group failed to topple the Roca government, it temporarily reentered politics during the administration of Diego Noboa (1850–1851). After the election of 1850, the supporters of one defeated candidate, General Antonio Elizalde, rebelled against the winner, Diego Noboa. When they failed to oust him, the new president retaliated with wholesale dismissals of officers hostile to his regime. Since Noboa's action decimated the officer corps, he attempted to rebuild the military by allowing the pro-Flores group to return and assume important positions in the armed forces. But Noboa was unable to forge an effective army in time to prevent his defeat.[29] In 1851 an ambitious political general, José María Urvina, relied on the partisans of the defeated Elizalde to help him oust Noboa. One of Urvina's first acts after gaining power was to rescind the law that permitted the pro-Flores group to return to Ecuador. A strong and distinguished general, Urvina managed to retain the support of enough military groups to maintain himself in power (1851–1855) and to elect his friend, General Francisco Robles, president in 1856.[30] Toward the end of the decade, however, an international crisis weakened the Robles government. Gabriel García Moreno, an aspiring young politician, used the opportunity to overthrow the Robles government in 1859 with the help of dissident military men, particularly the pro-Flores group.[31] This pattern of defeat, exile, rebellion, and restoration to power continued until well into the twentieth century.

The willingness of many groups to use force to attain political goals meant that national leaders, whether civil or military, had to rely on the army for support. The process gave distinct advantages to military politicians. But civilians, who formed enduring alliances with key groups in the military, also could survive. Thus authoritarianism became intertwined with militarism. The system favored strong and ruthless chief executives. Even today many Ecuadorians believe that only a "man of iron" can govern the country, but even such a man will fail if he lacks the support of the military.

Personalism

Ecuador, like most other Spanish American nations, emerged from the independence movement with shattered institutions. Only the church remained nearly intact. The new institutions of representative government had little opportunity to flourish. The pressures of war, economic decline, and political instability led to the rise of powerful individuals, such as Simón Bolívar, who could circumvent legal structures and personally settle national or local issues. Although the emergence of Ecuador as an independent nation coincided with Bolívar's demise, the pattern established by him and others continued. Individual leaders, rather than political parties or institutions, governed the country.

The failure to develop strong political institutions has strongly influenced Ecuador's political history. Men, rather than ideas or abstract political principles, were the basis of political movements. Although Ecuadorian politicians eventually coalesced around ideological tendencies forming the liberal and conservative parties, those organizations did not become the principal forces in national politics. Ecuadorian parties did not select leaders from within the ranks. Instead, men with strong personalities and political ambition took control of existing political parties or formed their own organizations. Political leaders might call themselves liberal or conservative, but it was Rocafuerte, Urvina, García Moreno, or Eloy Alfaro who governed the country, not a political party. Neither liberal nor conservative leaders managed to transfer their power to their parties; when they left office, their movements ended. Indeed, in some instances supporters identified themselves specifically with one person rather than with the party or ideology. This phenomenon has been present throughout the entire national period, but it has been most pronounced in the case of José María Velasco Ibarra who has been president of Ecuador five times (1934–1935, 1944–1947, 1952–1956, 1960–1961, 1968–1972). *Velasquismo* constitutes the most enduring personalist movement in Ecuadorian politics. Nevertheless, it failed to develop an institutional

structure. Although his following was extensive, there has been no effective Velasquista movement without Velasco Ibarra.[32]

Personalist politics have been dominant in Ecuador, but some individuals attempted to remedy this situation by creating political parties.
During the twentieth century, groups such as the liberals, conservatives,
and socialists sought to become effective mechanisms for selecting candidates and developing programs. However, the traditional patterns of social
relations, the patron-client and *compadrazgo* systems, managed to stymie
the formation of a modern political structure.

Liberal Politics

In the nineteenth century, liberals and conservatives agreed on many
issues. Both sought national development, which they generally interpreted to require an extended and improved network of communications,
a better and a larger educational system and, most of all, economic growth.
Significant differences, however, separated the two groups. Liberals
wanted to attain national development through the creation of a secular
state; conservatives considered the church an ally to whom they willingly
granted a privileged position in order to win its support. It was the role
of the church which generally divided liberals from conservatives and not
issues of development or civil rights. Nineteenth-century liberalism emphasized the secular state, individual rights, and a market economy. But
countries like Ecuador could not grant such guarantees when the over-
whelming majority of the population was illiterate and outside the money
economy. The realities of nineteenth-century society led some liberals to
embrace conservatism.[33]

Gabriel García Moreno provides the classic example of the liberal
turned conservative. He began his political career as a liberal insurgent
and the constitution of 1861 promulgated under his direction contains a
liberal bias. Once in power García Moreno realized that he needed to
maintain internal order before he could modernize the country. Like his
predecessor, Vicente Rocafuerte, he turned to authoritarian methods.[34]
García Moreno courted the military, which he used to bolster his regime.
Ecuador's history, however, demonstrated that the army was a necessary
but unreliable base of support. Therefore, he turned for assistance to a
highly politicized church, which he reformed and strengthened as coun-
terweight to the military. García Moreno's alleged religious fanaticism
obscures the fact that his manipulation of the church was the stroke of a

master politician. It was the only way that a civilian could achieve a modicum of political independence from Ecuador's endemic militarism. In contrast, the liberal Rocafuerte, whose administrative abilities, views, and authoritarian tendencies resembled García Moreno's, failed to establish a diversified power base. He was an avowed anticlerical governing a society with only two strong institutions. Since he eschewed the church, Rocafuerte had to depend on the military in the person of General Flores. When Flores opposed him, Rocafuerte could do little other than go into exile.[35] García Moreno, however, dominated Ecuadorian politics from 1860 to 1875. Only one other individual managed to retain power for a similar period, General Flores (1830–1845).

Toward the end of the century, economic rather than clerical issues became the main focus of contention between liberals and conservatives. The coastal export economy, with its center in Guayaquil, had grown rapidly during the last decades of the century. Coastal businessmen and bankers clashed with the highland elite whose economic base was the traditional subsistence economy. The growth of exports expanded the market economy and generated modern socioeconomic relationships. In the sierra, large landowners, including the church, retained their privileged position through traditional socioeconomic structures such as the patron-client system and concertaje. Politically, the conflict was expressed in opposing ideologies; the coast supported liberalism and the highlands conservatism.

Of course not all costeños were liberal nor were all highlanders conservative. For example, García Moreno, Ecuador's most successful conservative, was born in Guayaquil while General Urvina, a prominent liberal, was a highlander. Place of birth was not the principal determinant of political preference. Social ties, economic interests, education, and career development affected political affiliations. Highlanders engaged in modern economic activities, such as manufacturing and business, as well as professionals whose aspirations were restricted by the sierra's traditional social structure, became liberals. This occurred even though the economic interests of the modern sector of the coast and the highlands were sometimes in conflict. For example, sierra manufacturers favored protective tariffs and import restrictions while coastal importers supported free trade. Both liberal groups, however, put aside their conflicts temporarily to establish the secular state which they felt to be necessary for their future well-being.[36]

Political parties began forming in the 1870s when the economy was expanding and the country beginning to modernize. Three major political groups emerged between 1875 and 1878: the conservatives stressed García Moreno's authoritarian and proclerical policies. The progressives were moderates who favored limited reforms; the group included former conservatives who abandoned the Conservative party after García Moreno's assassination. Although men had called themselves liberals since independence, the Liberal party did not officially exist until organized in 1878 by General Ignacio Veintimilla, a self-styled "radical" who had captured the presidency. Even though he became the titular head of the Liberal party, Veintimilla soon alienated many liberals and eventually abandoned all pretense of liberalism by becoming a dictator. He was ousted during the civil war of 1883. The progressives then gained control of the presidency and retained power until 1895. During that period some liberals, who had helped oust Veintimilla, participated in the government as a minority faction. But other liberals refused to cooperate: instead they resorted to insurrection and subversion.[37]

The liberals gained power in 1895 and retained it until 1925. Many historians, believing that the liberal period ushered in a new era in politics and began the process of modernization, consider the year 1895 a turning point in Ecuador's history. The early liberal period coincided with the growth of the coastal export economy. During these years the government initiated railroads, sewage treatment plants, port facilities, and other public works projects. Not surprisingly the liberals attacked the church, long considered the chief bulwark of the traditional socioeconomic system, by secularizing education, abolishing the tithe, and establishing a civil registry for births, marriages, and deaths. They also confiscated church lands giving them to special committees, *juntas de beneficencia,* which were to use income from those properties to provide modern social services. These actions pleased many businessmen, bankers, and commercial agriculturalists who believed that Ecuador was becoming a modern nation.

Despite the liberals' impressive accomplishments, it would be wrong to consider 1895 a turning point. While important changes occurred, they did not constitute a break with the past. The liberals ruling Ecuador had to contend with the same forces that had shaped the nation's politics since independence—regionalism, militarism, authoritarianism, and personalism. Although the increase in world demand for cacao beginning in the 1860s and 1870s profoundly affected many aspects of Ecuadorian life, the rules of politics changed only slowly, if at all. The liberals first secured and then maintained political dominance by refining methods that had evolved during the nineteenth century. From 1895 until 1916, political disputes continued to be resolved on the field of battle and arbitrary and authoritarian measures were frequently used. Although political parties existed, they remained at a low level of institutionalization. Individuals rather than parties dominated politics. Regionalism also continued to exercise enormous influence. Several times during the early liberal period, the country disintegrated into warring factions. The liberals, however, attempted to contain regionalism via the politics of pork barrel legislation (see chapter 4 for a discussion of this phenomenon).

Some writers have criticized the liberals, arguing that they resorted to electoral fraud, controlled elections, and force to retain power. These critics maintain that the nation was overwhelmingly conservative and that as a minority party the liberals found such tactics necessary.[38] This explanation ignores the fact that conservatives and progressives also had employed the same methods when in power. The alleged difference in the size of the Liberal and Conservative parties is more apparent than real. Although a majority of Ecuador's population resides in the highlands where the conservatives were strong, only a small segment participated in politics. Economic and social differences between the two regions meant that a greater percentage of the coastal population was politically active. No one really knows the size of either party, but it is likely that they were more evenly matched than is generally believed. Political parties were only loose collections of small groups that owed primary loyalty to an individual or a region. When their party failed to select their candidate or favor their area, these subgroups often withdrew from the party to join the opposition. In such circumstances, and in the absence of a tradition of political compromise, all Ecuadorian governments regularly resorted to fraud and force to maintain their authority.[39]

From 1912 to 1924 liberal governments perfected the techniques of political control. Elections, however, remained a time of tension. The authorities employed violence and intimidation only in the countryside; in the larger urban centers, merely the presence of the police and the army near polling places proved sufficient to assure that elections would be orderly. If it appeared that the government's candidate would not win, the police or the military would be ordered to stuff the ballot boxes. By the 1920s electoral fraud and preelection persuasion methods became so refined that few opposition candidates remained in the race for the entire campaign. Opposition parties demonstrated their dissatisfaction with the government in other ways. They either refused to nominate candidates or convinced their supporters to boycott the elections. Only infrequently did they resort to traditional tactics of rebelling against liberal governments or attempting to subvert the military.[40]

Although the liberals eventually developed an orderly election process, the first years of liberal domination were a period of intense conflict. They gained power in 1895, as the result of a conservative-inspired rebellion that succeeded in forcing the progressive president, Luis Cordero, to resign, but which was unable to retain power. The provisional government in Quito rapidly lost control as insurrections erupted in Manabí, Latacunga, Ambato, El Oro, Los Ríos, Guayaquil, and even Quito itself. As in 1834 to 1835, 1859 to 1861, and in 1883, the country disintegrated into warring factions. Coastal liberals saw an opportunity to achieve national supremacy by inviting Eloy Alfaro to return from exile and assume command of their forces.

Alfaro had a great reputation as a liberal insurgent. A native of Manabí, he began his political career as a partisan of General Urvina. In 1864 Alfaro kidnapped a provincial governor in an abortive attempt to oust García Moreno, his first experience as a *guerrillero*. When the movement failed, Alfaro prudently fled to Panama where he became an extremely successful businessman. Later, he used his wealth to finance liberal insurrections against conservative governments. In some instances, as in 1883 to 1884, he even led montoneras from Manabí and Esmeraldas against the governments of Veintimilla and José Plácido Caamaño. By 1895 Alfaro had an international reputation as a soldier. Not only had he fought in the Ecuadorian civil wars but also participated in similar struggles in Central America and in the Cuban independence movement. Distinguished civilians, such as Lizardo García, Emilio Estrada, and José L. Tamayo, who would themselves later become presidents of Ecuador, invited Eloy Alfaro to lead the liberal forces in 1895.[41]

Alfaro commanded the support of other guerrilleros including Leonidas Plaza who had gained military experience in earlier insurrections. Plaza, who would eventually become president, had backed Alfaro in the abortive uprising in 1884. Like Alfaro, Plaza had escaped abroad where he also earned an international reputation as a liberal revolutionary. After fighting in Costa Rica and El Salvador, he, along with other guerrilleros, returned to Ecuador to command the coastal montoneras that decisively defeated government troops in August 1895. Like his predecessors—Flores, Rocafuerte, Urvina, Robles, García Moreno, and Veintimilla—Alfaro first assumed power and then convoked an assembly that wrote a new constitution and elected him "constitutional" president of Ecuador in October 1896.[42]

The liberal triumph, however, did not restore peace. Alfaro's government had to quash numerous armed challenges from church-backed conservative insurgents. Ironically, the liberals controlled the conservatives more easily than the opposition that emerged from their own ranks.[43] The process of selecting a presidential successor precipitated rebellions by competing liberal aspirants.

The first crisis over the presidential succession occurred in 1900 just prior to the expiration of President Alfaro's term. The Liberal party had to select a candidate in a tense atmosphere in which gossip and press speculation heightened public apprehension. Rumors circulated that elements of the armed forces might prevent the election of a civilian. Although a number of prominent civilian liberals enjoyed widespread support, Alfaro named General Plaza the official candidate. The president apparently considered Plaza an acceptable moderate whom he could control. The other leading military contender was General Manuel A. Franco, a rabid anticlerical and radical whom Alfaro recognized he could not dominate. When Alfaro realized that he would also be unable to dominate Plaza, he withdrew his support. Plaza, however, had won the backing of the leading military men and thus reached the presidential palace despite Alfaro's opposition and Franco's rivalry. Although Plaza avoided a public break with Alfaro, the division between the two liberal leaders never healed. Their rivalry was one of the major causes of the turbulence that lasted until 1916. At times, as in the years from 1912 to 1916, the antagonism erupted into civil war. On other occasions, such as in 1906 and 1911, it merely resulted in extraconstitutional changes in government.[44]

The second crisis over the presidential succession occurred in 1904 when the breach between the Alfaro and the Plaza wings of the Liberal party had become irreconcilable. Plaza, imposing a civilian, Lizardo García, as his successor, left Ecuador to serve as ambassador in Washington. His departure set the stage for García's ouster. The Alfaro group, outraged by Plaza's choice, began slandering the new president claiming that he was betraying the liberal cause by continuing Plaza's subversive policies. Because Plaza had encouraged conservatives to participate in his government, his rivals accused him of betraying liberalism. The charge was specious: Plaza (1901–1905) had enacted more liberal reforms than Alfaro (1895–1901). The campaign, nonetheless, weakened the García government. Many politically astute officers lost no time in joining the Alfaro group. García attempted to save himself by recalling Plaza, but the liberal general arrived too late to prevent the president's overthrow.

A military insurrection elevated Alfaro to power once more in 1906; García had been forced out after only four months in office.[45]

The 1906 revolution provides an excellent example of the way in which traditional political practices endured. Since independence, civilian presidents remained in office only as long as military leaders supported them. Like earlier military chieftains, such as Flores, Urvina, and Veintimilla, Alfaro willingly sacrificed orderly processes to satisfy his personal ambitions. Believing himself indispensable he was determined to retain power. Until his death in 1912, no liberal civilian president completed a term of office.[46]

Turbulence marked Alfaro's second term. After assuming power, he convoked a constituent assembly that wrote a new constitution and elected him to a second "constitutional" term (1907–1911). This, of course, was in keeping with Ecuadorian political traditions. The exercise failed to consolidate Alfaro's position; he faced growing opposition not only from conservatives but also from within his own Liberal party. Many former supporters viewed Alfaro as an opportunist who would sacrifice liberal ideals to retain power. The president reacted to the opposition by harshly suppressing dissenters, particularly the press, which had operated freely during the Plaza administration. This harassment confirmed the worst fears of Alfaro's critics who redoubled their attacks on the government. The threat of war with Peru in 1910 briefly united the country. Once an interim settlement was negotiated, the public turned its attention to the coming presidential campaign which coincided with Plaza's return after several years abroad. The stage was set for the final confrontation between the two liberal leaders.[47]

In 1911, Alfaro supported Emilio Estrada, a leading liberal businessman from Guayaquil. As the official candidate, Estrada easily defeated his two liberal opponents, Generals Plaza and Franco. But when the president-elect declared that he would pursue an independent policy and attempted to separate himself from Alfaro, the old chieftain tried to prevent Estrada's inauguration. Alfaro accused Estrada of not taking the conservative threat seriously and demanded that the president-elect resign because he had learned that Estrada suffered from a heart condition. Alfaro acted as he did because he had no desire to relinquish power. He had used the same tactic in an unsuccessful attempt to prevent Plaza from taking office in 1901, and he also used it to justify his insurrection of 1906. Yet Alfaro himself had appointed leading conservatives to cabinet posts and to sensitive diplomatic missions. They had been sound appointments that demonstrated his political skill, but they contradicted his alleged reasons for demanding Estrada's resignation. The tactic backfired and Alfaro was sent into exile.[48]

President Estrada's death in December 1911 unleashed a civil war that lasted five years. In Guayaquil, General Pedro Montero rebelled against the caretaker government announcing that he opposed both the Plaza faction of the Liberal party and the conservatives. General Flavio Alfaro, Eloy Alfaro's nephew, was appointed supreme chief in Esmeraldas. The rebel leaders agreed to recall Eloy Alfaro from Panama to head the insurrection. In Quito the government appointed General Plaza, who had been Estrada's minister of finance, commander of the national armed forces. It appointed another leading liberal general, Julio Andrade, second in command. Government forces defeated the insurgents in a series of bloody battles, and eventually occupied Guayaquil. Both sides were armed with the modern weapons that had been procured to meet the danger of a Peruvian invasion in 1910. Approximately 9,000 participated in the conflict: 3,800 regular troops remained loyal to the government, 2,700 regular soldiers joined the rebels, and 2,500 volunteers participated on both sides. During January 1912 more than 3,000 men died in the civil war. Ecuadorians were shocked by the extent of the carnage. Conspiracies, violence, and even civil war were relatively common in national politics. Major battles, however, were infrequent and seldom involved more than a few casualties. Public indignation turned against Alfaro and his supporters who were portrayed as unprincipled opportunists willing to destroy the nation to gain their selfish ends.[49]

Although the conflict ended with an armistice that permitted the rebel leaders to go into exile, the high emotional state of the populace in Guayaquil prevented them from leaving. The public outcry to punish the rebels became so great that local officials capitulated: General Montero was tried, found guilty, and sentenced to sixteen years at hard labor—the maximum penalty under Ecuadorian law. This sentence did not pacify the outraged public. A mob attacked and brutally murdered the prisoner in the courtroom. Government officials transferred the remaining rebel leaders to the García Moreno penitentiary in Quito for safekeeping. But the capital proved as insecure as Guayaquil. Mobs burst into the prison and murdered the prisoners, including Eloy Alfaro, with a savagery that eclipsed the Guayaquil episode.[50]

During the following weeks the country lived in a state of high emotionalism and near anarchy. The army was called out to maintain order, but the situation continued to deteriorate as the new presidential elections approached. Liberals were split between supporters of Generals

Plaza and Andrade. Each side believed only its candidate could save the country. In this tense situation, an unknown assailant killed General Andrade allowing Plaza to win the election. Serious insurrections threatened his administration: pro-Alfaro and pro-Andrade dissidents accused Plaza of having plotted the death of their leaders. As a result, during the years from 1912 to 1916, the government was plagued with a series of rural guerrilla uprisings, particularly in the coastal province of Esmeraldas. Hostilities finally ended in 1916 when President Alfredo Baquerizo Moreno (1916–1920) granted a general amnesty to the rebels.[51]

The years following the liberal triumph of 1895 did not witness a change in Ecuador's political culture. Personalism remained a crucial factor. Although there were several important personalist leaders, two men— Alfaro and Plaza—dominated the first thirty years of liberal rule. Unlike Alfaro, Plaza came to believe that personalism and authoritarianism hindered Ecuador's modernization. As the arbiter of national politics between 1912 and 1925, Plaza used his influence to strengthen political institutions and to peacefully transfer presidential power from the incumbent to the victor. Despite the incessant civil strife that marred his second administration, Plaza continued the progressive policies that had characterized his first regime. He implemented reforms while respecting civil liberties, particularly the freedom of the press. This increased his stature among the public. Plaza was also the most prominent survivor of the generation of liberals that came to power in 1895.[52]

Plaza achieved unparalleled political influence in Ecuador for two reasons. First, he possessed strong ties to both the sierra and the coast. The principal economic groups in those regions believed that Plaza would protect their interests. Coastal entrepreneurs supported him because he worked to control political violence. They favored orderly government and the peaceful transfer of power because it was important for the growth and well-being of the coastal export economy. At the same time, Plaza had the backing of sierra landowners. His marriage into a highland family and his ownership of large haciendas reassured wealthy serranos that Plaza would not threaten their interests. The urban professional and middle classes also supported him because his progressive administration provided them with new opportunities for advancement. Plaza managed to bridge the widening gap between the traditional and modern sectors and between urban and rural groups.

The military was the second pillar of Plaza's enduring political power. During his second presidency, he promoted men loyal to him. These officers dominated the Ecuadorian army until 1925. The army played an active and crucial role in liberal politics: it not only preserved order, it "made" elections and assured liberal victories. Plaza's authority, and the respect higher ranking officers had for him, assured the liberal leader power.[53]

Plaza attempted to use his power to promote the institutionalization of national politics. He believed that the country would remain politically immature as long as any individual retained power. He preferred to exercise influence from behind the scenes. Plaza also believed that the office of the president was too powerful, tending to reinforce personalism and authoritarian rule. This was particularly true in a nation like Ecuador with a poorly articulated sense of civic responsibility and weak institutions. Therefore, he supported civilian presidents who would respect the powers and prerogatives congress enjoyed under the constitution of 1906.[54]

From 1916 to 1925, it appeared that Plaza had created an orderly transition of government. Three liberal civilians—Enrique Baquerizo Moreno, José Tamayo, and Gonzalo Córdova—succeeded one another in controlled but peaceful elections. The congress functioned; its powers were not usurped by a powerful president. Civil liberties were generally respected. And a free and active press thrived. There were a few insurrections against the government by conservatives and disgruntled officers, but these movements were easily suppressed. It appeared that Ecuador was becoming politically mature and that its development was ensured.[55]

The liberal development program had two goals. The first sought to remove obstacles to social and economic progress which the attacks on the church had partially accomplished. The second part of the program required positive change. The liberals acceded to power promising that an active state would foster national development. This meant public works to build the social and economic infrastructure the country needed. The state replaced the church as the principal agent providing education, health, and other social services. The emergence of an active state in Ecuador provided a new arena for regionalist struggles. Liberal rhetoric strengthened regionalist tendencies by stimulating local desires for development and prosperity. The growing power of congress, which resulted from the Constitution of 1906 and from Plaza's policies, led to the enactment of extensive pork-barrel legislation. Nationally funded regional public works projects allowed local leaders to please their constituencies as well as deliver the votes for the national government. Liberal progress and prosperity was based on the growth of world demand for cacao, the nation's major export. Unfortunately, cacao was subject to wide fluctuations in demand and price.[56]

The advent of World War I initiated a production and marketing crisis in the cacao industry which in turn threatened the national economy. Because the government depended on export taxes for a major part of its revenues, the decline of cacao exports had important political and economic ramifications. National and local demands for public expenditures increased at a time when the government's revenues declined. Rather than curtail public works projects, liberal governments resorted to extraordinary means of financing their programs. Normally, this meant increasing the money supply through special loans from coastal banks. These policies and the effects of the world economic slump following World War I severely disrupted the economy.[57] (These issues are considered in greater detail in chapter 4.)

The combined effects of unsound liberal fiscal practices and the worsening economic crisis ended the political stability established by Plaza. The cooperation of coastal bankers with liberal governments led to widespread criticism of the banks. They were blamed for the growing inflation and, particularly, for the severe unemployment that culminated in a bloody strike in Guayaquil in 1922. The workers' actions convinced the more conservative serranos that social revolution was near. These events strengthened regionalism. Many highlanders viewed the progress of the coast with suspicion. Since 1895 all liberal presidents had either been costeños or closely identified with Guayaquil interests. The association between coastal banks and the national government convinced many highlanders that the port city dominated national politics. It was widely believed that a "corrupt coastal oligarchy" was exploiting the nation for its own selfish ends. In July 1925 a group of young military officers overthrew the government of Gonzalo Córdova and began what they believed to be a program of national regeneration.[58]

3. Nineteenth-Century Political Economy

The structural conditions that retarded Ecuador's political, social, and economic development—regionalism, isolated and largely self-sufficient highland markets, an extensive subsistence sector, geographic barriers that restricted the flow of goods and ideas, and the absence of political consensus—also disrupted its public finances. These factors, not ideology, have been the primary determinants of Ecuadorian fiscal practices. Since these conditions prevailed throughout the nineteenth century, it is not surprising that similarities existed in the financial problems confronting succeeding administrations and in the solutions advanced to resolve them. The persistence of such obstacles should not lead one to the conclusion that nothing changed in Ecuador's political economy. Government expenditures grew and became more diversified as attitudes toward the role of the state changed. At various stages in this evolutionary process, however, government attempts to balance the budget, collect and administer tax revenues, negotiate foreign loans, and implement other fiscal operations floundered as the result of geographic isolation, regionalism, poverty, and civil strife. In short, even as the system developed and became more complex, underlying physical, economic, political, and social conditions restricted the state's ability to formulate and implement financial policy.

As with other aspects of national life, regionalism affected government finances. The coast provided most of the central government's income. Since 1830, customs, particularly import duties, have been the most important source of ordinary state revenue (see Appendix C). The coast, and its chief city Guayaquil, were the principal source of national income because they produced nearly all the country's exports and received most of its imports. The money economy of the coast, in contrast to the primarily subsistence economy of the highlands, also provided the state with opportunities to impose a variety of direct and indirect taxes.

Thus, although the region contained few people, it yielded a much greater income to the government than the more populous highlands. In addition, coastal entrepreneurs supplied Ecuadorian regimes with most of their emergency funds prior to the founding of the Central Bank in 1927.

In the nineteenth century, governments frequently resorted to extraordinary means to finance their activities because ordinary revenues, including taxes and income from state services and property, did not provide enough funds to cover government expenditures. Until the creation of commercial banks in the 1860s, coastal capitalists contributed either voluntary or forced loans to cover budget deficits. While the government also sought such loans in the highlands, coastal businessmen seemed easy targets for such exactions because they possessed more liquid capital than their sierra counterparts. Wealth in the highlands generally consisted of land with which the national government did not interfere. Between the 1860s and 1925, the coastal banks replaced private individuals as the major source of government loans.

Taxes were the most significant segment of ordinary government income, but for a variety of reasons administrations were unable to formulate or implement an effective system of taxation. The country's poverty and low developmental potential, given contemporary technology, restricted the tax base. At the same time, politics limited the state's ability to tax. As the first two chapters have indicated, there were geographic, social, economic, and political obstacles to the development of a strong national government. Until well into the twentieth century Ecuador was less a nation than a series of loosely articulated regions. Effective taxation requires governmental authority and efficiency, but Ecuadorian regimes were generally weak and inefficient. The instability and civil strife characteristic of the Ecuadorian political system made taxation difficult and, on many occasions, impossible. Even in periods of comparative calm, individual attitudes hampered taxation. Ecuadorians were unwilling to pay taxes and the state did not have the power to enforce general compliance with the law. One of the country's most cherished beliefs has been that it is overtaxed. Without accurate data on the economy, the government could not refute such notions, formulate a rational tax code, or judge the effectiveness of its tax system. Finally, during the nineteenth century Ecuadorian regimes did not possess a trained bureaucracy to administer taxes. Consequently, the country relied on taxes that were easy to collect regardless of their equity, productivity, or economic rationality.

Efforts to increase the productivity of the tax system centered on the relatively simple and generally ineffective procedure of modifying tax laws rather than correcting the structural problems that made taxation difficult. When legislation proved unequal to the task, governments turned to borrowing to obtain necessary funds. Since foreigners would not provide Ecuador with funds because it had defaulted on earlier loans and was unable to resume debt service, internal borrowing offered the only alternative.

Government expenditures increased throughout the nineteenth century as its scope of activity broadened. At independence, the role of the state consisted principally of maintaining internal order and external security. This gradually expanded to include social welfare and economic development. The trend culminated in the multiplication of government functions as it attempted to solve some of the nation's most pressing and complex social and economic problems. The development of the active state, which required an increase in government expenditures, did not go unchallenged, however, nor did it evolve in a systematic fashion. Regionalists, for example, were often more successful in channeling the state's new resources into their own projects than the government was in fashioning a national consensus. The state often failed to achieve national goals if these required transferring resources from one region to another. Nevertheless, national government expenditures increased through time and the role of the state expanded.

The Struggle for Fiscal Control

Throughout the nineteenth century there was a struggle between regionalists and nationalists for the increasingly valuable resource that was the state. The conflict involved yearly confrontations among interest groups each claiming a larger share of the growing national budget as well as an ideological clash between those who sought to centralize fiscal control and those who championed decentralization. Ecuador inherited a decentralized financial system from Spain, which allocated specific revenues to fund individual projects or activities. After independence, regionalists sought to preserve and expand the old system, preferring that special agencies, local autonomous juntas created to fulfill specific functions, collect and disburse most government revenues. Conversely, nationalists sought to extend the power of the state through centralized control of government income. In general congressmen and local officials championed decentralization while the executive branch favored centralization. Each side believed that its system best satisfied the country's needs. Nationalists argued that a centralized system of finances would allow the government to allocate its scarce resources efficiently and thus overcome obstacles to national unity. Regionalists defended a decentralized system because the difficulties of communication and the continuing political instability made a centralized system impractical. They believed that decentralization assured uninterrupted funding for vital local projects and services.

The arguments of the regionalists and the nationalists cloaked more fundamental disagreements regarding national development. Regionalists judged the effectiveness and value of government expenditures according to the immediate impact it had on their areas. They, therefore, favored local projects and services and insisted that the funds be allocated in a way that would make their redirection to other goals impossible. Nationalists preferred an integrated and, in their view, a more rational allocation of national resources. They gave priority to projects that fostered overall national development regardless of their impact on particular regions. To undertake national development programs, the government needed centralized fiscal control that allowed the transfer of resources from one area to another. The conflict between these two views intensified in the second half of the nineteenth century when the growth of the cacao export economy engendered new expectations concerning the role of the national government. Regionalists and nationalists both sought to mold the emerging active state to their own purposes. Neither side achieved a lasting victory in the struggle that encompassed all aspects of government finances, including accounting, taxation, and budgeting.[1]

Ministers of finance attempted to gain control of local treasuries early in the national period. In 1831 the finance minister complained that the new nation was really four different states in terms of government finances: the departments of Quito, Guayaquil, Cuenca, and Cauca—at that time the latter was considered part of Ecuador. Each department was intensely regionalist, defending its own interests through an independent fiscal administration. The system may have worked well for Gran Colombia, when the national capital had been in distant Bogotá, argued the minister, but now it granted too much power to individual departments. Instead, he proposed a national fiscal structure in which the departmental treasuries would act simply as tax collecting offices. Only the national treasury would have the authority to disburse government funds. In the minister's view, unified fiscal control would not only strengthen the national state but it would also weaken and ultimately eliminate uprisings sparked by regionalist interest. In addition, the centralized system would permit the government to standardize bookkeeping procedures and simplify the auditing of state accounts.[2] Congress responded by instituting a centralized system of government finances. As always, it was easier to pass laws than to implement them.

Nineteenth-century ministry of finance reports are filled with complaints against local authorities who refused to comply with the law and with ministry directives. For example, efforts to introduce a single accounting system and to audit provincial treasury offices met with little success. Too few people outside of Guayaquil possessed sufficient accounting skills to implement the new methods. At the same time, many local officials ignored requests to submit their accounts for audit.[3] The drive to standardize accounting received new impetus in the 1850s when the ministry of finance introduced a simplified version of double-entry bookkeeping. Hailed as a notable advance by contemporaries, the system does not appear to have been successful. The first García Moreno administration had to reintroduce the system in the 1860s. In later years, ministers of finance continued to report that local accounts were irregularly kept, that many different methods were being used throughout the country, and that audits of local treasuries were extremely difficult. As a result, the government lacked an accurate picture of national finances. As late as 1897 the liberals found it difficult to implement a reformed accounting procedure because there was a shortage of personnel with adequate knowledge of double-entry bookkeeping in the interior provinces.[4] The struggle to achieve standardization and control of government finances continued well into the twentieth century.

Tax legislation constituted yet another source of conflict between regionalists and nationalists. Regionalist legislators introduced tax laws and altered old ones so that revenue was allocated to specific projects or functions. To prevent the diversion of these monies, they created autonomous juntas to collect and/or administer such funds. These types of laws resulted in a complicated tax system in which many surcharges were added to existing taxes. Tariffs, in particular, were burdened with countless and ultimately ridiculous additional charges despite government attempts to simplify customs procedures by consolidating the numerous surcharges into a single duty. For example, the reformed customs tariff of 1885 replaced many small surcharges with a single 20 percent additional levy, the proceeds to be subdivided among fifty-nine projects and services formerly funded through the additional charges. Such reforms provided only temporary improvement since the congress did not hesitate to create new additional taxes or subdivide the proceeds of existing ones.[5] Consequently, revenue collection and disbursement remained a tedious and complicated process well into the twentieth century.

Special interest tax legislation had negative long-range effects. Additional taxes proliferated because they were the principal source of development capital. Each region was determined to receive its share. For example, the nineteenth-century expansion of the transportation system discussed in chapter 1 was financed through special funding. Education, local water projects, public building programs, and sanitation also were funded in this manner. Inevitably special interest legislation undermined government attempts to gain control of national finances. It stripped the executive branch of authority to regulate tax collection and to allocate government funds. The cost of collecting taxes and administering programs increased as special agencies multiplied. The tendency to divide revenue among a growing number of autonomous agencies reduced the income of many juntas. On occasions some did not even have enough money to cover their administrative costs. In other cases, autonomous bodies had a surplus that they could not spend. The executive was powerless to correct such imbalances because the law prevented the transfer of funds from one agency to another. The problems of accounting and auditing also increased with the proliferation of juntas. Many bodies used their own bookkeeping procedures, ignoring government requests to standardize accounting methods. In some cases, agencies were not legally required to submit their records to the national government. As a result, the state had neither knowledge nor control of a large segment of national income and expenditures.[6]

Regionalists' efforts in congress to use the national government to capture the symbols of progress for their areas also had detrimental effects on national budget formation. As the scope of government activity expanded in the second half of the nineteenth century to meet the growing demands for material progress, legislators often approved expenditures incompatible with realistic projections of ordinary revenues. Rather than limit the number of projects to those the state could actually fund, congress arbitrarily increased official estimates of government income so that, on paper, revenue covered the expenditures they had voted for their districts. Ministers of finance urged unsuccessfully that the legislature adopt realistic projections of government income, based on past collections, so that the budgetary process could become more rational. The government required realistic budgets so that it would not have to seek extraordinary income from loans to pay for necessary ordinary expenses. Few legislators accepted these proposals, particularly during the cacao boom. As a consequence, the state continued to endure large deficits in the last years of the nineteenth century.

Taxation

The Ecuadorian tax system was both inadequate and unjust. Tax revenues never were sufficient to cover current ordinary expenses because Ecuadorians were loath to pay taxes. The nation's most productive levies were indirect taxes, such as customs duties, collected primarily on the coast. The Ecuadorian ruling class would accept only two significant direct taxes: Indian tribute and the tithe, imposts that fell principally on the poor and on the less populous coastal region. Ecuadorian governments tried to improve tax collection while vainly attempting to convince the highland landowners to pay their just share of taxes.

Nineteenth-century Ecuador relied principally on indirect taxes for ordinary government income. Customs duties were the most productive of these taxes (see Appendix C). Nontax income, such as revenue from state services and property, contributed only a small amount to ordinary government income. Direct taxes failed to generate substantial revenue (see Appendix K). This was in sharp contrast to the colonial period when Indian tribute, a direct tax on the native population, constituted the colony's major source of revenue (see table 4). The principal change in the post-independence tax structure was the increase in customs collections. In the late colonial period customs duties were assessed mainly in Spain or some other part of the empire upon export to Ecuador. Only a modest sum was collected upon entry into the Audiencia of Quito.[7]

The coast had benefited from the imperial changes in trade regulations of the late eighteenth century. At independence the region was in the midst of a cacao export boom while the highlands, the most populous area of the country, suffered a protracted depression. Textiles, its principal export industry, could no longer compete with the better and cheaper European cloths. Also its principal market, the mines of Peru, was in decline. As a result, the sierra consumed rather than produced government revenues. The national government, therefore, relied on the coast's growing export economy as the primary source of indirect taxes.[8]

TABLE 4

GOVERNMENT INCOME

Source	1807	1830
Indian Tribute	248,951	201,379
Aguardiente	91,727	39,618
Alcabalas	32,252	69,605
Temporalidades, Novenos, Vacantes Mayores y Menores	71,592	60,138
Tobacco	5,539	9,329
Papel Sellado, Habilitaciones, Timbres Moviles	11,317	15,892
Orden de Carlos III	---	1,000
Customs	81,663	311,500
Total	543,041	708,461

Source: Ecuador, Ministro Secretario de Estado, *Esposición, 1831, Cuadro* 1, 2.

Cacao exports were crucial to the nation's economy and fiscal system. Although cacao producers paid export taxes and *diezmos* (tithes)—the latter partially replaced by a special export charge levied on cacao in the 1890s—these did not provide the government large amounts of revenue. Instead cacao exports contributed to national revenues indirectly. Cacao exports earned the income that permitted Ecuadorians to purchase a relatively high level of imports.[9] When cacao production declined, or when market dislocations occurred, export earnings dropped. As a result, imports had to be reduced and government income fell. Cacao's spectacular performance as an export until the 1920s underwrote government expansion and the emergence of the active state in Ecuador. The cacao boom, however, did not transform the nation from a poor country, dependent on a single tropical export, into a wealthy state. Even during the best years for cacao, import taxes were not sufficient to overcome the obstacles to development that Ecuador faced.

During the nineteenth century Ecuadorian governments relied on tariffs for revenue and only incidentally to promote economic development. Of the twenty tariff laws enacted between 1830 and 1894, none was protectionist. In some instances the codes exempted machinery and goods needed for local industries and public projects from import duties or taxed them at reduced rates. Such exemptions, however, were generally short-lived. Since the country's political instability repeatedly engendered government crises, embattled regimes, faced with urgent needs for increased revenue, reimposed export duties on exempted goods and increased levies on imports.[10]

Nineteenth-century regimes tried various methods of assessing import duties in order to create a system of taxation that would be both productive and easily administered. Every government sought to maintain a duty equivalent to 25 percent of the market value of imported goods. In the nineteenth century, this goal was accomplished by tariffs that listed specific duties for each item imported. The system had two major difficulties. In spite of periodic revisions of the tariff schedules, customs officials could never keep abreast of either the increase in prices of imported goods or the introduction of new products into the country. The *aduana* was constantly embroiled in tedious disputes about the proper classification of imports not listed in the tariff. Consequently, those items on the lists that were charged fixed duties seldom paid the desired 25 percent ad valorem rate. At times, customs levies fell as low as 10 percent of market value before officials could raise the duties to reflect increased prices. In the 1860s when efforts were made to substitute a 25 percent ad valorem tax for the specific duty system, that reform and other efforts to modify the tariff structure failed. Defenders of the existing system argued that the state could retain the tariff's productivity by frequently revising the specific list. They believed that such administrative revisions were easier than attempting to control the fraud that an ad valorem system would invite.

By the 1880s the specific tariffs had become extremely cumbersome. In 1884, for example, legal imports valued at 15,416,163 pesos paid a duty of only 1,668,917 pesos in taxes, 10.8 percent of declared value. The collection of even that modest levy was a tedious operation. Before calculating the tariff, importers and customs officials had to agree on the proper classification of the articles being taxed. A disagreement often resulted in a protracted dispute that had to be resolved in the courts or by higher government officials. Once the authorities agreed on a classification, they had to compute the duty. Some charges were calculated on the basis of weight, others on the basis of the dimensions of the items imported, and still others according to the number of pieces in the shipment. After they established the basic duty, customs officials had to add the myriad additional charges levied to fund special projects or agencies. This often required a dozen separate calculations before arriving at the duty for an import, each step providing ample room for disagreement between the customs service and the importer.

The 1880s campaign to reform the aduana sought to simplify administration while increasing tariff productivity. The reformers concentrated on two issues: the establishment of a uniform general duty and the elimination of the numerous additional charges. Several ministers of finance proposed a single duty based on the gross weight of the imports, a system being used successfully in Colombia, Venezuela, Costa Rica, and Nicaragua. The reformers claimed that Mexico and Chile had decided to shift from an ad valorem duty to one based on gross weight owing to the difficulty in controlling fraud. They maintained it would be easier to administer this duty than a uniform ad valorem tax because the customs service was not required to establish the true value of imports, a difficult task since merchants could prepare false invoices.[11]

The government finally promulgated a new customs code based on weight in 1885. The new legislation, however, did not establish a uniform duty. Instead the code divided imports into nine classes each taxable at different rates. The old additional charges were consolidated into a single 20 percent levy. The national treasury received the basic duty; the proceeds from the additional charge were distributed among the projects and autonomous agencies authorized by congress to receive them. The new tax system temporarily increased customs revenue. By 1896, however, collections had declined to 21.69 percent of the declared value of legal imports. The minister of finance complained that Ecuador's revenues fell at a time when other nations had collected duties as high as 38 percent ad valorem. Furthermore, the 20 percent additional charge proved insufficient to fund the autonomous agencies. Congress, therefore, imposed additional new charges. By the turn of the century the new customs system had become as complex, as cumbersome, and as inefficient as the one it had replaced.[12]

In contrast to indirect customs duties, direct taxes diminished in importance during the nineteenth century. Only two direct levies, the Indian tribute and the tithe—a 10 percent tax on gross agricultural production—were significant. Although these taxes had been the major sources of revenue in the colonial period, they declined relative to other levies after independence. Critics of these taxes argued that they were inequitable and a hindrance to national development. Nevertheless, Indian tribute persisted until 1857 and the government did not abolish the diezmos until 1889. Many middle- and upper-class urban Ecuadorians refused to pay direct taxes, but were quite willing to countenance levies that fell on the indigenous population. The Indians not only had to pay tribute, but in the sierra they also contributed a disproportionate share of the diezmos. The heavy tax burden on this segment of the population was directly related to its powerlessness in Ecuadorian society.

Indian tribute, the nation's most productive direct tax, was collected only in the highlands. The levy had not been collected on the coast since 1820.[13] During the first decade of national life Indian tribute provided between one-third and one-fifth of total ordinary government income. Its importance declined in the following years and it was ultimately abolished in 1857 (see table 5).

The campaign to abolish Indian tribute and the counterstruggle to retain the tax constituted one aspect of the regionalist conflicts that divided the nation in the nineteenth century. Local conditions and social values molded the conflicting attitudes of the coast and the highlands toward Indian tribute. Costeños opposing the tax argued that coastal Indians freed of this onerous burden produced more than their sierra counterparts. Abolition of the tribute, they claimed, would stimulate highland production and integrate the natives into the market economy. Their arguments failed to consider two important issues. Only a few Indians lived on the coast, and the region's population was more integrated economically because there was a shortage of labor and because the coast was the center of the export economy. These conditions did not exist in the highlands. Sierra politicians and landowners argued that the tax was necessary because the Indians were lazy and would not work unless forced to pay tribute. They also warned that the state could not afford to lose such an important

TABLE 5

INDIAN TRIBUTE 1830–1857

Year	Amount in pesos	% of Ordinary government revenue
1830	201,379	28.4
1831	205,652	26.4
1832	197,000	35.6
1839	176,845	20.3
1847	168,188	15.2
1855	150,558	15.2
1856	156,995	14.9
1857	147,289	12.6

Sources: Calculated from data in Ecuador, Ministro Secretario de Estado, *Esposición, 1831;* Ecuador, Ministro de Hacienda, *Memoria, 1833;* Ecuador, Ministro de Hacienda, *Esposición, 1847, 1855, 1857, 1858.*

source of revenue. Serrano congressmen managed to stymie the attempts of several governments to abolish the Indian tribute. It required the combined efforts of the Urvina (1851–1856) and the Robles administrations to abolish tribute in 1857.[14] These presidents accomplished their goals because both were military men with strong ties to the coast. Highland dissatisfaction over the abolition of tribute constituted an important component in the overthrow of the Robles government and the subsequent rise to power of García Moreno and the conservatives.

As predicted, tax revenues declined dramatically in the highland provinces after the Indian tribute was abolished. In 1858 the minister of hacienda noted that interior provincial treasuries could no longer meet their obligations. To remedy the situation the government had to transfer funds collected by the Guayaquil customs to the treasuries of Pichincha, Cuenca, and Loja (see table 6). Since the administration viewed the transfer of revenues from Guayaquil to the interior provinces as an unpalatable but necessary solution, it urged congress to provide the sierra provinces with their own permanent sources of funding.[15] The dilemma of raising taxes in a heavily populated but economically backward region continued to frustrate generations of government officials. As long as highland industry and agriculture remained stagnant and as long as the area continued to be isolated from the coast, the sierra would have to rely upon tax transfers from the coast to pay for needed services. This situation convinced costeños that their area was being exploited in order to support

TABLE 6

EFFECTS OF THE ABOLITION OF INDIAN TRIBUTE 1857

Province	Income	Expenditure[1]	Deficit[2]	Surplus
Pichincha	3,499	12,588	9,089	
Imbabura	1,857	1,721		136
León	1,636	1,232		404
Chimborazo	1,949	1,259		690
Cuenca	1,436	3,289	1,862	
Loja	573	681	108	
Total	10,950	20,779	11,059	1,300

Source: Ecuador, Ministro de Hacienda, *Esposición, 1858*, p. 5.

[1]Only figures for Quito include expenses for the military.

[2]These deficits would have been larger, and more provinces would have had deficits, were it not for the fact that some late collections of Indian tribute were included in the 1857 accounts.

an unproductive interior. Their complaint became part of the regionalist rhetoric and remained a source of conflict well into the twentieth century.

The tithe was the other important direct tax of the nineteenth century (see table 7). The diezmos replaced a colonial levy called the *novenos*. Income from the tithe was divided between the church and the state. Until 1867 two-thirds of the amount collected went to the church and one-third to the government. Subsequently, as a result of amendments to the Concordat of 1862 negotiated by Antonio Flores Jijón, the government's share increased to half. The Vatican also ceded to the Ecuadorian government a special tithe donation for 1863 to 1866 that temporarily raised the state's share to two-thirds. From 1872 the government received 60 percent of the diezmos. In all these arrangements the state agreed that the church would have priority and the government would return part of these funds when the church's share could not meet its needs.[16]

Since the state did not possess the bureaucracy to administer the tithes, it relied on tax farmers to collect the levy. The system was inefficient and riddled with numerous abuses. The government only received a small portion of the amount actually collected while tax farmers frequently stole from the Indians and small rural proprietors. The government repeatedly warned the collectors to assess only 10 percent of agricultural production and to refrain from taking chickens, *cuyes*, and other products that could not be divided into tenths. But ministers of finance charged that tax farmers ignored their regulations and that these abuses damaged agriculture.[17] The tax proved especially onerous for the Indians of the sierra who were forced to relinquish goods the value of which often exceeded the total yearly profit from their small parcels of land. Since diezmos were calculated on the basis of gross rather than net agricultural production, in good years landowners might pay as much as 20 to 30 percent of their income. In bad years, tithe obligations could force small agriculturalists from the land. Given the socioeconomic structure of nineteenth-century Ecuador, the Indians were particularly vulnerable to exploitation by tax gatherers. On occasion these exactions resulted in bloody clashes between native communities and the tithe collectors. In other instances the overburdened Indians abandoned their lands and fled to the coast to escape taxation.

The tithe yielded more revenue in the highlands than in the coast in the first half of the nineteenth century. Until 1850 the largest amount produced by the diezmos in the diocese of Guayaquil amounted to 34,761 pesos, but after mid-century the situation changed dramatically. In 1854

TABLE 7

GOVERNMENT REVENUE FROM THE TITHE 1830–1889

Year	Absolute amount[1]	% Ordinary government revenue
1830	60,138[a]	8.5
1832	37,820	6.9
1846	37,634	3.4
1854	57,075	5.6
1855	43,107	4.1
1857	81,334	6.3
1861	117,723	8.1
1862	92,537	8.2
1863	200,518[b]	14.9
1864	152,881[b]	10.6
1865	431,089[b]	27.2
1866	66,109[b]	4.8
1867	326,279	20.2
1868	36,166	2.5
1869	100,712	6.1
1870	118,666	5.3
1871	181,632	7.3
1872	228,478	7.8
1873	296,882	9.6
1874	347,039	11.2
1875	141,007	4.9
1876	367,496	15.4
1877	224,497	10.4
1878	266,269	10.8
1882	187,132	8.5
1884	308,223	9.7
1885	390,008[c]	15.5
1886	448,378	14.1
1887	451,656	10.1
1888	392,150	9.7
1889	363,754	11.7

Sources: Calculated from data in Ecuador, Ministro Secretario de Estado, *Esposición 1831;* Ecuador, Ministerio de Hacienda, *Informe 1833, 1847, 1855, 1857, 1858, 1863, 1867, 1880, 1885, 1887, 1888, 1890; El Nacional* (Quito), no. 327 (1868).

[1]Pesos through 1884 and sucres thereafter.

[a]Estimate by minister of state in 1831.

[b]Government income from the diezmos for these years was increased by a special donation from the Church required by the amendments to the Concordat of September 26, 1862.

[c]Estimated government revenue. Total diezmos collections for 1885 were 686,663.

the Guayaquil tithe produced 43,842 pesos and by 1857, it had increased to 127,589 pesos while the Quito and Cuenca tithes only yielded 88,226 and 28,188 pesos respectively. Since the 1857 diezmos for the entire country had amounted to 244,004 pesos, Guayaquil alone contributed more than half. Thereafter, tithe collections increased slowly in the highlands but rose dramatically in the coast as a result of the cacao boom. Since this coincided with the abolition of Indian tribute, which constituted the sierra's major tax, the coast's role as the principal source of government revenue became even more pronounced. In an attempt to increase its income, the government took direct control of tithe collection on the coast in 1869. Tax farmers, however, continued to collect the diezmos in the highlands until the levy's abolition in 1889. After 1869, the state benefited directly from the coast's economic expansion because through the tithe it collected a substantial portion of the nation's major export crop, which it sold abroad. Loans from the Banco del Ecuador financed the marketing of the government's cacao exports.[18]

Many Ecuadorians criticized the tithe as a regressive tax that harmed agriculture. But its importance as a source of revenue and the absence of an alternative impost in the sierra hamstrung its opponents. On various occasions, reformers had suggested that the government replace the diezmos with income and property taxes, but no one seriously accepted such alternatives. In addition, the church opposed its abolition until it could acquire a new method of financing its activities. Finally, in the 1880s economic self-interest induced the conservative, proclerical sierra landowners to join their liberal, anticlerical coastal counterparts to suppress the tithe. On November 16, 1889, the Ecuadorian government reached an agreement with the Vatican that abolished the diezmos and provided church support through a three sucre per thousand valuation tax on rural property.[19] As in the case of the Indian tribute, the abolition of the tithe reduced government income, forcing the state to cover deficits with bank loans and additional taxes on cacao. The suppression of the diezmos did not end the abuses associated with that levy in the sierra. The collectors of the new tax still exploited the poor who carried a disproportionate share of the new tax burden. Those who could not pay had their goods confiscated and sold.

The low yields from the new direct tax on rural property demonstrated the unwillingness of large highland landowners to pay taxes. They used their influence to avoid payment or greatly undervalued their holdings and therefore their tax liability. The government could not overcome entrenched local interests. Attitudes toward taxation had not changed since the 1850s when the state failed in its attempt to replace Indian tribute with a direct tax on rural property. Since wealthy Ecuadorians rejected the principle of progressive taxation, the colonial practice of shifting the cost of government to those least able to pay continued until the twentieth century.[20]

Tax administration has presented serious problems to the Ecuadorian state. During the nineteenth and early twentieth century, virtually every minister of finance complained that existing regulations were inadequate and that tax collection would improve if proper legislation were enacted. Nearly every administration modified the tax laws convinced that its predecessors had failed. In spite of many changes, tax yields remained low and governments could barely finance even basic services. The history of *aguardiente* (the local alcoholic beverage made from sugar cane) taxation is an excellent example of the problems.

Ecuadorian officials were torn between their desire to limit the use of aguardiente and their need to tax the product. Most administrators deplored the widespread consumption of aguardiente, which they viewed as a vice afflicting the lower classes and crippling them as workers. Yet they could not abolish the tax because they considered it a potentially lucrative source of income. Indeed, government officials sought ways to increase revenue from liquor taxes. They justified their actions by allocating aguardiente income to worthy enterprises, such as the manumission of slaves, *lazaretos* (hospitals for contagious diseases), schools, and public welfare projects.

The Flores government established the pattern of seeking ways to maximize aguardiente revenue. In September 1830 it abolished the existing state liquor monopoly, substituting licensing requirements for producers. The law made no provision for adequate enforcement and the country's rugged topography made it easy for unlicensed distilleries to flourish. Not unexpectedly, the system proved unworkable. By June 1831 the Flores government admitted defeat and abolished the system. It subsequently introduced a sugarcane tax. The levy, collected at the local level, was based on the amount of land under cultivation. To encourage effective administration, the law authorized cantonal authorities to collect the tax and to retain 5 percent of the revenues. The new method floundered when property owners refused to register their lands. Since cantonal officials had social and economic ties with local landowners, they could not enforce the law. Congress suspended the regulation in November 1831. Thereafter, known distillers, importers, and distributors of alcohol were assigned a monthly fee ranging from one to six pesos, depending on the size of their operation and local circumstances. The new arrangement, however, did not generate much income. In 1835, only five years after its abolition, the Rocafuerte government reinstated the *estanco* (state monopoly) of sugar production in the highlands, while retaining a modified fee system on the coast. But the estanco also failed and was again abolished in 1837. Thereafter, the government returned to a policy of regulating the production and sale of aguardiente.[21]

In the following decades governments tried, discarded, and later reinstated a variety of approaches in their search for the best method of extracting aguardiente revenues. Congress enacted fourteen laws restructuring liquor taxes between 1830 and 1893. All were ultimately judged inadequate. Succeeding finance ministers called for changes in the laws regulating alcohol in the vain hope that they could end fraud and contraband while increasing government income. Most administrators believed that if they could discover a way of taxing the aguardiente actually produced and consumed in Ecuador, they could raise income second only to customs.[22] Consequently, many governments devoted an inordinate amount of time and effort attempting to increase a source of revenue that rarely produced as much as 5 percent of state income (see table 8).

Even perfect laws could not have ensured the efficient collection of aguardiente levies. The problem lay in public attitudes toward taxation and in the inability of public officials to implement tax laws. The government simply did not have the personnel to enforce tax laws and collect revenues. Inadequately trained and poorly paid, such employees found it more rewarding to accede to the wishes of those whom they regulated than to obey government instructions. In addition, because of local influence aguardiente officials were often relatives and friends of the clandestine distillers. Family ties and patron-client relationships made it unlikely that influential persons would be punished or large scale illicit production ended. Instead enforcement was likely to be directed toward the smaller producer and the petty offender. But even in those cases in which officials were intent on enforcing the law, they were hindered by a shortage of personnel to regulate production and collect taxes in the isolated regions. Even under ideal conditions government regulations were likely to be enforced only near the major cities and along the main roads.

To surmount these difficulties, many administrations farmed out the aguardiente tax since experience indicated that tax farmers were more efficient. When the national government attempted to collect taxes, revenue declined substantially. Tax farming, however, also suffered from defects. Since the state lacked data on the production and consumption

TABLE 8

GOVERNMENT REVENUE FROM AGUARDIENTE 1830–1924

Year	Absolute amount[1]	% Ordinary government revenue
1830	39,618	5.6
1832	15,400	2.8
1836	27,150	3.6
1837	37,942	4.9
1838	30,370	3.8
1839	27,841	3.4
1846	44,007	4.0
1852	14,483	1.8
1853	50,170	4.8
1854	31,468	3.1
1855	40,170	4.8
1856	51,636	4.9
1857	56,127	4.4
1861	52,517	3.7
1862	72,036	6.4
1863	56,291	4.1
1864	62,744	4.4
1865	69,258	4.3
1866	71,440	5.2
1867	71,400	4.4
1868	66,493	4.6
1869	90,687	5.5
1870	100,404	4.4
1871	100,844	4.1
1872	112,074	3.9
1873	118,410	3.8
1874	122,632	4.0
1875	121,408	4.2
1876	134,627	5.7
1877	97,667	4.5
1878	122,436	5.0
1879	124,165	4.1
1882	83,425	3.8
1884	180,633	5.7
1885	149,558	5.9

TABLE 8 (Continued)

GOVERNMENT REVENUE FROM AGUARDIENTE 1830–1924

Year	Absolute amount[1]	% Ordinary government revenue
1886	154,198	4.8
1887	146,234	3.3
1888	112,794	2.8
1889	112,714	3.6
1890	132,643	3.2
1891	171,827	4.8
1892	185,834	4.9
1893	176,679	4.1
1895	75,430	---[a]
1896	267,822	---[a]
1897	322,106	4.7
1898	330,205	4.2
1899	337,553	4.4
1900	379,826	4.7
1901	339,093	3.2
1902	356,786	3.8
1903	343,758	3.4
1904	355,861	4.2
1905	254,161	2.2
1906	541,525	4.2
1907	384,678	3.1
1908	586,900	4.6
1909	832,361	5.2
1910	721,323	5.4
1911	752,404	5.6
1912	797,847	4.0
1913	962,265	4.8
1914	1,023,099	6.0
1915	928,297	6.2
1916	1,048,251	6.5
1917	1,035,865	6.3
1918	1,260,761	9.1
1919	1,020,461	6.7
1920	976,480	5.7
1921	743,401	4.7

TABLE 8 (Continued)

GOVERNMENT REVENUE FROM AGUARDIENTE 1830–1924

Year	Absolute amount[1]	% Ordinary government revenue
1922	953,563	5.1
1923	1,511,240	8.2
1924	1,485,824	7.0

Sources: Calculated from data in Ecuador, Ministerio de Hacienda, *Informe, 1833, 1847, 1855, 1857, 1858, 1863, 1867, 1880, 1885, 1887, 1888, 1890, 1892, 1894, 1898, 1901, 1902, 1904, 1906, 1912, 1913, 1915, 1916, 1917, 1919,* and *1921*; Ecuador, Ministerio de Hacienda, *Boletín de estadística fiscal y comercial* III (1912); VII (1917); *El Nacional* (Quito), no. 327 (1868); Ecuador, Ministerio Secretario de Estado, *Exposición 1831*; Ecuador, Ministerio de Hacienda, *Libro de balances,* 1919–1920, *1922–1925*; Ecuador, Ministerio de Hacienda, *Balance general y sus anexos,* 1920.

[1]Pesos through 1884 and sucres thereafter.

[a]Incomplete income data for this year makes it impossible to compute the percentage.

of aguardiente, it could not establish a minimum bid based on a realistic estimate of the tax yield. Instead it had to accept the highest bid tendered. Thus the government acted without knowing the amount of profit made by the tax farmers, which posed a serious problem in outlying areas. Tax farmers also had the power to prevent the government from regulating them or from creating competition. Many tax farmers, who engaged in large-scale purchase and distribution of aguardiente, would buy and store large quantities of alcohol. If the state attempted either to collect liquor taxes directly or to auction the contract to someone else, the outgoing tax farmer would dump his stock of aguardiente on the market. This sale not only glutted the market but, since the liquor had already been taxed, it cut deeply into the profit of the new tax farmer and into government income. Thus a few individuals monopolized the bidding for the aguardiente tax and the state could seldom succeed in challenging their privileged position.[23]

Experimentation with approaches to increase the effectiveness of taxation was not limited to one item. Legislators continuously modified tax laws in an effort to augment government income. As in the case of aguardiente, these efforts failed because they did not address the real obstacles. Legislation could not change public attitudes toward taxation, and the congress never created the adequate, well-paid, and well-trained bureaucracy necessary to impose taxes on an unwilling population.

The Foreign Debt

Many nineteenth-century Latin American governments turned to foreign loans as a way of meeting extraordinary expenditures, particularly in the early independence period. But Ecuador could not negotiate loans because it had not paid its share of the sums contracted by Gran Colombia during the war of independence.[24] In 1838 Ecuador assumed 21.5 percent of the debt, £1,424,579 (7,122,896 pesos).[25] It paid nothing during the next decade because internal conflicts consumed both the attention and the funds of Ecuadorian governments. By 1848 the foreign debt had grown to 17,210,475 pesos, including principal and unpaid interest.[26]

The Ecuadorian government began renegotiations with the representatives of the English bondholders of the Gran Colombian debt in 1850. After four years of difficult bargaining, the parties reached an understanding for debt repayment. Ecuador agreed to issue £1,824,000 (9,120,000 pesos) in new bonds in September 1855 to refund the original debt and £399,421 (1,997,105 pesos) of back interest. These *bonos ecuatorianos de la deuda extrangera consolidada* earned an annual interest of 1 percent as long as the Guayaquil customs revenues remained below 400,000 pesos a year. Thereafter, the rate of interest would rise incrementally with collections until it reached a maximum of 6 percent. The government pledged one-quarter of the Guayaquil customs income to pay the capital and interest. The new bonds did not refund all the unpaid interest that had accrued to the original debt. Ecuador canceled a portion of the interest when it relinquished some Peruvian securities it held to the British bondholders. The remaining debt was to be amortized by ceding large tracts of land in Esmeraldas and in the Oriente to the creditors. This portion of the debt did not bear interest and was covered by a special bond issue, *bonos ecuatorianos provisionales,* in the amount of £996,646 ½ (4,983,232 ½ pesos). The bondholders had twenty-one years from the date the agreement went into effect to exercise their option on the land. If they failed to do so, the bonds were automatically canceled.[27]

The 1854 agreement, like all subsequent arrangements between Ecuador and her foreign creditors, became the target of severe and increasingly bitter criticism. From the moment debt agreements were ratified, they came under attack from domestic critics of the government who believed that the terms were too onerous. Ecuador's neighbors, Colombia and Peru, also objected to the treaty because they claimed title to some of the lands ceded to the bondholders.[28] These protracted and vociferous attacks on the debt agreement provided a rationale for subsequent default.

Between 1855 and 1891, Ecuador made only a few payments under the 1854 settlement. Initially, it suspended debt payments during periods of internal upheaval and foreign invasion, as in 1859–1860, 1863, and 1864. García Moreno tried unsuccessfully to renegotiate the debt during his two administrations (1861–1865 and 1869–1875) in hopes of securing a new loan to build a railroad from Guayaquil to Quito and to liquidate the government's debt to local banks. In 1869 he ordered a suspension of payments until a new agreement was ratified. Ecuador's representatives could not renegotiate the old debt or obtain a new loan because neither congress nor the public had realistic expectations. They refused to take into account their country's history of political instability, its poor credit rating, and its limited potential for short- or medium-term development. Instead, they insisted on gaining terms similar to those obtained by the larger and more stable European nations. For example, Ecuadorians proposed a fifty-year loan at 6 percent interest with only a 14 percent discount to be guaranteed by 25 percent of the country's customs revenues. The terms were unacceptable to foreign financiers, and Ecuador remained in default. Besieged with internal difficulties, most governments simply ignored the foreign debt. Although the creditors formed the Ecuador Land Company Ltd., their efforts to implement the agreement to transfer lands to the foreign bondholders failed.[29]

In 1888 President Antonio Flores Jijón gave priority to restoring the nation's foreign credit because Ecuador required foreign capital to develop a modern transportation system. Obviously, it could not obtain the capital as long as the debt was in default. After two years of negotiations, congress approved a new accord in 1890. Ecuador agreed to issue £750,000 (3,750,000 sucres) in new bonds to replace the £1,824,000 (9,120,000 sucres) of the 1854 consolidated bonds and the £442,560 (2,112,800 sucres) of unpaid interest that had accrued in the twenty-three years the government had been in default. Since only £1,753,500 worth of old bonds were presented for conversion by the bondholders, Ecuador issued new bonds worth only £713,900 (3,569,500 sucres) bearing an interest of 4.5 percent for the first five years and 5 percent thereafter. An additional 10 percent tax on imports secured amortization of the debt. In the event the new tax did not produce sufficient revenue to pay the debt, the government agreed to cover the difference from other income.

Although the new accord benefited Ecuador, some of the public and some government officials argued that the administration had acknowledged too much of the original debt, that the repayment schedule was too long, and the interest too high. The critics failed to consider that the new agreement refunded the debt at approximately 40 percent of its original value and completely canceled the unpaid back interest. Nevertheless, the critics succeeded. In 1894 after making only three semiannual payments, congress suspended debt payments pending a resolution of the world monetary crisis and a revision of the 1890 agreement. The Cordero administration managed to obtain a new and more beneficial accord that went into effect in March 1895. The new arrangement proved as transitory as its predecessors. When the liberals came to power they halted foreign debt payments in March 1896 on the grounds that the 1895 revision did not serve the national interest.[30] The old problem of the foreign debt remained unresolved.

The Internal Debt

Unable to cover its expenses through taxation or to negotiate new foreign loans, Ecuador relied on internal borrowing to meet its perennial budget deficits. In 1836 Vicente Rocafuerte described the public treasury as exhausted by war, the lack of exports, and the underdeveloped state of agriculture. This situation remained true for the rest of the century. Although government resources increased, particularly after mid-century, as a result of the expanding world demand for tropical agricultural products, they could not defray state obligations that also had expanded. The effects of political instability on government finances were heightened in 1852 when congress enacted a law making the state responsible for damage to private property resulting from foreign invasion, insurrections, and other violent political acts. Thereafter, individual claims for these losses added substantially to the internal debt.[31]

Nineteenth-century public financial records were chaotic, resulting in losses to both individuals and the government. Creditors or their heirs often were unable to establish the validity of their claims. The disorder, however, favored unscrupulous persons who successfully pressed fraudulent claims or who collected several times for the same debt. Numerous ministers of finance tried valiantly to impose control over the records of the internal debt, but they enjoyed limited success. Ecuador possessed neither the financial resources nor the trained personnel to set its financial house in order. Thus it is impossible to determine the exact size of the nation's internal debt at independence. During the first Flores administration (1830–1834), official estimates of the internal debt ranged from 500,000 to 800,000 pesos. Despite determined efforts to reduce the internal debt, by 1864 it had increased to an estimated 3,903,201 pesos. Although the debt continued to grow throughout the rest of the century, the government's expanded revenues from cacao reduced the debt's rate of growth so that it only increased to 5,528,929 sucres by 1891 (see table 9).[32]

The internal debt consisted of a variety of obligations. The debts inherited from Gran Colombia constituted the most significant item at independence. This obligation consisted of Gran Colombian bonds issued in 1827 which Ecuador assumed when it became independent. Although the new government only slowly amortized this debt, its importance diminished rapidly as other obligations grew. Unpaid salaries, pensions, and retirement benefits, forced and voluntary loans, interest, and the value of requisitioned goods and services quickly supplanted the Gran Colombian bonds as the most significant items in the internal debt. In the second half of the nineteenth century, loans from local banks further contributed to the mounting internal debt.[33]

Unpaid civil and military salaries became a particularly troublesome form of public indebtedness. The government failed to recruit capable civil servants because salaries were inadequate and frequently in arrears. Those who entered the bureaucracy became so concerned with collecting their pay that the government was nearly paralyzed. High officials in the ministry of finance had to devote such an inordinate amount of time considering requests for back salaries that their other duties suffered. The situation produced other problems since unpaid civil servants often had no choice but to turn to corruption to survive. Clearly an unpaid army posed the greatest threat to the government and public order. Destitute soldiers resorted to rioting and looting while their officers plotted revolution. In spite of these dangers, most nineteenth-century governments periodically suspended the army's salary.

The state tried to cope with the problem of salaries in a variety of ways. In the short run, it resorted to paying its employees with bills of credit that could be used to pay taxes or exchanged for public lands in the disputed Oriente. The practice began in 1830 when the government issued 100,000 pesos in bills of credit and continued for the rest of the century. Few civil servants were either in a position to use the bills for such purposes or wait for their eventual redemption. Since they had to sell the bills to survive, their value depreciated rapidly. Importers purchased them at huge discounts and used them to pay custom duties, thereby reducing government income. In periods of financial crisis the state, desperate for hard currency, either refused to accept the bills or only accepted them as partial payment for taxes, further depressing their

TABLE 9
INTERNAL PUBLIC DEBT 1831–1891

Year	Absolute amount
1831	800,000[a]
1865	3,903,201[a]
1877	4,432,995
1888	4,981,985
1889	5,424,398
1891	5,528,929

Sources: Calculated from data in Ecuador, Ministro de Estado, *Esposición, 1831*, p. 16; Ecuador, Ministro de Hacienda, *Esposición, 1865*, p. 12–13; Ecuador, Ministro de Hacienda, *Memoria, 1880*, p. 26; Ecuador, Ministro de Hacienda, *Informe, 1890, Cuadro R*; Ecuador, Ministro de Hacienda, *Informe, 1892, Cuadro P*.
[a]Estimate.

value. The state's only long run solution was to amortize the debt. Although most budgets included allocations for back pay, the funds proved generally insufficient to cancel the debt or were diverted to defray other costs. It was not unusual for internal debt payments to be decades in arrears. For example, on August 15, 1855 the president of the Dirección Jeneral del Crédito Público announced with great pleasure that the administration had amortized a substantial portion of the internal debt incurred before March 6, 1845. But more than 500,000 pesos in government obligations, incurred between March 1845 and August 1855, when the report was written, remained outstanding and were not paid for another decade. As late as the 1890s, budgets included provisions for funding back pay.[34]

During the first three decades of national life, loans from individuals constituted the major source of extraordinary government revenue. In periods of internal disorder these loans often became the only source of government income because rebel activity prevented the administration from collecting taxes.[35] Yet despite their importance, most Ecuadorians considered the extraordinary loans harmful to the state. Ecuador's first two presidents, Juan José Flores and Vicente Rocafuerte, severely criticized the cost of borrowing from private individuals. During those turbulent years, coastal businessmen demanded interest rates of up to 3 percent per month on short-term loans to the government. These rates were not excessive when weighed against the risk assumed by the lenders. Although a few individuals made considerable fortunes loaning money to the state, others, such as Miguel Anzoátegui who helped finance the independence movement and who also guaranteed the loan for the 1832 war against

Colombia, died paupers. Governments generally repaid their creditors very slowly. But in addition, after a change of government, the new rulers often forced creditors to renegotiate the terms of their agreements, particularly if they had been political adversaries. The claims of such unfortunate individuals were usually reduced sharply and sometimes disallowed altogether. Thus, in view of those circumstances, high rates of interest were justified. The official literature on government finances in the early national period of Latin America is filled with references to *agiotistas* (loan sharks) who bled governments dry with their high rates of interest. Generally delivered by heads of state or ministers of finance, these condemnations failed to note that governments had abysmal credit records and that the lenders provided regimes funds when no other source of revenue existed.[36]

Banks and Politics

Given the chronic insolvency of the state and its limited ability to increase ordinary revenue or to obtain foreign loans, it was natural that the government would use its power to approve bank charters as a means of securing new funds. The enabling legislation of the early banks linked approval of their charters to the granting of loans and other services to the government. In the 1830s and 1840s several administrations attempted unsuccessfully to promote the establishment of a bank in Guayaquil. While they sought to enhance the nation's economic development, they also wished to create an institution that would refinance the internal debt and lend to the government at 9 percent a year. These efforts failed until the 1860s when the expanding coastal export economy had grown sufficiently to support new financial structures. Although governments continued to incur debts to individuals by their failure to meet payrolls or live up to their obligations, after the 1860s they turned increasingly to Guayaquil banks to help them cover budget deficits.[37]

A relationship of mutual dependency existed between the Ecuadorian government and the banks. The banks supplied funds to the government and the state set the limits of banking activity. Banking was as much a political as an economic enterprise in Ecuador. Credit expansion or contraction generally depended more on the demands of the government for loans than on the economic conditions of the country or the lending institutions.

Gabriel García Moreno, for example, demanded that the Banco Luzarraga, established in Guayaquil in 1860, lend his administration 100,000 pesos in return for the right to emit 500,000 pesos in bills. The state agreed to accept the paper as legal tender in all public transactions, including the payment of customs duties.[38] Similar agreements preceded the founding of two other Guayaquil banks: El Banco Particular and El Banco del Ecuador. Between 1860 and 1861 the García Moreno administration borrowed 500,000 pesos from the banks to defend itself from its enemies. Since the political conflict lasted for some time, the government could not meet its debts, forcing the banks to renegotiate the payment schedule. In 1863 and 1864 the regime borrowed an additional 800,000 pesos to cover budget deficits and to repay the earlier debt. Thereafter, repayment of bank loans became an important part of the national budget.[39] The payment of bank loans generally was given priority over other government obligations because the state needed further loans to continue functioning. But banks, like earlier individual lenders, had no guarantee of government loyalty or support. During the nineteenth century several Guayaquil banks floundered when the state, which had once depended on them, abandoned the institutions.[40]

Ecuadorian governments did not always negotiate loans with banks; on a few occasions they simply seized the funds. In 1867 García Moreno compelled the Banco Particular to relinquish 3,902 pesos deposited by the municipality of Guayaquil. This practice reached an extreme in 1882 to 1883, during the struggle against the Veintimilla government. At that time Guayaquil remained under President Veintimilla's control while Quito was in the hands of a coalition of liberals and conservatives who called themselves the provisional government. The highland coalition financed its campaign in two ways. First it seized 174,000 pesos from Veintimilla's personal account at the Banco de la Unión in Quito claiming that he had probably stolen the funds from the national treasury. Then the provisional government forced the Banco de la Unión and the Banco de Quito to lend it 130,000 pesos and 125,000 pesos respectively. Veintimilla responded by claiming that the Banco de la Unión had transferred the money to the Banco del Ecuador in Guayaquil where it had an account with a balance of 115,000 pesos. The Guayaquil bank refused to relinquish the money without authorization from the bank in Quito. Thereupon General Veintimilla sent his soldiers to collect a 200,000 peso loan. He was considering "borrowing" additional funds from the Banco de Crédito Hipotecario when his opponents overthrew him in mid-1883.[41]

Governments generally used more subtle coercion to secure bank loans. For example, the state had the right to accept or reject a given bank's bills at government offices. Those institutions whose bills the tax office would accept succeeded; those denied acceptance faced disaster. The government-granted charters limited the banks' right to issue currency. Thus banks naturally curried government favor to obtain the right to issue more money. On November 7, 1871, the administration introduced a uniform banking law that, among other things, required that a bank retain a reserve of gold and silver equal to one-third the amount of bills the institution had issued. The law also provided for government regulation through periodic inspection of bank records. Although the legislation was revised in 1878 and again in 1886, the reserve requirement and the provision for government inspection were not altered. The state used its regulatory power selectively to foster its own interests. Banks that supported the government received preferential treatment. In some cases bank inspectors interpreted "bills in circulation" to mean only the currency actually in the hands of the public, whereas in others they also included bills deposited in the bank vaults. This was important because nineteenth-century banks often printed more bills than allowed by law. Government reaction ranged from demanding an immediate recall of all improperly backed bills, whether or not the bank was in a position to increase its metallic reserve, to ignoring the over-issues, giving the institution unlimited time to withdraw unbacked paper from circulation, or to increase its reserves. The government's response to such over-issues varied according to the bank's relationship with the regime.[42]

The government deliberately used a flexible banking policy to enhance or erode the position of individual banks. Financial institutions, therefore, found it expedient to cooperate fully with the state and to extend loans that were an integral part of government fiscal policy. The high price of failing to meet an administration's demands and the rewards of compliance were apparent by 1870. It also had become clear that past services to the government did not guarantee a bank's position. Much more important was the ability to provide future aid to regimes perennially short of funds. These lessons were not lost on succeeding generations of bankers. Accordingly banking policy reflected the understanding that the only institutions in Ecuador that were not expendable were those maintaining close government ties. Bankers had to be willing and able to subordinate prudent banking policy to political expediency.

The relationship of mutual dependency between the government and the successful banks that characterized the Ecuadorian banking system was established as soon as modern banking began in the 1860s. Two Guayaquil banks, the Banco Particular and the Banco del Ecuador, typify that relationship. The Banco Particular constituted the financial mainstay of the García Moreno administration in the years from 1862 to 1864, loaning the government 800,000 pesos. In return the administration agreed to accept the bank's bills at par at all public offices as payment for taxes and fees. Since money was often discounted when it moved from one region to another, the state's acceptance of the bills at face value strengthened public confidence in the institution. But the regime's support did not last. In 1865, García Moreno decided not to accept the bank's bills at par in the highlands. This action undermined the Banco Particular and contributed to its demise in 1870.[43]

The failure of the Banco Particular was directly related to García Moreno's campaign to secure another large loan. In 1865 the government decided that the institution was not large enough to provide the state another big loan. The administration, therefore, supported the formation of a new bank with sufficient capital and reserves to lend the government 800,000 pesos and to convert its bills to specie upon demand. After several unsuccessful attempts, a group of Guayaquil businessmen formed the Banco del Ecuador in 1867 with considerably greater capital and reserves than the Banco Particular. One of the new corporation's first actions was to grant the government a 500,000 peso loan in 1868 in return for a contract granting the bank sole right to present its bills at par at public offices. This sealed the fate of the Banco Particular. The Banco del Ecuador became García Moreno's principal source of extraordinary revenue until his death in 1876. At the end of 1873 the government owed the bank 1,254,263 pesos and held an additional line of credit of 1,000,000 pesos, which it could use upon demand. García Moreno guaranteed the loans by mortgaging 90 percent of the nation's customs revenues, the tithes from the diocese of Guayaquil, and half of the government's revenue from the salt monopoly. In essence García Moreno bartered away the state's principal sources of future revenue in return for unlimited credit from the Banco del Ecuador.

A rapid expansion of the money supply through bank currency issues and large government loans precipitated a monetary and financial crisis. Between 1872 and July 1874 the value of the peso declined from 1.02 pesos to the dollar to 1.63. As a result the public lost confidence in Banco del Ecuador and began redeeming its bills for gold and silver. To save the bank the government prohibited the export of bullion and limited the public's right to redeem bills, giving the Banco del Ecuador an opportunity to reduce the volume of its currency in circulation and strengthen its financial position. The bank recalled many of its private loans, but it did not request that the government repay its debt even though the state was by far the largest debtor. In this instance, government actions protected the bank, because the government continued to depend on it for credit. The Banco del Ecuador survived and continued to extend credit to other administrations. It remained the dominant bank in the country during the rest of the nineteenth century and the principal source of government credit. In 1890 the state owed the Banco del Ecuador 1,183,710 of the 2,046,148 sucres it had borrowed from Ecuadorian banks.[44]

The amount of interest paid to banks in the period from 1883 to 1889 (see table 10) indicates the continuing importance of loans to government and their regional character. Guayaquil banks, Ecuador's largest and best-capitalized institutions, whose strength derived from access to gold and foreign currency generated by the coastal economy, held the bulk of the government debt. This strength emphasized the region's importance as the primary source of government revenue, a reality that heightened regional antagonisms.

The Emergence of the Active State

Nineteenth-century budgets reflect the increased scope of state activity. The secular trend rose both in government income and expenditure for the period 1830 to 1895 (see Appendixes K and L). The growth of the coastal export economy made possible the increased scale of state activity. In 1830 estimated income and expenditures were 708,000 and 692,000 pesos respectively, exclusive of extraordinary military expenditures. By 1893 government income had increased to 4,326,000 sucres and expenditures to 4,433,000. This growth in expenditures went hand-in-hand with the multiplication of government functions.

In the first decades of national life, military expenditures and debt service consumed nearly the entire national budget. In those years, the government limited itself largely to self-preservation. For example in 1830, 73.9 percent of the budget went to the military. During the next three decades, military expenditures continued to be the most important item in the budget, absorbing at least 30 percent and frequently exceeding 50 percent of the budget. These figures underestimated the true level of military expenditures because large extraordinary wartime expenditures were not included in the budget. Although military expenditure dropped

TABLE 10
INTEREST PAID TO BANKS 1883–1889

Year	Guayaquil institutions[1]	Quito institutions[2]	Total
1883	74,257	9,665	83,922
1884	80,071	13,222	93,293
1885	80,071	3,466	83,537
1886	88,145	7,352	95,497
1887	306,552	10,561	317,113
1888	116,242	8,460	124,702
1889	166,834	6,191	173,025

Source: Calculated from data in Ecuador, Ministro de Hacienda, *Informe, 1890.*
[1]Includes Banco del Ecuador, Banco Internacional, and Corporación Comercial.
[2]Includes Banco de Quito and Banco de la Unión.

as a percentage of budget allocations in the 1860s, it remained the single most important item in the national budget for the rest of the century. During the second half of the nineteenth century the armed forces consumed between one-quarter and one-third of all ordinary government revenues. Periods of civil strife and political instability increased military expenditures. When they occurred, governments had to borrow substantial extraordinary revenues. Since internal borrowing was a political necessity, debt service became a significant part of the budget in the nineteenth century. In the years from 1830 to 1878 debt service normally accounted for one-quarter to one-third of ordinary expenditures. But in a few instances it rose to 40 percent of budgeted expenditures.

Ecuadorian rulers, beginning with Flores and Rocafuerte, aspired to expand government activity in education, public works, and public welfare. Their speeches, reports, and legislation served as an ideal for the future. Rocafuerte, for instance, maintained that roads would not only improve communication and transportation but also aid economic development. He believed also that education was necessary if the country was to have an enlightened and productive population.[45] Although these views were widely accepted, there was little chance of implementing them in the first half of the nineteenth century. The nation's poverty and continuous political turmoil prevented governments from allocating resources in significant amounts for those purposes. During the first two decades after independence the government allocated less than 10 percent of its revenue to education, public works, and welfare (see Appendix L).

The potential for state action began to change in the second half of the nineteenth century as a result of the rapid growth of the export sector. The government also increased its revenues by introducing a more efficient system of tax collection on the coast. The rise in government income coincided with increased public demands that the state take a more active role in expanding the socioeconomic infrastructure of the nation. Coastal businessmen, in particular, demanded the introduction of better systems of communication and an expanded educational system.[46]

Most historians have accepted the notion that García Moreno was the principal architect of the active state in Ecuador. Frederick B. Pike, a distinguished scholar who carefully reviewed the secondary literature, recently summed up that view when he wrote: "Despite the bitter opposition he evoked, García Moreno brought greater progress to Ecuador than any president before him—or since him, for that matter."[47] Such views are widely held because of the paucity of research in nineteenth-century Ecuadorian history. An analysis of government actions in education and in communications, however, demonstrates that García Moreno did not act differently from other national leaders. Although the country's leading conservative president did make important contributions in both areas, he was neither the first to do so nor did his death bring an end to such endeavors.[48]

A study of the period from 1841 to 1894 indicates that primary education expanded in direct relation to the growth of the cacao export economy. The number of schools increased from 166 in 1841 to 254 in 1857. After García Moreno assumed office in 1861, education continued to expand at about the same rate. It did not decline after his death in 1875. Indeed by 1894 just before the liberals took power, there were twice as many schools with two-and-one-half times as many students as there had been in 1875 when García Moreno was assassinated (see table 11).

The figures in table 11 obviously cannot assess the quality of education. Without a detailed analysis of education in nineteenth-century Ecuador, one is confined to elementary conclusions from the scant data available. Nevertheless, the increased emphasis placed on education, the growth of the school system, and the rapid expansion of government funds allocated to education, all testify to the importance of the state in providing the social services necessary for the development of a modernizing urban sector in late nineteenth-century Ecuador (see table 12).

During the second half of the nineteenth century the government was also concerned with public works, particularly communications (see table 13). In 1839–40 it spent 1,256 pesos for public works, whereas public works expenditures increased to 638,005 sucres in 1891. As indi-

TABLE 11

PRIMARY EDUCATION 1841–1894

Year	Number of schools	Number of students
1841	166	4,769
1854	212	5,862
1857	254	10,348
1867	343	13,495
1873	433	22,448
1875	526	31,795
1885	800	51,000
1890	853	56,126
1892	1,106	68,274
1894	1,209	76,152

Sources: Calculated from data in Ecuador, Ministro de Instrucción Pública, *Informe, 1890, 1894*; Ministro de Interior, *Esposición 1857.*

TABLE 12

GOVERNMENT EXPENDITURES FOR EDUCATION 1847–1893

Year	Amount[1]	Year	Amount[1]
1847	3,052	1884	244,638
1855	7,639	1887	284,397
1857	15,234	1888	317,570
1863	35,307	1889	336,174
1865	50,952	1890	459,902
1871	151,189	1891	491,492
1879	191,624	1893	379,005

Source: Calculated from data in Ecuador, Ministro de Hacienda, *Informe, 1847, 1855, 1858, 1865, 1873, 1880, 1885, 1888, 1890, 1892, 1894.*

[1]Pesos through 1884 and sucres thereafter.

cated in chapter 1, the government devoted a considerable portion of its resources to the building of roads and later to the construction of railroads. In fact, the renewed efforts to refund the foreign debt in the 1860s and the 1880s were directly linked to administration desires of securing money for road and railroad projects. Although the García Moreno and the Antonio Flores administrations made important contributions to road building in the highlands, they proved unsuccessful in constructing a railroad. To accomplish such a major project, Ecuadorians needed foreign

TABLE 13

GOVERNMENT EXPENDITURES FOR PUBLIC WORKS 1839–1891

Year	Amount
1839–40	1,256
1846–47	3,776
1854–55	20,517
1863	110,731
1865	139,017
1871	430,025
1879	512,254
1887	588,695
1891	638,005

Source: Calculated from data in Ecuador, Ministro de Hacienda, *Informe, 1847, 1855, 1865, 1867, 1880, 1888,* and *1892.*

capital which they could not obtain on acceptable terms. Telecommunications projects, however, were economically feasible. The government installed a telegraph system between the coast and the sierra during the 1880s and 1890s. The increased speed of communication had a tremendous impact on the country by dramatically expanding government authority. The telegraph made possible a degree of fiscal control over centralized funds hitherto unimagined. If improved communications made the national government stronger and more efficient, it also led to an increased public demand for state services which the nation's late nineteenth-century prosperity seemed to make possible.[49]

The expansion of education and the improvements in communications provide only the most prominent examples of the rise of the active state in Ecuador. By the end of the century, the scope of government action was highly diversified. Ecuadorians increasingly perceived the state as having an important role in promoting social and economic development. Their view derived much impetus from the continuing economic expansion of the coast and the parallel growth in the complexity of society. It was also linked to regional desires for local improvement. Guayaquil and the coast were the first to benefit from new government programs in health, sanitation, and urban beautification projects. But within a short time Quito and other highland centers aspired to similar modern comforts. By the 1880s and 1890s urban Ecuadorians widely accepted the notion that the state had a responsibility for promoting economic and social well-being, although they disagreed about the degree of necessary government involvement. For example, welfare expenditure increased from 615 pesos in 1854–55 to 249,299 sucres in 1893 (see table 14). By 1893, education, social welfare, and public works accounted for 26.8 percent of government expenditures (see Appendix L). Nevertheless, the principal cost of government continued to be the maintenance of internal order and external defense. Not until the twentieth century would there be a successful drive to achieve an effective diversification of state activities through the allocation of a larger share of public resources to nonmilitary functions.

TABLE 14

GOVERNMENT EXPENDITURES FOR WELFARE 1854–1893

Year	Amount[1]
1854–55	615
1863	6,574
1871	20,921
1878	79,479
1884	91,826
1888	139,473
1890	124,874
1893	249,299

Source: Calculated from data in Ecuador, Ministro de Hacienda, *Informe, 1855, 1865, 1873, 1880, 1885, 1890,* and *1894.*

[1]Pesos through 1884 and sucres thereafter.

4. Government Finances, 1895–1925

Many of the problems that characterized nineteenth-century finances plagued the public finances of the liberal era (1895–1925). Liberal governments, unable to fund expenditures from ordinary revenue, continued to rely on loans from local banks. Foreign loans, generally, were unattainable on politically acceptable terms because of the country's poor credit history. Indirect taxes, particularly customs duties, remained the main source of ordinary revenue. Cacao retained its position as the country's most valuable export, and its market performance determined the level of government revenue. The erratic performance of cacao, particularly in the 1920s, contributed significantly to the financial problems of liberal administrations.

The demands of the military in the face of political and regional upheavals also disrupted government finances. Throughout the liberal period, military expenditures remained high, generally outstripping the funds allocated for that purpose (see table 15 and Appendix L). Military outlays generally comprised the largest single item in liberal budgets, although sometimes payments for the public debt surpassed military expenditures. Military needs disrupted the budgeting process in three ways. First, governments had to fund large, extraordinary expenditures for defense in order to quell insurrections. Second, governments often could not collect taxes in the regions that were in conflict. Finally, the recurrent instability convinced many Ecuadorians that only a decentralized fiscal system could ensure the maintenance of vital services. Thus a rapid decentralization of the fiscal system coincided with periods of civil war, such as 1912 to 1916. (See chapter 2 for discussions of militarism and liberal politics.)

Regionalism and the desire of localists that their areas reap the benefits of liberal progress, however, were the most significant factors in the progressive decentralization of the nation's fiscal system. Liberal ideology

TABLE 15
MILITARY EXPENDITURE 1895–1927

Year	Amount[1]	Year	Amount[1]
1895–96	2,629,099	1914	7,599,823[b]
1898	2,048,125	1915	6,593,320[b]
1900	3,148,408	1916	5,112,062[b]
1901	3,413,440	1917	4,764,067
1902	2,384,723	1918	5,861,940
1903	2,496,501	1919	4,568,245
1904	2,354,758	1920	5,343,206
1905	2,293,626	1921	5,501,804
1907	4,043,923	1922	5,892,007
1908	3,276,624	1923	6,214,767
1909	3,614,416	1924	6,709,679
1910	5,885,432[a]	1925	8,132,284[c]
1911	3,585,531	1926	9,230,501
1912	3,758,178	1927	10,143,578
1913	3,933,521		

Sources: Calculated from data in Ecuador, Ministro de Hacienda, *Informe, 1896–97, 1899, 1901–06, 1908–09, 1912, 1915–18, 1925–28*; Ecuador, Ministerio de Hacienda, *Boletín de estadística fiscal y comercial*, III, (1910); VII (1914); Ecuador, Ministerio de Hacienda, *Balances generales y sus anexos, 1919–20; 1920; 1922–25.*

[1]Amount in current sucres.

[a]Border dispute with Peru.

[b]Period of civil war.

[c]Coup of July 9, 1925.

stressed the necessity to establish a secular state to promote Ecuador's social and economic development and modernization. Liberals believed that the state should stimulate growth by creating the needed economic and social infrastructure, particularly an improved and enlarged communication network to foster the development of an integrated national market. Their program also included expanded public services, such as education, sanitation, and health care to augment the productive capacity of the population.[1]

The public eagerly embraced the concept of an active state. Sections of the nation, which had been content to allow the sun to make trails passable after the rainy season, demanded all-weather roads and railroads. Those regions fortunate enough to obtain such improvements soon considered the new communications systems necessities, viewing any interruption of traffic, even when caused by floods or earthquakes, as an unacceptable burden. As in other countries once development started, demand increased for more and better services. Liberals acceded to these demands by passing laws that approved numerous public works projects and by increasing expenditure on education and welfare (see tables 16 and 17 and Appendix L).

The liberal era was a time of visible progress. The government expanded the country's communications network by constructing telegraph lines, roads, bridges, and railroads. Urban life, particularly in the major cities, was enhanced through the building of water and sewage systems, the introduction of electric lighting, and the expansion and improvement of the postal services. Education became available to increasing numbers of Ecuadorians (see table 18). Still, these real advances were achieved inefficiently since the country's economic weakness and regional loyalties restricted the government's capacity to meet these demands.[2]

TABLE 16
EDUCATION EXPENDITURE 1895–1927

Year	Amount[1]	Year	Amount[1]
1895–96	267,459	1913	2,180,013
1898	349,318	1914	1,730,809
1899	438,848	1915	1,401,670
1900	524,865	1916	1,944,016
1901	841,403	1917	1,854,284
1902	906,796	1918	2,510,461
1903	872,792	1919	2,858,065
1904	959,956	1920	3,615,812
1905	957,764	1921	3,672,644
1907	1,050,962	1922	3,830,302
1908	1,285,201	1923	3,129,071
1909	1,501,434	1924	3,588,914
1910	1,507,106	1925	3,089,210
1911	1,885,356	1926	3,638,904
1912	1,835,592	1927	4,028,065

Sources: Calculated from data in Ecuador, Ministro de Hacienda. *Informe 1896–97, 1899, 1900–06, 1908, 1909, 1912, 1915–19, 1922 Anexo*; Ecuador, Ministerio de Hacienda. *Boletín de estadística fiscal y comercial*, III (1910); Ecuador, Ministerio de Hacienda. *Boletín*, no. 5 (October 1928).

[1]Amount in current sucres.

TABLE 17

WELFARE EXPENDITURE 1895–1927

Year	Amount[1]
1895–96	98,792
1898	124,272
1900	199,711
1904	256,853
1908	318,532
1911	388,390
1915	380,857
1920	629,774[a]
1924	667,049[a]
1927	665,600

Sources: Calculated from data in Ecuador, Ministro de Hacienda, *Informe, 1896–97, 1901, 1905, 1909, 1912, 1916*; Ecuador, Ministerio de Hacienda, *Balance general y sus anexos, 1920*; Ecuador, Ministerio de Hacienda, *Boletín*, no. 5 (October 5, 1928).

[1]Amount in current sucres.

[a]Includes fire departments.

TABLE 18

PRIMARY EDUCATION 1894–1928

Year	Schools	Enrollment	Attendance
1894	1,209	76,152	- - -[a]
1902	1,317	83,648	- - -[a]
1909	1,355	85,237	- - -[a]
1914	1,411	86,981	- - -[a]
1915	1,231[b]	95,091[c]	- - -[a]
1916	1,400	97,395	85,241[d]
1919	1,630	99,254	85,014
1921	1,716	103,344	89,895
1924	1,488	112,219	101,376
1928	1,771	128,746	111,699

Sources: Calculated from data in Ecuador, Ministro de Instrucción Pública, *Informe 1894, 1902, 1909, 1915, 1916, 1919, 1921, 1928*.

[a]Information not available.

[b]Decrease due to civil war in Esmeraldas and Manabí.

[c]School age population in Ecuador estimated at 254,400 individuals.

[d]Most of the absenteeism is in rural areas.

Realizing that the growth of the state could benefit their provinces, regionalist leaders insisted that all areas simultaneously receive a share of public projects. In this manner they prevented establishing national priorities for construction based either on the economic impact of the proposal or on the limits of government resources. Since national poverty prevented the simultaneous completion of the numerous projects authorized by congress, the legacy of the liberal era remained one of uncompleted public works. In the 1920s regionalism, as well as economic dislocations, contributed to a growing dissatisfaction with the government's performance. During the post-1920 period currency rapidly depreciated, resulting in higher levels of government expenditures that were more apparent than real. Although the state appeared to enjoy growing revenues, the declining value of the sucre actually reduced the government's ability to act. Nevertheless, the public became increasingly intolerant of regimes that did not fulfill its rising expectations. In such circumstances it became politically impossible to reduce the scope of government activity, even during periods of severe fiscal stringency. Forced to maintain acceptable levels of public expenditures, liberal administrations turned to banks for loans, thereby strengthening the symbiotic relationship between Ecuadorian banks and the government which first emerged in the nineteenth century. In this as in other ways the Liberal era (1895–1925) represented the logical culmination of nineteenth-century trends rather than a sharp break with the past.

Decentralization

Fiscal decentralization constituted one of the most intransigent problems inherited by the liberals. Two kinds of decentralization characterized Ecuadorian public finances: autonomous agencies had the authority to collect and disburse public revenues and the congress allocated income collected by the national treasury through statutes to specific programs. These practices were indicative of the strength of regionalism, as represented by the congress, and the public distrust of the national government, particularly the executive branch. The congress froze appropriations by law and created innumerable autonomous agencies because Ecuadorians believed that no president could be trusted to administer national revenues honestly and equitably. Fiscal disunity, therefore, became institutionalized. Cognizant of the waste and inefficiency inherent in decentralization, liberal presidents attempted to introduce centralized fiscal control; but no chief executive had sufficient strength to subjugate regional interests successfully.

Throughout the liberal era, ministers of finance led the struggle to establish executive control of national finances against congresses determined to defend and extend the decentralized system. The first liberal minister of finance, Serafín S. Wither S., argued in 1896 that the national budget was the best and most efficient mechanism for allocating national resources. The practice of creating taxes, the proceeds of which were specifically linked to particular services or projects, and enacting laws, which allocated a portion of an existing tax to a particular function, was inefficient and frequently counterproductive. The system of special treasuries, authorized to collect and disburse public funds, prevented the national government from regulating public finances and auditing public accounts. Numerous autonomous treasuries also required a larger bureaucracy than a unified system, thereby increasing the cost of government. Abuses were inevitable in these circumstances; government funds were either lost or diverted from their intended purpose. Accounts were fragmentary or nonexistent not only because there were few trained accountants in the country but also because special treasuries refused to submit their accounts for audit. Minister Wither proposed that the congress abolish the earmarked additional taxes that burdened foreign trade and complicated customs collections as a first step in reforming government finances. His plan would consolidate the many special taxes with the basic import levy to form a single tax that would be deposited in the national treasury and assigned through the national budget rather than by a specific statute. The new procedure could eventually be extended to encompass all forms of taxation thereby restoring flexibility to public expenditures. The liberal congress rejected his recommendation as it would many similar reforms.[3]

In 1900 a new minister of finance charged that the system of decentralized taxation was the principal cause of the government's financial difficulties. Although the number of taxes had increased since 1895, the funds controlled by the president had diminished because the laws creating the new levies also legislated their disposition, forcing chief executives to seek extraordinary funding, particularly bank loans, in order to meet ordinary administrative expenses. The growth in the internal debt demonstrated the poverty of the executive branch. The minister rejected regionalist assertions that statutory allocation of revenue served the public interest by maintaining services and protecting the budgets of public projects. His successor agreed that there was an urgent need to centralize national income and expenditure, not only to provide adequate funding for administration but also to ensure that the services and projects that were currently funded by decentralized monies actually received the support that congress intended. Rather than protecting these activities, the existing system left most underfunded and the rest with more money than they could reasonably invest. Under this system many public works were abandoned and public employees were paid late or not at all.[4]

The extent of fiscal decentralization of Ecuador was incredible. In 1900 the national government collected 8,137,161 sucres, but 4,837,692 sucres were either controlled by autonomous agencies or assigned by law to specific programs. The president had no authority over 59.5 percent of ordinary government revenue. If the 3,148,408 sucres absorbed by the military are subtracted, the chief executive controlled only 151,061 sucres. The year 1900 was not unusual. From 1901 to 1907 the centralized portion of government income amounted to less than 50 percent of total revenues. In 1907, for example, 68 percent of ordinary government revenue was decentralized.[5] It is not surprising that Ecuadorian presidents found it necessary to obtain bank loans to operate their administrations.[6]

Nationalists were also dismayed because they believed most of the funds were wasted supporting a redundant bureaucracy. In their opinion decentralization actually hurt local interests since multiple treasuries and bureaucracies consumed much of the income collected. Few, if any, of the funds were left after the costs of collection and administration were deducted.[7] The congress remained unconvinced by these arguments and continued to earmark taxes as well as subdivide existing taxes to fund particular services. These practices resulted in a tax code that was extremely difficult to interpret and administer. By 1911 the tax system had become so complex and chaotic that the congress occasionally inadvertently pledged the revenues from a single source to two or more programs.[8]

The financial problems of the national government during World War I provide an example of the fiscal straitjacket created by institutionalized decentralization that deprived the government of flexibility during a crisis. The disruption of international trade during the war resulted in a drop in Ecuadorian government income. Revenue collections in 1914 fell 19 percent below budget projections; the following year, income was 29 percent less than projected by the administration. In addition, the Plaza administration had to increase military expenditures to quell a civil war that raged in the coastal provinces. Budgetary inflexibility crippled the administration's efforts to maintain vital public services in the face of the dual financial and political emergency. To meet mounting budget deficits the government resorted to internal borrowing while ignoring its external obligations.[9]

Financial control by the executive branch deteriorated from 1914 to 1924 as congress authorized 83 public works projects to be funded with special taxes. In 1916 when ordinary government revenue reached 16,544,960 sucres, the congress allocated 13,126,185 sucres (79.3%) through special legislation to education, debt service, welfare, sanitation, and to railroads and other public works leaving only 3,418,775 sucres (20.7%) for other administrative costs, including military expenditures. In the budget those sectors were assigned 8,623,475 sucres; therefore the government faced a deficit of 5,204,699 sucres. In addition the congress voted four million sucres in special grants to the police, public works, the postal and telegraph services, the army, education, the government pension fund, and the diplomatic corps raising the 1916 deficit to over nine million sucres, or more than 50 percent of ordinary government revenue.[10]

The problems created by the proliferation of autonomous agencies were most apparent in the area of public works. In 1905 there were 253 special public works projects authorized by statute plus 93 more funded through the national budget. Eighty-four autonomous juntas, each with its separate organization and bureaucracy, administered the decentralized projects. A few juntas fulfilled their responsibilities conscientiously, but most were less scrupulous, wasting funds or using them for nonauthorized expenditures, ignoring government requests for accountability. The state could neither supervise the juntas nor determine if they were complying with their charter, because their autonomous legal status protected agency members from public scrutiny. The multiplication of these juntas retarded national development because most failed to complete their projects. Some agencies failed because they received insufficient funds; some lacked the resources even to initiate their projects although they usually managed to pay the salaries of the directors; and some started and subsequently abandoned the project. Only 55 of the 346 authorized public projects were under construction in 1905, including works administered directly by the national government. The remainder had either been abandoned or were never begun.[11] During the next seventeen years the executive branch unsuccessfully sought to gain control of public works expenditure. The few hard-won advances, such as the creation of a central directorate in the province of Pichincha to unify activities of all juntas established to oversee road construction in the province, were quickly submerged by the growing number of projects approved by the congress. Despite the demise of many works and the consolidation of a few, 257 projects, including 21 railroads, had legislative sanction in 1922. Rather than evaluating the proposals submitted by the provinces, cantons, and parishes and approving only those serving the national interest (however defined) that could be funded adequately, the congress rubber-stamped most projects with disastrous consequences for national finances.[12]

Officials who wanted centralized fiscal control argued with great urgency as the economy faltered in the 1920s when the export of cacao began to decline. The long series of deficit budgets, partially funded by bank loans, accelerated the currency depression that resulted from the nation's declining productivity. In an unsuccessful effort to shame the congress into action, the minister of finance wrote his annual report in 1921 almost entirely by linking together quotes from earlier ministerial reports. He demonstrated that the nation's fiscal difficulties stemmed from long-standing, much-discussed, problems. Just as previous ministers of finance had accurately diagnosed the national ills, he contended, they also had prescribed the proper solutions. The minister concluded that the congress' decision to subordinate fiscal responsibility to political expediency had caused Ecuador's fiscal crisis.[13]

The congress continued to avoid tax reform but because of the deteriorating financial situation it appointed a Permanent Legislative Commission in 1921 to study national economic and fiscal problems and to recommend reforms. The commission issued a series of detailed reports and projects of laws in 1922, 1923, and 1924 that concluded the tax system was unjust and unproductive; the multiple decentralized treasuries created financial chaos; the national accounting system was outmoded and inefficient; the internal debt escalated because the government lacked sufficient income to meet urgent needs and was forced to seek bank loans; resources were wasted because expenditures were unplanned; the foreign debt was growing because the government did not provide funds for its service; and, finally, the nation's depreciated currency was subject to wild fluctuations. The commission believed that the process of decentralization had advanced to the point at which the authority of the state had not only eroded but had been abridged with autonomous agencies usurping the legitimate prerogatives of the state. The commission, therefore, recommended that the congress restore the national government's authority by centralizing the collection and expenditure of national revenue. It should also authorize the sixty-six general treasury offices to collect all government revenue and order the suppression of the fifty-seven special treasuries that received decentralized revenues. Each autonomous junta should be examined and those judged unnecessary abolished. It recommended that the congress also reform the general statute (*ley orgánica*) of public finance and most tax legislation as well as draft budgets on the basis of realistic estimates of income and expenditure. It urged the creation of a national public works plan to establish construction priorities and procedures for monitoring expenditure. Although the legislators generally agreed on the need for reform, they could not resist regionalist demands and thus they continued to vote for new decentralized taxes and agencies. By 1924 the legislature had decentralized over 80 percent of ordinary government revenue, pledging it by statute to special programs. When the military ousted Gonzalo Córdova in July 1925, this decentralized system remained essentially intact.[14]

The failure to reform the tax and budgetary systems had profound effects as the economy deteriorated in the 1920s. The sucre declined in value as cacao exports diminished, falling from 2.5 sucres per dollar in 1920 to 5.05 sucres per dollar in 1926. The cost of imports more than doubled (see table 19). Yet the same years brought a decline in customs receipts because tariff rates were fixed charges based on the weight of imported items. Duties originally set to produce a 44 percent ad valorem equivalent raised only 11 percent by 1924. Escalating government costs and declining revenues ensured continuous and worsening deficits that seriously affected the internal economy (see Appendix M). The depreciation of the sucre and government deficits led to a serious inflation. Imports, as well as local products increased in price, driving up the cost of living 145 percent between 1913 and 1925 (see table 20). The inflation severely

TABLE 19

OPEN-MARKET EXCHANGE RATE OF THE SUCRE 1920–1926[a]

Year	Average rate	Range
1920	2.25	2.11 – 2.60
1921	3.45	2.70 – 3.90
1922	4.20	3.73 – 4.80
1923	4.80	3.60 – 5.80
1924	5.05	4.14 – 5.60
1925	4.35	4.10 – 4.70
1926	4.45	4.45 – 5.56

Source: Calculated from data in Luis Alberto Carbo, *Historia monetaria y cambiaria del Ecuador* (Quito: Imprenta del Banco Central del Ecuador, 1953), 106, 110.

[a]Stated in sucres per dollar.

hurt public employees because their salaries lagged substantially behind the increases in the cost of living, leading to discontent and increased inefficiency in government services. Although salaries in the private sector rose at a faster pace than in the government, Ecuadorians believed they still did not keep pace with inflation. Newspapers continually reported increases in the cost of food and other necessities and generally painted a dismal picture of the nation's economic state, intensifying the widespread discontent and worker militancy. This unrest culminated in the strikes and riots of November 1922 in Guayaquil that left scores of workers dead and caused considerable damage to property. Thereafter, employers adjusted the salaries of workers in the private sector more quickly to reflect the declining purchasing power of the sucre. Government employees, however, remained poorly paid.[15]

Ecuador's grave economic and political condition prompted President Tamayo to take action. He hired an American financial adviser, John Hord, to assist in reforming the country's fiscal system. (His activities are discussed in greater detail in chapter 5.) The minister of finance also initiated an internal reorganization of the ministry to encourage efficiency

TABLE 20
COST OF LIVING INDEX 1913–1925[a]

Year	Cost of Living Index
1913	100
1915	130
1916	170
1917	204
1918	238
1919	214
1920	193
1921	194
1922	215
1923	208
1924	242
1925	245

Source: *El Comercio,* no. 7657 (December 13, 1926).

[a]From 1913 to 1917 the index is based on the cost of 14 local commodities in Quito; from 1918 to 1925, it is based on the cost of 25 local commodities. The commodities are: rice, peas, sugar, barley, sweet potatoes, meat, charcoal, beans, eggs, wheat flour, barley flour, large beans, lentils, lard, large kernel corn, small white corn, carrots, two types of local tubers, men's suits, and shoes.

and to improve financial control. Ministry personnel were required to keep exact accounts, to collect taxes when due, and to deposit collections daily in designated banks. Failure to comply with the new requirements led to dismissal. These reforms improved tax collection. In addition, the administration convinced the Banco del Ecuador and the Banco Comercial y Agrícola to lower the interest rate on government indebtedness. President Tamayo also took preliminary steps to rehabilitate the nation's external credit by briefly resuming payment on the railroad bonds that had been in default since 1913 as part of an abortive plan to negotiate a large foreign loan to pay the internal debt and for public projects. In its most far-reaching attempt at reform the Tamayo administration presented the congress with a unified budget for the next fiscal year of 1924.

The Permanent Legislative Commission, the minister of finance, and John Hord cooperated in framing the centralized budget project, which placed the collection and distribution of national revenues in the hands of the national government. The proposal sought to rationalize government expenditure and control public works and autonomous agencies. The congress agreed to centralize collections, but it blunted the intent of the budget project by requiring that autonomous agencies and special projects receive 80 percent of the proceeds of the formerly decentralized taxes. The compromise essentially retained decentralized expenditures. Still, the adoption of this budget initiated the process of centralization and established the basis for later reforms.[16]

Trade and Taxation

As the country's principal export throughout the liberal era (1895–1925), cacao's performance in the international market ultimately determined the level of government income, regulated the foreign exchange available to Ecuador and, in turn, set the limit for imports. Since taxes on imports were the single most important source of ordinary government income, declines in export earnings rapidly translated into decreases in public revenues. Internal or external market disruptions not only affected government income but also made reliable budget projections impossible. Public finances were at the mercy of fluctuations in world cacao markets.

Ecuador, the world's largest cacao producer during the nineteenth century, lost its preeminent position in the twentieth because other countries expanded production and because Ecuadorian cacao trees were destroyed by disease. In 1894 the country grew 28.3 percent of world production, but by 1903 the Ecuadorian crop represented only 18.3 percent of world output (see table 21). From 1894 through 1903 world production expanded 83.5 percent from 69,096 metric tons to 126,795 metric tons, while Ecuadorian output increased only 19 percent from 19,560 metric tons to 23,238 metric tons. The country's two leading competitors were Brazil and San Tomé. Brazilian cacao production expanded 114.3 percent from 10,148 metric tons to 21,738 metric tons; San Tomé, which grew 6,133 metric tons in 1894, harvested 22,450 metric tons in 1903, an increase of 289.8 percent. Ecuador's position continued to erode during the following decade despite increases in output (see table 22). Average yearly production, which reached 37,400 metric tons, represented only 16.2 percent of world output. Between 1903 and 1910 the Gold Coast became the world's leading cacao grower, followed by Brazil. By 1925, when Ecuador raised 34,200 metric tons, its crop constituted only 6.8 percent of world production. The situation did not improve until World War II when other exports supplanted cacao. During the 1920s and 1930s the country began the difficult search for a new major product to export.

TABLE 21

ECUADORIAN CACAO PRODUCTION AS A PERCENTAGE OF
WORLD PRODUCTION 1894–1925

Year	Percentage	Year	Percentage
1894	28.3	1911	15.2
1895	24.9	1912	14.4
1896	23.9	1913	15.4
1897	21.9	1914	15.3
1898	24.8	1915	11.1
1899	27.7	1916	14.7
1900	18.4	1920	11.7
1901	21.6	1921	10.9
1902	20.1	1922	10.8
1903	18.3	1923	6.7
1904	18.9	1924	6.5
1903–1910	16.2	1925	6.8

Sources: Calculated from data in Ecuador, Secretaría de Instrucción Pública, *Memoria*, *1905*, 26; Luis Alberto Carlo, *Historia monetaria, y cambiaria del Ecuador* (Quito: Imprenta del Banco Central del Ecuador, 1953), 467; Luis Eduardo Laso, "Contribución al estudio de la economía política ecuatoriana," *Revista jurídica y de ciencias sociales*, no. 4 (1930), 57; Lois Weinman, "Ecuador and Cacao: Domestic Response to the Boom-Collapse Monoexport Cycle" (Ph.D. diss. University of California, Los Angeles, 1970), 347.

TABLE 22

ECUADORIAN CACAO PRODUCTION 1894–1931

Year	Amount[1]	Year	Amount[1]
1894	413,632	1913	782,332
1895	385,384	1914	971,678
1896	377,036	1915	769,752
1897	358,198	1916	1,079,252
1898	453,192	1917	1,008,767
1899	578,426	1918	819,099
1900	411,349	1919	826,580
1901	513,114	1920	865,010
1902	536,213	1921	884,989
1903	499,213	1922	877,404
1904	613,392	1923	642,694
1905	472,213	1924	663,159
1906	496,049	1925	701,768
1907	429,187	1926	447,711
1908	692,089	1927	483,424
1909	690,620	1928	516,025
1910	798,556	1929	356,212
1911	853,679	1930	417,041
1912	782,332	1931	300,845

Source: Luis Alberto Carbo, *Historia monetaria y cambiaria del Ecuador* (Quito: Imprenta del Banco Central, 1953), 449.

[1]Quintales.

The price of Ecuadorian cacao remained high from 1894 to 1914 despite the expansion of world production because world consumption increased rapidly. In the decade 1894 to 1903, consumption expanded more rapidly than production; it grew 97.5 percent from 64,507 metric tons to 127,452 metric tons. The balance between supply and demand continued until 1916, despite market disruptions caused by World War I (see table 23). Although the large 1914 harvest caused some downward pressure on the price of Ecuadorian cacao, the country's exporters weathered the early war years with relative ease by transferring sales to the United States market. In 1916 the situation changed. Increasing world output and marketing difficulties resulted in huge stockpiles of unsold cacao, a glut that lowered prices the following year (see table 24).

Ecuadorian growers, concerned with changing world marketing patterns for their product, formed an association in 1912 to maintain the

TABLE 23

WORLD CACAO PRODUCTION AND CONSUMPTION 1894–1924[a]

Year	World production	World consumption
1894	69,096	64,507
1895	76,212	72,532
1896	72,180	75,868
1897	80,168	83,545
1898	85,174	88,246
1899	99,886	99,376
1900	102,076	100,993
1901	105,820	109,081
1902	123,939	122,185
1903	126,795	127,452
1911	245,043	230,000
1912	232,500	248,800
1913	256,700	254,100
1914	276,900	255,900
1915	296,200	288,900
1916	307,500	260,400
1920	368,385	374,188
1921	380,095	403,180
1922	400,363	421,809
1923	454,270	436,446
1924	499,794	474,212

Sources: Calculated from data in "Informe acerca del cacao," in Ecuador, Secretario de Instrucción Pública, *Informe, 1905*, 25,28; Luis Alberto Carbo, *Historia monetaria y cambiaria del Ecuador*, 467, 468; Lois Weinman, "Ecuador and Cacao: Domestic Response to the Boom-Collapse Monoexport Cycle" (Ph.D. diss., University of California, Los Angeles, 1970), 347, 438.

[a]In metric tons.

price of cacao, the Asociación de Agricultores. The group obtained permission from the government to charge a tax of one sucre per quintal on cacao exports. In an effort to control prices the association used the revenue to purchase the national crop and withhold it from the market when there was a big price decline (see table 25). The association succeeded in bolstering the price of Ecuadorian cacao in 1914, but its success proved short-lived. The association lacked sufficient resources and controlled too small a percentage of world output to regulate world cacao prices. To meet deteriorating market conditions in 1916, the group obtained a tax

TABLE 24

CACAO EXPORTS 1913–1926

Year	Quantity[1]	Price[2]	Value[3]
1913	92,305	.1082	9,989
1914	100,408	.0984	9,880
1915	81,611	.1152	9,399
1916	94,063	.1231	11,580
1917	99,633	.0881	8,779
1918	84,691	.0783	6,631
1919	98,502	.1391	13,704
1920	103,131	.1539	15,873
1921	94,487	.0611	5,769
1922	97,551	.0735	7,173
1923	68,077	.0557	3,789
1924	73,284	.0804	5,893
1925	72,517	.1084	7,864
1926	47,994	.1105	5,303

Source: U.S. Bureau of Foreign and Domestic Commerce, "Ecuador: Tabular Guide to Economic Conditions," P. J. Stevenson to Wilbur J. Carr, Washington, April 25, 1929, NA, 822.50/16.

[1]Thousands of pounds.
[2]U.S. cents per pound.
[3]Thousands of U.S. dollars.

TABLE 25

CACAO PURCHASED BY ASOCIACIÓN
DE AGRICULTORES 1913–1917

Year	Percent purchased
1913	23
1914	35
1915	31
1916	77
1917[a]	81

Source: Luis Alberto Carbo, *Historia monetaria y cambiaria del Ecuador* (Quito: Imprenta del Banco Central, 1953), 472.

[a]Seven months.

increase to three sucres per quintal. Ironically, the association exacerbated the crisis by acting as a commodity broker that exported cacao on consignment. In 1916 for example, 87 percent of the cacao controlled by the association was exported in this manner. Because of market disruptions and world overproduction, large unsold stockpiles of association-owned cacao accumulated in New York and in European markets. The postwar deflation further imperiled the association; the price of cacao fell from 26.75 cents per pound in March 1920 to 12 cents in December 1920. The decline continued and by June 1921 the price was 5.75 cents per pound. Since the association eventually sold most of the cacao at a loss, it incurred large foreign and domestic debts, which finally forced its liquidation at the end of 1925. By that time many cacao producers considered the Asociación de Agricultores a monopoly and an impediment to trade.[17]

Since liberal governments derived between 53 percent and 81 percent of their ordinary revenue from customs duties, they were concerned with the effectiveness of the customs service (see Appendix C). The liberals believed that the government should appoint and promote customs officials on the basis of merit rather than by political patronage, but low salaries as well as political realities obstructed that laudable goal. Lax administration and contraband significantly diminished collections throughout the liberal era. Although the liberals passed many laws and issued innumerable administrative orders between 1895 and 1923 designed to improve customs administration, political appointees with little or no training continued to fill most positions. Smuggling also continued to drain government revenue severely.[18]

The liberals inherited a cumbersome and unproductive tariff structure. Despite earlier revisions, the aduana code was burdened with additional charges that no longer reflected the value of imports because the sucre had depreciated. Although ministers of finance beginning in 1895 urged that customs duties be unified, additional import levies continued to proliferate. By 1915 imported items had to pay over twenty different taxes, some calculated on weight and others based on value.[19] Despite the experience of nineteenth-century regimes, the liberals still believed that they could increase collections by revising tariff schedules on individual items at a fixed rate of return. Dissatisfied with the 21.7 percent ad valorem equivalent placed on imports in 1897, the Alfaro administration attempted to increase collections to a rate of 34 percent. As in the past, customs officials could not revise the tariffs fast enough to keep abreast of price increases or the introduction of new products into the country. In addition, they failed to adjust the fixed rates to offset the declining value of the sucre. This problem became acute between 1920 and 1925 when the value of the sucre fell by half. Customs levies declined to 16 percent ad valorem in 1921 and 11.5 percent in 1923, precisely at a time when the national government desperately needed greater revenues.[20]

Since the liberals, like their predecessors, believed that the aguardiente tax might provide a major source of income, they sought to revise liquor laws to bring tax collection into line with the suspected high level of production and consumption of aguardiente. Between 1899 and 1919 they modified these laws 134 times; only customs duties received more legislative attention. Despite these efforts, alcohol taxes never provided more than 10 percent of ordinary revenue. The government also failed to control contraband. Local officials constantly complained that geography; small, poorly paid staffs; and the complicity of important local residents obstructed their efforts. Indeed, some individuals holding aguardiente tax concessions charged that local officials and local courts cooperated with residents to encourage smuggling and to protect tax evaders.[21]

Liberals tried a variety of methods to tax alcohol. The early regimes taxed the private producers and/or sellers of aguardiente. Some officials urged the formation of a state liquor monopoly or estanco. The second Plaza administration seriously considered forming a state monopoly on production but did not because of the large initial investment required to establish an estanco and the difficulty of setting fair prices for purchasing sugarcane and selling alcohol in the absence of reliable data.[22] When the Tamayo administration established a state monopoly in 1922, it leased to private companies the right to control the production and sale of aguardiente.[23] On July 1, 1922, the Sociedad Estanco del Chimborazo signed a six-year contract with the government to administer an aguardiente monopoly in that province. The company agreed to pay the state a fixed monthly sum for the concession, to pay the projected taxes for the life of the agreement, and to post a cash performance bond.[24] In other instances, estanco contracts were much larger ventures. The Compañía Ecuatoriana de Estancos collected taxes on articles on which they held a monopoly, including aguardiente, salt, and tobacco, in the coastal provinces of Los Ríos, El Oro, Guayas, Manabí, and Esmeraldas.

The estanco contracts generated only a modest increase in revenue from alcohol, but they produced massive discontent. The new monopolies disrupted traditional aguardiente marketing arrangements that were controlled by the local elite. When the estanco law went into effect in mid-1922, some large sugarcane producers reduced production, hoping that public discontent over the increased cost of sugar, which accompanied the new arrangement, would force the government to abolish the monopolies. Estanco officials, generally perceived as rapacious representatives of the Quito government, also aroused hostility among small sugar growers who produced aguardiente as a sideline. In some cases, armed confrontations ensued between the monopoly's employees and small producers. Such disorders became commonplace in Azuay province, culminating in an Indian uprising in the vicinity of Cuenca. Tensions subsided when the government revised the law to exclude sugar not destined for aguardiente from controls. The exception provided many individuals with opportunities to evade the law and created insurmountable enforcement problems in isolated regions.[25] In some instances estanco companies succeeded. In Chimborazo province the annual production of aguardiente increased from about 400,000 liters in 1922 to 680,000 liters in 1925, when the provisional government, established after the July 1925 coup, canceled the estanco contracts. Sugar producers in Chimborazo, pleased with the monopoly's administration, lobbied unsuccessfully to retain the estanco.[26]

Despite this notable success, resistance to the monopolies was generally widespread. Some opposed the idea of a privately controlled estanco, others disliked the concept of monopolies, but the majority of the population strongly resisted any effective taxation. Opponents harnessed regionalist sentiment in the highlands, claiming that estancos harmed agricultural development and were responsible for the area's backwardness.[27] On balance the political costs of increasing revenues from alcohol far outweighed their limited economic gains. Local highland elites, inconvenienced by the estancos, supported the ouster of the Córdova government in 1925.

The Foreign Debt

Like their predecessors, liberals had an ambivalent attitude toward Ecuador's external debt. They believed that it was important to reach an accord with their foreign creditors because they wanted additional loans to develop the nation. But like most Ecuadorians, the liberals also thought that their country had never received fair treatment from its creditors and supported unilateral action to guard the national interest. Eloy Alfaro suspended debt payment and ordered an investigation of the entire debt history as a prelude to future negotiations. Emilio M. Terán's report, *Informe al Jefe Supremo General Eloy Alfaro sobre la deuda anglo-*

ecuatoriana, criticized all nineteenth-century debt negotiations, charging that earlier Ecuadorian representatives failed to protect the nation's interests. He recommended that the Alfaro administration repudiate the existing agreement to save the country from irreparable harm. The *Informe* subscribed to the general belief that Ecuador had been victimized by the actions of unscrupulous creditors and dishonest or inept national representatives, and that therefore the country's lengthy defaults were really patriotic acts. The report also accepted the widely held Ecuadorian notion that the country should not have to repay loans if the projects they were to finance failed.[28]

The need for new funds to complete the railway from Guayaquil to Quito forced the Alfaro regime to renegotiate the foreign debt. In 1897 the government signed a contract with Archer Harman authorizing the American to form the Guayaquil and Quito Railway Company. The company had the right to raise funds to construct the line, but the foreign bondholders in London objected to any new bond issues as long as payments on their bonds remained unpaid. If the holders of the old Consolidated Debt Bonds did not obtain satisfaction, their opposition would depress the price of Ecuadorian railroad bonds. With the President's permission, Harman traveled to England to settle the question. He arranged to purchase the old debt at 35 percent of its value (£242,606) with Ecuadorian Condor Bonds, a proposed government bond issue paying 4 percent interest and amortized at 1 percent per year. Congress, however, rejected the agreement, claiming it favored Harman and his associates as well as the foreign bondholders. Harman negotiated a new contract with the government and returned to London to reopen talks with the bondholders. They reached a new accord entailing a 70 percent diminution of the debt; each 100 pounds of Consolidated Debt Bonds with accrued interest were exchanged for £36 of First Mortgage Bonds of the Guayaquil and Quito Railway, bearing 6 percent interest and redeemable at 1 percent per year, and a cash bonus of £2.10.[29] The foreign bondholders acquiesced to the arrangement, which constituted the third major reduction in their claims, because they considered the agreement their only hope of avoiding a complete repudiation of the debt by the government. They gauged Ecuadorian attitudes correctly. In his message to the congress in 1900, for example, President Alfaro declared that the English creditors had reaped a splendid profit from the accord because Ecuadorian bonds had never sold for more than 25 percent of face value and were selling for less than 20 percent when the settlement was reached.

He failed to mention that the bonds commanded such low prices because the country repeatedly defaulted on its obligations; between 1834 and 1898 Ecuador was in default for 53 years.[30]

The new understanding permitted Harman and the Guayaquil and Quito Railway Company to begin work. Between 1899 and May 1906 the company issued $12,282,000 of special series First Mortgage Bonds backed by the railroad and the Ecuadorian government that guaranteed service on the bonds. The issues included $1,041,000 in Special Series Bonds bearing 6 percent interest and redeemable at the rate of 1 percent per year. The foreign bondholders in England received these bonds.[31] Contract revisions in 1900 required that the railway company deliver to the government the Consolidated Debt Bonds which the company had acquired from the foreign bondholders. The administration agreed to pay the company $750,000 in railway bonds which the government owned and £77,900 of new Condor Bonds, bearing 4 percent interest and redeemable at 1 percent per year. To comply with these new terms Harman had to frame a new agreement with the foreign bondholders because the accord with the company stipulated that the Consolidated Debt Bonds remain in London with the Council of Foreign Bondholders for security. The council agreed to relinquish the old bonds in return for $250,000 of the railway's First Mortgage Bonds.[32]

President Alfaro strongly supported Harman and the railway company, but many Ecuadorians complained that the American had unduly influenced the government and wielded inappropriate power. In 1906 a disagreement between the railway company and the government quickly resulted in a suspension of debt service. The minister of finance's 1906 report rejected any government responsibility for the railway bonds, even though the contract between the company and the government clearly stated that the government guaranteed bond service with a lien on customs revenue. He conveniently ignored the law authorizing the issue of the railway bonds that required each bond bear a statement of the government's responsibility. Relations between the company and the government became more strained when the company failed to meet the 1907 construction deadline. Critics demanded that the contract be canceled and the company confiscated. Public criticism briefly turned to praise with the completion of the line in 1908.[33]

The government, the railway company, and the railway bondholders reached an agreement in 1908 which provided for the resumption of payments and the refunding of back interest as part of a new bond issue to provide working capital for the company. The railway bondholders accepted a new bond issue of 2,309,016 sucres secured with income from the salt monopoly for part of the interest due them. The bondholders also relinquished their interest due July 1907 in return for noninterest-bearing certificates, also backed by income from the salt monopoly. The owners of the general series First Mortgage Bonds approved a reduction in their interest from 6 percent to 5 percent and an issue of $2,486,000 of Prior Lien Bonds, bearing 6 percent interest and redeemable at 2½ percent per year. The new bonds permitted the government to reduce the original railway debt from $12,282,000 to $10,808,000, by retiring the Special Series Bonds. In addition, the railway company used funds from the Prior Lien Bonds to purchase equipment and provide working capital. The Ecuadorian government benefited from a reduction in its obligations while the railway bondholders once again obtained from the government formal recognition of its promise to guarantee service of the debt. All parties agreed to use arbitration to resolve future disputes.[34]

Although the Ecuadorian government failed to fulfill the terms of the 1908 accord, the agreement was not revised during the remainder of the liberal period. The government made only a partial remittance to the sinking fund in July 1909, the due date of the first payment, and had completely defaulted by July 1910. The liberals made only six semiannual interest payments on the First Mortgage Bonds, which constituted 95 percent of the country's foreign debt, between July 1910 and July 1925. The government owed twelve years' interest on the First Mortgage Bonds and sixteen years of amortization payments, when it was ousted from power by the military. Service on the Salt Bonds, issued in 1908, had been sporadic; only the Prior Lien Bonds had been paid with some regularity (see table 26).[35]

Ecuador's international reputation for fiscal irresponsibility grew with its repudiation of two French bond issues sold in 1909 and 1911 for railroad construction. The government had guaranteed both issues by pledging income it already had mortgaged to other creditors! Seven million francs in Bahía Railway Bonds—bonds of the Compagnie Francaise de Chemins de Fer de l'Equateur—were secured by the customs receipts of the Province of Manabí, while £200,000 of Central Railway Bonds—Manta to Santa Ana—sold in Paris were backed by one-third of the duty on the export of tagua nuts from the Province of Manabí. But in the 1908 accord, Ecuador already had pledged the customs revenue to the holders of the Guayaquil and Quito Railway Bonds. The government also agreed to guarantee the French bonds provided the railroad companies fulfilled certain conditions. Since the wording of both contracts was vague, disputes

TABLE 26

EXTERNAL DEBT JANUARY 1, 1925[a]

Debt	Original capital	Unredeemed capital January 1, 1925	Interest arrears	Total debt January 1, 1925
First Mortgage Bonds of Guayaquil and Quito Railway	10,808,000	10,732,000	6,707,500	17,439,500
Prior Lien Bonds of the Guayaquil and Quito Railway	2,486,000	742,000		742,000
Salt Certificates	1,075,000	636,480	239,882	876,362
Cóndor Bonds	389,500	337,000	176,940	513,940
Total	14,758,500	12,429,480	7,124,322	19,553,802

Source: Calculated from data in Ecuador, Ministerio de Hacienda, Boletín (November 1929).
[a]Figures in dollars.

quickly arose over each party's rights and obligations. The government voided the contracts, refusing either to service or recognize the debts. Whether justified or not, that action damaged the country's credit.[36]

A dispute between the Asociación de Agricultores and the Mercantile Bank of the Americas further damaged Ecuador's credit rating. The association had begun to function in 1913 to provide price supports for cacao. During its first year of operation the association marketed 17 percent of Ecuador's cacao exports; by 1916 it was purchasing 77 percent of production and exporting 55 percent of the cacao crop. The association paid growers half the value of their crop in cash and covered the remainder with a promissory note. Although the association financed its activities through a tax on cacao exports, that income proved insufficient and it began to fund its transactions by borrowing from the Banco Comercial y Agrícola and advances from foreign consignees. During World War I large stockpiles of unsold association-owned cacao built up in Guayaquil and in New York along with the debt to the Banco Comercial y Agrícola and the Mercantile Bank of the Americas, which had begun representing the association in New York in December 1916. The Mercantile Bank advanced the association up to 80 percent of the market value of the cacao it received. In 1917 England and France prohibited cacao imports and the United States imposed higher taxes. These war measures, in addition to world overproduction, reduced both the demand for and the value of cacao. When the association proved unable to pay, the Mercantile Bank sold the organization's cacao to collect some of its debts. The Asociación de Agricultores and the bank failed to reach an agreement on the balance of the debt. The dispute lasted for years and confirmed foreign bankers' belief that Ecuadorians could not be trusted to meet their contractual obligations.[37]

Foreign banks were understandably reluctant to offer Ecuador loans on advantageous terms in light of the country's dismal credit history. Yet congress, ever mindful of public opinion, refused to grant liberal chief executives authority to make the necessary concessions in order to float a large loan. The 1910 emergency loan of $1.5 million from Speyer and Company to purchase armaments during a threat of war with Peru was the last foreign loan the government floated during the liberal era. The Alfaro administration also attempted to negotiate a thirty- to forty-million, dollar loan from Speyer to reorganize the nation's finances. But the company would only consider the proposal if the loan was guaranteed by Ecuadorian customs receipts and if their collection and disbursal were administered by a foreign expert. These demands do not seem unreasonable given the country's credit history. Moreover, international bankers frequently insisted that debtor nations revise or reform their financial structures to ensure the repayment of the loans. In the early 1920s Peru, Bolivia, Panama, Nicaragua, and Guatemala employed foreign financial commissions or individual foreign experts to restructure their finances and restore their external credit. Ecuadorians, however, rejected the imposition of a foreign expert to guarantee loan payments as an infringement of their sovereignty.[38]

After World War I various presidents attempted to secure loans but the congress continued to demand terms which foreign interests considered unrealistic. For example, in 1921 the congress authorized President Tamayo to seek a foreign loan of up to 100,000,000 sucres ($48,600,000) and to offer as a guarantee of payment revenues from items covered by the state monopoly and proceeds from taxes assigned to public works. The security the congress offered was inadequate and unproven. Ecuador had only one source of dependable income that could service a large loan: customs revenue. The government contacted a number of U.S. firms, including Blair and Company, Bankers Trust Company, and Speyer and

Company. None would consider providing a loan with such inadequate security.[39]

Ecuadorians continued to believe that they could eventually obtain foreign capital on their own terms because foreign speculators frequently offered to negotiate loans abroad in return for a contract to build a railroad, a sewage facility, or some other public project. These speculative proposals inevitably failed, but they convinced Ecuadorians that their country was attractive to foreign investors.[40] In 1922, for example, the congress considered the proposal of a representative from the Foundation Company of New York to build a railroad between Sibambe and Cuenca. In return for the contract, the company agreed to secure an American loan to finance construction of the railway. Although the company had failed to obtain a similar loan for Peru, the Ecuadorian congress considered the offer, one of several proposals submitted by foreign speculators to the legislature in 1922. No serious lender, however, would lend Ecuador money without insisting on significant fiscal and monetary reform. Foreign bankers agreed that Ecuador could only receive new loans if it accepted a mixed commission of foreign financial experts, representing the creditors, and national experts, representing the government, which would recommend reforms. Some bankers even suggested specific reforms, such as the creation of a central bank, as well as administrative reform. Most agreed with the commission of chambers of commerce of Quito and Guayaquil which declared in 1917 that administrative inefficiency cost the government 40 percent of its income.[41]

In an attempt to come to terms with the demands of international lenders, the Tamayo administration made a number of concessions not authorized by the congress. In October 1923 the government signed a contract with the Ethelbuga Syndicate of London for a loan of $18,250,000 securing the contract with the nation's customs revenues and agreeing to permit a foreign expert to administer customs collections to ensure debt service. Congress rejected the arrangement and insisted that only part of customs receipts guarantee the loan and that at least two agents administering the revenue assigned to loan repayment be representatives of Ecuadorian banks. These conditions lessened the security which the lenders desired. It is unlikely that the loan could have been signed under any conditions because the syndicate was speculating that New York bankers would buy their contract. But the Mercantile Bank of the Americas demanded that the debts owed to it by the Asociación de Argicultores be recognized before New York banks grant further credits to the government. Given the circumstances no accommodation was possible and foreign money markets remained closed to Ecuador.[42]

Budgets and Banking

Budget deficits, the norm between 1895 and 1925, forged a close bond between liberal administrations and coastal banks (see Appendix M and tables 27 and 28). Their relationship was neither the creation of the liberals nor a conspiracy by coastal bankers to control the state. Rather it characterized Ecuador's political economy from the time banks were established in the 1860s. Although both sides profited from the arrangement, it was the government that instigated the symbiotic relationship and that benefited the most. Bank loans, supplied mainly by two Guayaquil banks—the Banco del Ecuador and the Banco Comercial y Agrícola—contributed significantly to government revenue from 1895 to 1926 (see table 29).[43]

Since Ecuadorian governments failed to adopt adequate budgets, they had to rely on deficit spending and internal bank loans. The country remained dependent on a single major source of ordinary revenue, customs. Cacao exports, therefore, determined the level of government income. Disruptions in world trade, such as occurred in World War I, increased world competition, and crop diseases affected government income negatively. In addition, internal political instability and external threats required extraordinary military expenditures not included in the budgets.[44] The threatened military confrontation with Peru in 1910, for example, consumed extraordinary funds for mobilization that were funded through bank loans. From 1913 to 1925 military expenditures exceeded amounts allocated for that purpose every year. The budget process itself contributed to deficits because it subordinated economic reality to political expediency by overestimating revenue and underestimating expenditures (see Appendix M).[45] Between 1896 and 1925 government income exceeded budget projections in only six of the twenty-nine years; in all but one of those years, the surfeit was eliminated by expenditures. Liberal regimes could not control expenditures; between 1910 and 1925, real expenditures exceeded budget projections for thirteen years. Had the debt service been paid, expenditures would have exceeded the budget in all but one year.[46] The problem was exacerbated because budgets frequently remained in effect for several years because legislators could not agree on new estimates. The projected budget for 1920, adopted in 1919, is illustrative.

TABLE 27

GOVERNMENT DEBT TO BANCO DEL ECUADOR 1869–1926

Year[1]	Amount[2]	Year[1]	Amount[2]
1869	447,099	1899	1,357,498
1871	817,999	1900	1,142,433
1872	876,171	1901[c]	1,103,227
1873	1,254,263	1902	1,867,432
1874	1,088,604	1903	2,663,942
1875	1,024,726	1904	2,787,274
1876[a]	824,076	1905	2,918,812
1877	969,223	1906	2,951,042
1878	921,076	1908	2,896,904
1879	895,261	1909	2,714,258
1880[b]	865,174	1910	2,799,110
1881	798,771	1911	2,724,598
1883	1,229,616	1912	3,059,197
1884	1,132,020	1913	3,023,197
1885	1,660,675	1914	3,122,914
1886	2,185,763	1915	3,300,051
1887	816,880	1916	3,548,124
1888	973,408	1917	3,752,528
1889	1,286,095	1918	4,015,205
1890	1,115,570	1919	4,296,269
1891	1,056,899	1920	4,597,008
1892	1,289,527	1921	4,924,430
1893	1,306,280	1922	5,849,341
1894	1,442,760	1923	5,596,800
1895	1,660,675	1924	5,825,514
1896	2,185,763	1925	6,095,608
1897	1,823,749	1926	6,095,609
1898	1,507,059		

Sources: Calculated from data in Ministro de Hacienda, *Informes, 1873, 1880, 1888, 1913*; Ministerio de Hacienda, *Balance general y sus anexos, 1920*; Banco del Ecuador, *Historia de medio siglo 1868 a 1918*, 66, 92, 153; Banco del Ecuador, "Balances," in Julio Estrada Ycaza, *Los bancos del siglo XIX*, (Guayaquil: Archivo Historica del Guayas, 1976), 66, 83, 87, 127–128, 133–134, 136, 142, 146.

[1]As of December 31.

[2]Pesos through 1884 and sucres thereafter.

[a]July 1876.

[b]June 1880.

[c]June 1901.

TABLE 28

GOVERNMENT DEBT TO BANCO COMERCIAL Y AGRÍCOLA 1895–1926

Year	Amount	Year	Amount
1895	977,959[a]	1912	3,825,497
1896	939,919	1913	4,907,039
1897	809,955	1914	6,706,684
1898	669,595	1915	6,715,409
1899	518,006	1916	7,251,897
1900	354,289	1917	7,712,852
1901	1,332,273	1918	8,402,276
1902	1,622,879	1919	9,390,547
1903	• 1,556,301	1920	9,936,868
1904	1,430,119	1921	10,334,813
1905	1,287,981	1922	11,218,259
1906	2,362,390	1923	11,909,612
1908	2,519,708	1924	12,678,304
1909	2,547,293	1925	27,262,496
1910	2,471,635	1926	23,370,000
1911	3,586,274		

Sources: Calculated from data in "Balances del Banco Comercial y Agrícola," reprinted in Julio Estrada Ycaza, *Los Bancos del Siglo XIX,* (Guayaquil: Archivo Historico del Guayas, 1976). 234, 243, 253–54, 262, 275, 280. Figure for 1911 is an estimation based on information in Great Britain, Department of Overseas Trade, *Report on the Economic and Financial Conditions in Ecuador, September, 1923,* 7; figure for 1909 is from Ministro de Hacienda, *Informe, 1910.*

[a]Includes consolidated government debt to Banco Internacional which merged with Banco Comercial y Agrícola.

That financial act remained in force, with only minor modifications, through 1924! Government income, however, equaled expected revenues only in the last year.[47]

The growth of the active state under the liberals engendered an increased public expectation which became one of the chief causes of budget deficits. The sizeable amounts of money the congress allocated to public works and autonomous agencies diverted needed revenue from essential government operations. In these circumstances the administration could function only with internal bank loans. In periods of political instability or declining revenue the situation worsened. The first liberal budget illustrates this process. Ordinary government revenue in 1895–96 reached 5,128,624 sucres, 3,974,586 of which derived from customs revenues.

TABLE 29
INTERNAL PUBLIC DEBT 1896–1945[a]

Year[1]	Amount	Percent owed to Banks[2]
1896	7,500,000[b]	41.7[c]
1903	7,060,154[d]	59.8[c]
1909	12,418,845	42.4[c]
1910	13,060,509	51.7
1911	12,570,238	55.2[c]
1912	12,579,838	61.8
1913	14,221,778	57.1
1914	15,229,459	65.9
1915	17,127,497	65.1
1916	18,658,988	64.7
1917	18,827,826	66.8
1918	20,720,518	59.9[c]
1919	22,624,481	66.9
1920	25,647,345	60.4
1921	28,521,573	61.3
1922	32,572,972	63.4
1923	36,032,920	48.6[c]
1924	39,834,542	46.5[c]
1925	49,353,427	67.6[c]
1926	42,412,055	72.0
1927	19,892,188[e]	- - -[g]
1928[f]	18,628,059	74.1
1929	11,949,629	79.2
1930	10,800,000	- - -[g]
1931	11,349,392	79.6
1932	21,700,000	- - -[h]
1933	34,761,910	- - -[h]
1934	36,984,733	91.6
1935	19,600,000[e]	- - -[g]
1936	16,885,006[e]	92.4
1937	26,830,600	96.9
1938	25,624,525	97.3
1939	24,631,416	97.7

TABLE 29 (Continued)
INTERNAL PUBLIC DEBT 1896–1945[a]

Year[1]	Amount	Percent owed to Banks[2]
1940	23,709,289	98.2
1941	37,062,646	99.6
1942	36,335,928	_ _ _[h]
1945	113,904,000	90.8

Sources: Calculated from data in Ecuador, Ministro de Hacienda, *Informe, 1896; 1910; 1913; 1925–28*; Ecuador, Ministerio de Hacienda, *Boletín Estadístico*, no. 7 (1914); Ecuador, Ministerio de Hacienda, *Balance general y sus anexos 1920*; Ecuador, Dirección Nacional de Estadística, *Ecuador en cifras 1938–1942*; Great Britain, Department of Overseas Trade, *Report on Economic and Commercial Conditions in Ecuador, 1932; 1934*; Ecuador, Banco Central, *Boletín Mensual*, año 21, no. 239–241 (June-August 1947).

[1]December 31 unless noted.

[2]Prior to founding of Banco Central del Ecuador in August 1927 these debts were owed to various banks of issue. After founding of the Banco Central the debts were owed to that institution.

[a]Sucres.

[b]Estimated.

[c]Includes only government debt to Banco Comercial y Agrícola and Banco del Ecuador.

[d]Includes only bonds issued for registered internal debt and debts to Banco Comercial y Agrícola and Banco del Ecuador.

[e]Reduction results from government using the profits from revaluation of gold reserves to pay debt to bank.

[f]October 9, 1928.

[g]Incomplete data.

[h]Over 90 percent.

That year government expenditure amounted to 8,779,520 sucres, leaving a deficit of 3,650,896, much of it the result of extraordinary military expenditures. Guayaquil banks funded 3,294,068 sucres of the deficit.[48] From 1897 to 1900 budget deficits fluctuated between 1.6 and 3.6 million sucres a year, primarily financed through bank loans.[49] From January 1901 through December 1913 aggregate deficits amounted to 4,280,339 sucres, while bank loans to the government equaled 4,130,391 sucres. During World War I the dramatic decline in government revenue from customs and the extraordinary military expenditures caused by the civil wars increased the government's dependence on bank loans. In 1914 the administration borrowed two million sucres, principally from the Banco

Comercial y Agrícola.[50] Starting late in 1915 the Banco del Ecuador contracted credit drastically, leaving the Banco Comercial y Agrícola as the
main government lender. In the decade from 1914 to 1924 the Banco del
Ecuador increased its loans to the government from 3.1 million to 5.8
million sucres while the Banco Comercial y Agrícola's portfolio of government securities rose from 4.9 million sucres to 12.7 million (see tables
27 and 28).[51] Government debt to the Banco Comercial y Agrícola rose
in 1925 to 27,262,496 sucres when the administration borrowed heavily
to buy controlling interest in the Guayaquil and Quito Railway.[52] The
bank paid a heavy price for financing budget deficits; it became the main
target of sierra regionalists who gained control of the government in the
military coup of July 1925.

Banking Politics and the Coup of 1925

World War I profoundly affected the financial system of the West. News
of the outbreak of war sparked a worldwide financial panic. Individuals
protected their wealth by converting paper currency into gold, thereby
threatening the financial stability of banks as well as national currencies
throughout the Western world. Governments enacted emergency legislation to protect their financial and banking systems; the belligerents and
their trading partners either abandoned or relaxed the gold standard. They
suspended specie payment, prohibited the export of gold, and took other
emergency measures to protect national financial integrity. In Latin
America the war forced Chile and Brazil, which were contemplating a
return to the gold standard, to postpone it, while Ecuador, Argentina,
and Bolivia, which based their currencies on the gold standard, instituted
inconvertibility. Without these measures the financial institutions of the
Western world would have collapsed.[53]

    An executive decree promulgated August 7, 1914, suspended convert-
ibility of Ecuador's currency for thirty days. The order also prohibited
the export of gold, pledged government assets to back currency issues in
the amount of government debt to the banks of issue, and decreed that
no new currency be emitted while inconvertibility was in effect. Congress
ratified the executive decree on August 31, 1914, and extended it for an
indefinite period. These actions came to be known in Ecuador as the
Ley Moratoria. When it became clear in September 1915 that a complete
prohibition on currency issue was unrealistic in the protracted worldwide
economic crisis, the congress modified the statute to permit banks to

issue currency if they had proper reserves. The revised law introduced a needed flexibility into the monetary system because it allowed the banks to increase the money supply in proportion to bank held government debt as well as metallic reserves (see table 30). The law also set the stage for currency depreciation since the government continued the practice of deficit financing through bank loans. The inflationary impact of this policy did not become apparent as long as productivity increased, particularly in the export sector. The sucre had been relatively stable between 1900 and 1916 when the exchange rate fluctuated around 2 sucres per dollar (see table 31). In 1916, Ecuador raised its largest cacao crop, but production began to decline the next year and by 1920 it was 20 percent below the record harvest (see table 22). By 1924 the crop had fallen 39 percent below 1916 figures, and world overproduction had diminished the price

TABLE 30

BANCO COMERCIAL Y AGRÍCOLA: MONETARY
CIRCULATION AND GOVERNMENT DEBT 1913–1926[a]

Year	Total bank issues	Bank issues backed by government debt[1]	Government debt to bank
1913	4,440,093	2,121,233	4,907,039
1914	6,304,937	5,989,817	6,247,045
1915	7,406,229	2,386,749	6,685,409
1916	11,564,599	6,378,979	7,199,286
1917	13,085,100	5,903,120	7,312,852
1918	14,709,912	7,527,972	8,347,196
1919	15,427,449	8,245,589	8,975,982
1920	13,083,910	5,902,030	9,636,347
1921	12,680,638	5,498,958	10,334,813
1922	16,725,703	9,543,843	11,218,259
1923	19,020,115	11,838,255	11,909,612
1924	23,063,943	15,882,123	12,578,304
1925	25,242,597	18,060,777	27,262,496
1926	25,627,099		

Sources: Calculated from data in Julio Estrada, *Los bancos del siglo XIX* (Guayaquil: Archivo Histórico del Guayas, 1976) and Ecuador, Ministero de Hacienda, Comisión Fiscalizadora de Bancos del Litoral, *Las Instituciones de Crédito del Ecuador en 1925: Banco Comercial y Agrícola (Guayaquil)*, (Quito: Talleres Tipográficos del Ministerio de Hacienda, 1926), 41–42.

[1]Issues not backed by gold in Guayaquil vault of Banco Comercial y Agrícola. Amounts in this column would be reduced if the bank's foreign funds were considered part of total reserves for the years 1914–1921, 1923–1926.

TABLE 31

EXCHANGE RATE 1900–1926[a]

Year	Average annual exchange rate[1]	Yearly high	Yearly low
1900	2.05		
1901	2.04		
1902	2.01		
1903	1.99		
1904	1.96		
1905	1.93		
1906	1.91		
1907	2.06		
1908	2.15		
1909	2.08		
1910	2.10		
1911	1.99		
1912	2.12		
1913	2.15		
1914[b]	2.10	2.15	2.08
1915[b]	2.12	2.36	1.91
1916[b]	2.27	2.50	2.12
1917[b]	2.50	2.50	2.45
1918[b]	2.58	3.20	2.43
1919[b]	2.15	2.43	2.11
1920[b]	2.24	2.60	2.11
1921[b]	3.53	4.00	2.65
1922[b]	4.05	4.85	3.65
1923[b]	4.86	6.20	3.40
1924[b]	5.13	5.65	4.50
1925[b]	4.32	5.10	3.85
1926[b]	5.05	6.20	4.25

Sources: Calculated from data in Luis Alberto Carbo, *Historia monetaria y cambiaria del Ecuador* (Quito: Imprenta del Banco Central del Ecuador, 1953), 68; Ministerio de Previsión Social y Trabajo, Dirección General de Estadística, *Comercio Exterior de la República del Ecuador en los años 1925 y 1926* (Quito: Talleres Tipográficos Nacionales, 1928).

[a]Sucres per dollar.

[b]Average annual exchange rate for 1914 through 1926 calculated by taking an average of the bimonthly high and low rates of the Banco de Descuento of Guayaquil, rather than averaging the yearly high and low rates. Therefore, column 2 for 1914–1926 is not an average of columns 3 and 4.

of cacao.[54] In such circumstances the return to the gold standard (convertibility) was out of the question.

Ecuador was not alone in facing a protracted fiscal crisis. World economic instability of unprecedented proportions prevented most countries, which had suspended the gold standard, from returning to it until the mid-1920s (see table 32). The period from 1914 to 1924 was characterized by violent shifts in trade and marketing patterns, price levels, currency values, and the distribution of wealth. Prices tripled between 1915 and 1921; then they fell 33 percent in fourteen months! For most countries, including Ecuador, this decline, the sharpest price deflation in modern times, was followed by a shorter cycle of rising and falling prices before the Great Depression. The extreme fluctuations of foreign exchange rates hindered international trade throughout this period. In Ecuador these fluctuations were particularly violent from 1917 through 1926, prompting

TABLE 32

CURRENCY STABILIZATION IN THE POSTWAR PERIOD 1922–1928

Country	Year of stabilization
Argentina	1927
Austria	1922
Belgium	1925, 1926
Bolivia	1928
Brazil	1927
Chile	1926
Czechoslovakia	1926
Ecuador	1927
England	1925
France	1928
Germany	1924
Hungary	1924
Italy	1927
Poland	1925, 1927
Russia	1924

Source: Information taken from chart prepared by Donald L. Kemmerer, University of Illinois, and submitted during hearing on Gold Reserve Act Amendments before a subcommittee of the Senate Banking and Currency Committee, March 29, 30, 31 and April 4, 1954, United States Congress, session 2 on Bills S.13,2332, 2364, and 2514 (Washington: U.S. Government Printing Office, 1954) 301–302.

governments to experiment with official fixed exchange rates, import controls, and restrictions on the sale of foreign drafts in an effort to shore up the sucre (see table 31). While these actions failed to moderate the fluctuations in the exchange rate or even to influence their direction, they succeeded in arousing the concern of Ecuadorians, even those who were not normally involved with external trade. Indeed the press and the public, overly concerned with the international value of the sucre, believed its decline resulted from speculation. They failed to realize that these changes were caused by declining productivity, budget deficits, and changing world market conditions. They fixated on the fluctuations of the exchange rate and demanded government action to stabilize the sucre through legislation, while overlooking the real solutions to the nation's economic problems: stimulating productivity and balancing the budget.[55]

Sierra regionalists used the country's financial plight to undermine their coastal rivals. They maintained that the Ley Moratoria—inconvertibility—and the government debt to Guayaquil banks were manifestations of a successful conspiracy by port bankers to dominate Ecuadorian politics. In their view a corrupt coastal oligarchy had selfishly exploited the country. The serranos concentrated their criticism on the Banco Comercial y Agrícola, the government's principal banker, and its manager, Francisco Urvina Jado. They chose to ignore the national and international conditions that were the primary cause of Ecuador's economic crisis.[56]

Regional jealousies, aggravated by personal antagonisms, clouded the economic and financial debate in Ecuador. Luis N. Dillon, a highland businessman and politician, emerged as the leading critic of what he termed the corrupt relationship between Guayaquil bankers and liberal administrations. He not only shared the northern highland's antipathy toward the more prosperous coast, his hostility was also fueled by the belief that his financial and political ambitions had been thwarted by Guayaquil bankers, particularly Urvina Jado. In 1922 Dillon had organized the Sociedad de Crédito Internacional in Quito, an institution established to issue currency in the highlands. The Sociedad had already printed and registered its notes when Urvina Jado learned that the bills had no backing. As the manager of one of the leading banks in the country, Urvina Jado considered it his responsibility to protect the nation's currency. He, therefore, complained to Minister of Finance Alfonso Larrea who, after investigating the matter, prohibited the circulation of the Sociedad's notes.

Dillon interpreted Urvina Jado's action both as a personal attack and as an example of regional animosity. Convinced that Guayaquil bankers dominated the country's banking and currency structure, he failed to notice that Urvina Jado acted in the same fashion when the prestigious Guayaquil Banco de Descuento also attempted to circulate improperly backed bills. The banker again protested to Minister Larrea and succeeded in having the notes recalled. In both instances, Urvina Jado acted to protect the nation's currency. Dillon, nevertheless, came to loathe the manager of the Banco Comercial y Agrícola. Dillon's enmity toward the coast intensified in 1924 when he failed to receive the post of minister of finance in the Córdova government. He, as well as the highland press, accused coastal regionalists of vetoing the appointment. Although Córdova offered Dillon another portfolio, the highlander rejected it believing that he deserved to be minister of finance since he was the manager of La Internacional, the country's largest textile factory, and because he was one of the most influential members of the highland business community.[57]

Dillon became the leading and most visible northern highland critic of the coast. Quito journalists, intellectuals, and politicians blamed a corrupt Guayaquil banking oligarchy for the country's problems. Disturbed by the ascendancy of the coast and what they perceived to be the diminishing status of Quito, the country's capital, northern highlanders charged that a small group of Guayaquil oligarchs ran the country. It was widely asserted, for example, that the president followed the orders of the manager of the Banco Comercial y Agrícola because the government owed so much money to that bank. Serranos interpreted the bank loans to the government as buying off the administration to retain the Ley Moratoria. They considered inconvertibility a plot by unscrupulous bankers to exploit the country, rather than a necessary measure to protect the currency. Serranos believed that Guayaquil bankers had vetoed Dillon's candidacy for minister of finance because the highlander opposed evil coastal practices. Dillon actively cultivated that image, speaking frequently on finances and national problems to organizations as varied as the Quito Chamber of Commerce and the military academy. Although a capitalist entrepreneur and a member of the liberal party, he did not hesitate to ally himself with socialists and militarists to propagate his regionalist views. Indeed, he donated funds, purchased advertising, and contributed articles to *La Antorcha*, a Quito socialist paper with a strong anticoastal bias.

Northern highland intellectuals and the Quito press in general argued that the coast exploited the rest of the country, but two sierra publications, *La Antorcha* and *El Abanderado*, a military oriented paper, were to play a key role in future events. As a socialist newspaper, *La Antorcha* published articles on socialism, but its hostility toward the "corrupt coastal plutocracy" and its demand for social reform made the paper acceptable to many Quiteños, both civilian and military. The paper often cooperated with *El Abanderado,* a journal that had a primarily military readership, published by retired Lieutenant Colonel Victor M. Naranjo. Naranjo published articles decrying the state of the country and condemning the plutocrats who had ruled too long. He argued that the army, the government, the courts, and the universities had all been corrupted to serve the interest of a few great capitalists in Guayaquil. *El Abanderado,* however, was primarily concerned with military reform. The paper distinguished between two types of officers: the professional and the political. It called political generals, like former president Leonidas Plaza, not only a cancer on the body politic but also a major impediment to the reform and modernization of the army. The paper considered General Francisco Gómez de la Torre, inspector general of the army, who had been educated in foreign military academies, the perfect example of a professional officer. In *El Abanderado's* view, political officers concerned themselves only with promotion and spoils while professional officers considered the country and the army's interests first. The paper exhorted the young officers, the first generation to be educated in a national military academy and presumably therefore professional, to abandon the old politics and to forge a new army and a new country. *El Abanderado* promoted regionalist antipathy by continually reminding the young officers that the old political officers, like Plaza, had grown rich by permitting coastal oligarchs to despoil the country.[58]

In 1924 *La Antorcha* and *El Abanderado* cooperated in advancing their common aims. *La Antorcha,* for example, falsely asserted that the Banco Comercial y Agrícola wanted the government to sell the Galápagos Islands; *El Abanderado* supported this allegation, claiming to possess official documents that proved the charge. Similarly, the two papers collaborated to discredit Free Masonry, a popular movement among coastal businessmen, but viewed with suspicion by the more conservative highlanders. The papers maintained that the Grand Lodge in Lima dominated Ecuadorian masons, and members therefore were agents of the country's ancient enemy, Peru. These arguments aroused the fears of young officers, most of whom were highlanders, and justified their regionalist sentiments. Starting in December 1924 the papers launched a campaign to convince the young officers that only they could save the country from the impending crisis. The papers publicized the recent military coup in Chile and praised its reforms. They also reminded the young officers that a Chilean mission had reorganized the Ecuadorian army and established the military academy where the officers had only recently studied. The conclusions were obvious; the young officers should take power, crush the corrupt coastal oligarchs, and reform the country. The articles and the exhortations of men like Dillon had the desired effect. Many young officers, writing under pseudonyms, submitted essays on national and military reform to the two papers. Their writings indicate that they blamed Guayaquil banks for the nation's problems. The fears of highlanders and, particularly, the concerns of the military men increased when President Córdova became ill and traveled to Guayaquil to recuperate. Serranos were convinced that the coast would dominate the president and that their interests would be forgotten.[59]

In October 1924 a group of lieutenants formed a *Liga Militar* in Quito to resolve the nation's crisis. Their plotting culminated in the overthrow of the Córdova government on July 9, 1925. The officers justified their actions in a twelve-point reform program which they prepared after consultation with Luis N. Dillon, the man whom they considered Ecuador's leading economic expert. Predictably they called for the repeal of the Ley Moratoria. They arrested Francisco Urvina Jado, the manager of the Banco Comercial y Agrícola, and named Dillon to the provisional governing committee that ran Ecuador after the coup. The young officers believed that they represented national not regional interest. Nevertheless, Urvina's death in exile and the subsequent destruction of the Banco Comercial y Agrícola symbolized the regional prejudices and economic misperceptions that triumphed in the 1925 coup.[60]

5. The Politics of Reform

The period from 1925 to 1931 is widely regarded as a time of national reform and regeneration in Ecuador. The traditional interpretation holds that the lieutenants who overthrew President Córdova on July 9, 1925, initiated a period of change that ended the domination of the "corrupt coastal oligarchy," and the creation of the central bank symbolized the rational restructuring that supposedly ended the old regionalist politics.[1] This interpretation, like other aspects of Ecuadorian history, reflects sectional bias, since most historians have been serranos. Idealistic young officers started the Liga Militar, but power rapidly passed to majors, colonels, and generals as well as to prominent Quito politicians. The reforms, which they advocated in the name of national unity and rehabilitation, returned power to the highlands. The new regime invited a team of American advisers led by Edwin W. Kemmerer to recommend changes to modernize Ecuadorian public finances. But the leaders of the July movement would not wait for the unbiased, apolitical recommendations of the foreign experts. Their activities prior to the arrival of the Kemmerer Mission intensified public distrust of the country's financial institutions and promoted their version of solutions appropriate for the nation's ills. Determined to end the financial power of the coastal elite, the highland leaders sought to establish the central bank in Quito and destroy the Banco Comercial y Agrícola, the largest and most prominent of the Guayaquil banks, the institutions that had financed a significant portion of Ecuador's early twentieth-century development.[2]

Banks and Revolutionary Politics

The Military League, which overthrew the government of Gonzalo Córdova, included military men from all sections of the country, but the young officers in Quito and Guayaquil were its principal leaders.

Although the coup began in Guayaquil on July 9, 1925, the Quito group took over the government in the capital. Without waiting for the Guayaquil representatives to arrive, they named a six-man Supreme Military Junta that in turn appointed a Provisional Governing Committee including two generals and two civilians from Quito, prominent among them Luis N. Dillon. These appointments concerned the guayaquileños who believed quiteños, hostile to the coast, had usurped control of the government. After considerable protest, one of the generals resigned and three representatives from the coast arrived to join the Provisional Governing Committee. The change did not affect the new balance of power. The coastal members received appointments to less important ministries such as education, public works, and social welfare, while highlanders filled those of interior, foreign affairs, finance, and war. Indeed General Francisco Gómez de la Torre, minister of war, and Luis N. Dillon, minister of finance, dominated the government with the support of the young officers and the Supreme Military Junta.[3]

The first Junta de Gobierno Provisional ruled Ecuador from July 10, 1925, until January 9, 1926, a period of great instability and regional conflict. Given the propaganda that preceded the coup, the young officers demanded the incarceration and later the exile of former president, General Leonidas Plaza, and bank manager, Francisco Urvina Jado. In addition, they closed the Banco Comercial y Agrícola and imposed restrictions on Guayaquil banks. Dillon, the new minister of finance, was only too happy to harass his former adversaries. The governing junta formed two commissions on July 21, 1925, to investigate the practices of the banks of issue. Although each of the investigative groups were to have three members, including two accountants, the Primera Comisión Fiscaliza dora, which examined the Banco Comercial y Agrícola, also included two army lieutenants.[4]

The first investigatory committee submitted its findings to Dillon on August 22, 1925. The report contained precise tables on all aspects of the Banco Comercial y Agrícola's activities, but clearly the auditors acted with bias. They concluded that the bank had illegally circulated improperly backed currency throughout the period from 1914 to 1925. To reach this determination the commission adopted an extremely restrictive definition of legal reserves and a very liberal construction of currency emission. It considered only gold actually deposited in the Guayaquil vault as the bank's reserve and it ignored the bank's overseas gold and government assets mortgaged to the bank. The commission considered all notes in circulation and uncirculated bills held in the bank's vaults as currency

emitted by the Banco Comercial y Agrícola. These interpretations significantly increased the quantity of the bank's improperly backed bills.[5]

The data necessary to evaluate the report of the Primera Junta Fiscalizadora is presented in table 33. If one considers, as did the new
government, that legal issues of currency had to be backed by 50 percent
gold reserves held locally, then the Banco Comercial y Agrícola was guilty
of overemission in every year from 1914 through 1926. The bank's metallic
reserves fluctuated between 2.5 percent following the run on the bank
precipitated by World War I, and 33.9 percent. If, however, one includes
the bank's overseas gold as part of its reserve, then illegally secured bills
circulated only in 1914, 1916, and from 1921 to 1926. But the picture
changes dramatically if one takes into account, as did the bank and previous
liberal governments, the 1914 legislation authorizing banks of issue to
include government debt to the institution as part of its reserves. In that
case, the reserves of the Banco Comercial y Agrícola were always
sufficient, and frequently exceeded the 50 percent requirement originally
established in 1898.

The commission's report carefully avoided any consideration of the
relationship between the 1914 reserve requirement legislation, the bank's
loans to the government during the period 1914 to 1925 and the "illegal"
emissions of currency. Yet, despite their adverse findings, the auditors
concluded that the Banco Comercial y Agrícola was solvent. Upon receipt
of the report, Minister of Finance Dillon fined the bank 2,237,093.33
sucres and then urged its liquidation. Since the institution was the country's largest bank with branches in several highland cities and since it had
been a major factor in the modernization of Ecuador during the preceding
twenty-five years, the minister urged that the government replace it with
a central bank.[6]

Ecuadorians had long considered the establishment of a central bank
a prerequisite for modernizing and reforming the nation's finances. Indeed
coastal bankers, as the individuals most concerned with monetary reform,
had publicly discussed such a move since 1920. They favored the creation
of a central bank, believing that it should be founded on a sound economic
basis and organized to respond to the country's special needs. The sierra
supported a central bank for political reasons. Highlanders wanted the
institution established only in Quito to end the financial hegemony of
the coast.

By the spring of 1925 the nation's economy had deteriorated so
drastically that Guayaquil bankers urged President Córdova to invite
Edwin Kemmerer, a Princeton economist with wide experience in advis-

TABLE 33

BANCO COMERCIAL Y AGRÍCOLA: MONETARY
CIRCULATION AND RESERVES 1913–1926[a]

Year	Gold reserves	Funds abroad	Government debt to bank	Bank note circulation	"Illegal" issues
1913	1,159,430	1,577	4,907,039	4,440,093	2,121,233
1914	157,560	2,807,930	6,247,045	6,304,937	5,989,817
1915	2,509,740	2,852,410	6,685,409	7,406,229	2,386,749
1916	2,592,810	2,782,006	7,199,286	11,564,599	6,378,979
1917	3,590,990	4,009,123	7,312,852	13,085,100	5,903,120
1918	3,590,970	7,966,184	8,347,196	14,709,912	7,527,972
1919	3,590,930	9,125,937	8,975,982	15,427,449	8,245,589
1920	3,590,940	2,535,091	9,636,347	13,083,910	5,902,030
1921	3,590,940	1,216,976	10,334,813	12,680,638	5,498,758
1922	3,590,930	1,225,630	11,218,259	16,725,703	9,543,843
1923	3,590,930	859,265	11,909,612	19,020,115	11,838,255
1924	3,590,910	80,192	12,578,304	23,063,943	15,882,123
1925	3,590,910	323,789	27,262,496	25,242,597	18,060,777
1926	3,590,910	720,158	23,370,000	25,627,099	18,445,279

Sources: Compiled from information in Julio Estrada Ycaza, *Los bancos del siglo XIX*, (Guayaquil: Archivo Histórico del Guayas, 1976), 248, 274–275, 280–281, and Ecuador, Comisión Fiscalizadora de Bancos del Litoral, *Las Instituciones de crédito del Ecuador en 1925: Banco Comercial y Agrícola (Guayaquil)*, (Quito: Talleres Tipográficos del Ministerio de Hacienda, 1926), 41–42.

[a]In sucres.

ing governments on currency stabilization and central bank operations, to study Ecuador's financial situation and recommend reforms. The bankers believed the services of a distinguished foreign expert were so vital that they offered to pay the cost of the advisory mission if the government did not have the money. Córdova was negotiating with Kemmerer when his government was overthrown. Dillon, the new minister of finance, opposed inviting a foreigner to advise the Provisional Governing Junta, therefore he terminated negotiations with Kemmerer. The junta chose to act without a thorough study.[7]

Dillon proposed forming a central bank by expropriating the metallic reserves of the country's banks of issue. This action would have severe repercussions among coastal banks that held the bulk of the nation's metallic reserve. Since the minister of finance intended to pay the banks less than half the world market value for their gold, the affected financial institutions understandably criticized the scheme. The bankers also were concerned because an extralegal government was ordering them to transfer their gold reserve to a new institution that they feared would promote parochial rather than national interests. In their view, the prudent and legal course would be to elect a constitutional government that would hire and implement the suggestions of disinterested foreign financial experts. The discussion concerning the technical aspects of establishing a central bank soon degenerated into a regional dispute, as the national press reported and analyzed the disagreement between the provisional government and the financial community. Highland papers defended the government, while the Guayaquil press so ardently supported the coastal bankers that the government imposed press censorship. Guayaquil papers struck to defend their right to publish. As a result of growing public discontent with the government, as well as disputes among the junta members, the Supreme Military Junta forced the resignation of the government.[8] It then appointed a new Junta de Gobierno Provisional that governed from January 10 to March 31, 1926.

To obtain backing for government policies, Humberto Albornoz, the new provisional minister of finance, hosted a banker's conference during February and March. He asked the bankers to examine the country's economic conditions and recommend solutions to national problems. The bankers reported that the fundamental causes of the financial crisis— government deficit spending and declining economic productivity—had been building for years. Since July 1925 government hostility to the banks and the loss of public confidence in financial institutions, which that hostility engendered, had exacerbated the crisis. Bankers urged consistent and supportive government policies toward the banks and their currency. They also argued that the government's campaign against the Banco Comercial y Agrícola threatened normal financial transactions since the bank had issued most of the currency then in circulation. The government's restrictive definition of reserve requirements had forced some banks to recall their bills, resulting in a currency shortage. To alleviate the scarcity, banks with insufficient "legal" notes to pay drafts presented at their windows issued checks drawn on their accounts at other banks in lieu of currency. The first provisional government originally had approved the use of these "circulating checks" as currency. Without warning it changed its policy, declaring them illegal and demanding their immediate withdrawal. The administration threatened to jail bankers who failed to comply promptly with the new policy. To alleviate the continuing scarcity of paper money, the bankers recommended that the government authorize an emergency emission of bills backed by government assets, mortgage bonds, or a reduced metallic reserve. As a temporary expedient to restore confidence, some bankers suggested that the government create a central office for currency emission as an appendage of the Ministry of Finance. The bankers, however, believed that Ecuador needed to bring a foreign advisory mission to propose definitive solutions for the nation's financial problems.[9] The government rejected most of the bankers' advice, but reopened negotiations with Kemmerer. At this point the Supreme Military Junta replaced the second provisional committee with a single executive, the Minister of Social Welfare Isidro Ayora who concluded an agreement with Kemmerer on April 1, 1926.

The Supreme Military Junta, the final arbiter of Ecuadorian politics, opposed a "premature" return to constitutional government. The costeños in the provisional government and politically active groups in the littoral favored the prompt convocation of a constituent assembly to defend their interests. The military, mainly from the highlands, believed national reforms could not be implemented through normal political means. By naming Ayora, a respected physician with strong ties both to the coast and the highlands, provisional president, they forestalled elections. The Ecuadorian army probably agreed with the British minister who reported to his government that "the real solution of Ecuador would be a man of the stamp of Porfirio Díaz of Mexico to run the country with an iron hand, assisted by foreign and honest officials." The minister of interior later defended the military's action before the 1929 constituent assembly, declaring that all who desired real change after July 9, 1925, concluded that it could only be accomplished by an honorable "dictator" who could organize and discipline the government. Parliamentary methods, he argued, could not have reformed the nation.[10]

The new Ayora administration also opposed Guayaquil banks. Indeed, it appears that it deliberately undermined public confidence in the banking system and aggravated the economic crisis. As a result, the weakened financial institutions could not reject government-imposed solutions to the monetary crisis. The Ayora government closed numerous banks and jailed their officers because they had failed to comply with orders recalling the illegal "circulating checks." Yet the regime failed to stem the contraction of paper money in the post-coup period. Of the many reasons for the growing scarcity of legal currency, most sprang from government actions. Restrictions on emissions even prevented banks from issuing new bills to replace worn and mutilated notes. Political and economic uncertainty further reduced the volume of money in circulation as the public began to hoard "legal" bills. Government plans to fund a central bank by transferring bank bullion reserves to the new institution at rates far below fair market price also prompted banks to restrict currency emissions. The treatment of the Banco Comercial y Agrícola did little to dispel the financial gloom. The bank remained closed pending a satisfactory arrangement concerning the public debt held by the institution. Late in April 1926 the Ministry of Finance and bank representatives announced an agreement that recognized 26,757,060.36 sucres of government indebtedness to the institution; the debt was reduced to 23,370,000 sucres by the fines former Finance Minister Dillon had imposed on the bank for its "illegal" currency issues. The government pledged to pay the bank two million sucres within thirty days so that it could reopen. Of the remaining debt, 2,980,000 sucres bearing 6 percent interest would be amortized at 2 percent per year, while 18,390,000 sucres, which corresponded to loans funded with improperly backed notes, would bear no interest and would be repaid in annual installments of two million sucres. The Banco Comercial y Agrícola did not reopen because the government reneged on its agreement. Untimately Ecuador's leading bank was liquidated.[11]

The financial crisis forced Provisional President Ayora to act. On June 16, 1926, he froze the metallic reserves of the banks of issue; on June 23, he decreed the establishment in Quito of a Caja Central de Emisión y Amortización. The new Central Office of Emission and Amortization was, ostensibly, a private institution with government representation on its board of directors. Although the Caja's board included a representative from each former bank of issue as well as Humberto Albornoz, the government representative—a quiteño banker and minister of finance in the second provisional governing junta, the administration controlled the institution because it approved the Caja's bylaws and organization. The minister of finance dominated the organizing sessions that were held in his office! The government authorized the Caja to issue currency with a 25 percent metallic reserve, in contrast to the old 50 percent requirement. The banks' gold reserves were transferred to the Caja at the tentative value of 10 sucres per pound sterling, or less than half their actual market price. The new consolidated metallic reserve provided backing for all bills then in circulation as well as for the new notes to be issued by the Caja. The government also transferred its indebtedness to banks to the Caja, agreeing to amortize the consolidated debt with one-half the revenues from export duties. (This new commitment violated the agreement between the Ecuadorian government and the Guayaquil-

Quito Railway bondholders.) The banks of issue cooperated in the formation of the Caja because they too wished to resolve the monetary crisis and because the government assured them that the Kemmerer Mission would establish the final value of the metallic reserves. Nevertheless, on October 18, 1926—the same day that the American advisers arrived in Guayaquil—Ayora decreed that the definitive price for the confiscated gold was 10 sucres per pound sterling. He also informed the banks that all bank notes, even those never released to the public, formed part of a bank's legal emissions, thereby significantly increasing the gold which the banks of issue had to transfer to the Caja.[12] These actions presented the foreign advisors with a *fait acompli* (see table 34).

From November 1926 through August 1927, the Caja limited itself to emitting "validated" paper currency from the former banks of issue and replacing worn out or damaged bills. This was consistent with the government's view of the Caja's role. It had been founded essentially to prevent an open discussion of how and where the central bank should be established. Most bankers, including Francisco Urvina Jado, had been willing to transfer their gold reserves to a central bank at fifteen sucres per pound sterling, or about 75 percent of its market value. This would have provided the government a significant profit and started the institution on a strong footing. Understandably the bankers opposed the payment of only ten sucres offered by the government. Since coastal banks held most of Ecuador's gold reserves, the sierra politicians easily portrayed the bankers' attitude as a nefarious example of coastal regionalism and avarice. Furthermore, the government opposed the bankers' demand that the new central bank be headquartered in Guayaquil, the nation's commercial capital. The Ayora government, supported by a pro-sierra military, wanted the nation's political capital also to be its financial center. Therefore, it acted decisively to preempt any possible conflicting recommendations from the Kemmerer Mission.[13]

The Role of Foreign Advisers

Since independence presidents like Flores, Rocafuerte, García Moreno, and Alfaro, to name only the most prominent, had relied on foreign experts to advise their governments on finance, technology, education, sanitation, transportation, agriculture, industry, and military reorganization. Ecuador drew foreign experts from England, France, Spain, Germany, Italy, Chile, Japan, and the United States. American advisers

TABLE 34

GOLD RESERVES TRANSFERRED TO CAJA CENTRAL
DE EMISIÓN Y AMORTIZACIÓN

Bank	Amount of gold reserves required by Caja Central de Emisión y Amortización
Banco del Ecuador	2,572,883.70
Banco Comercial y Agrícola	3,716,174.05
Banco del Pichincha	2,901,507.00
Banco del Azuay	737,750.00
Banco de Descuento	330,000.00
Compañía de Credito Agrícola e Industrial	346,000.00
Total	10,604,314.75

Source: Decree, no. 476 (October 20, 1926), Ecuador. *Anuario, 1926*, vol. 24, tomo 2, 962–964.

became more prominent as the United States expanded its economic and political role in the world, particularly after World War I.[14] In some instances the foreign advisers provided technical expertise which Ecuadorians did not possess, but in most cases the foreigners were invited to support or legitimize the views held by a faction within the country. Given the regional and political divisions in Ecuador, nationals could not command sufficient respect to obtain the consensus necessary to implement change. A pattern emerged in the late nineteenth and early twentieth century: Ecuadorians would discuss intensely an issue and then invite foreign experts to propose solutions. Governments employed foreign advisers with known views who would recommend policies they favored. The government that implemented the suggestions could argue that it had acted on the apolitical advice of foreign experts. Foreign advisers were most effective when involved with short-term projects. Specialists hired as long-term consultants or advisors soon lost their special status as they became involved in local politics.

Ecuador also used foreign experts to convince foreign investors and creditors that the country respected the principles of international finance and would establish internal financial order. Ecuadorian governments capitalized on the self-interest of the wealthy nations to achieve their own ends. Ecuadorians employed advisers in a conscious effort to direct their own future. Foreign missions were not an example of imperialism imposed on an unsophisticated and vulnerable nation, as some contemporary observers have argued.[15]

John S. Hord's experience as a foreign adviser exemplifies the role of external experts in Ecuador. José L. Tamayo was elected president in 1920 promising to reform government finances. Once in office he proposed obtaining the services of a foreign financial adviser but internal political and economic problems delayed the hiring. In 1923 the Tamayo administration negotiated an agreement with John S. Hord, who had more than twenty years of experience as a foreign financial adviser. The agreement granted Hord a four-year contract at fifteen thousand dollars per year, round-trip transportation between the United States and Ecuador, and funds for travel and office expenses within Ecuador. Hord was to advise the minister of finance and to serve on the Comisión Técnica Financiera Consultiva in the ministry. The commission, which had been created by the congress in October 1922 to revise existing regulations and to draft new legislation on taxes, tariffs, budgets, tax collection, fiscal control, loans, and other aspects of government finances, had not begun to function by mid-1923.[16]

The press reacted favorably to Hord's appointment. When he arrived in Guayaquil on August 20, 1923, the city's papers urged politicians, bankers, and businessmen to put aside private interests and traditional prejudices to assist Hord with their expertise and insights. The press cited his experience in Mexico, Puerto Rico, the Philippines, Cuba, and Haiti. The biographical sketch strengthened his credibility as a financial expert. In an interview with Guayaquil papers, Hord showed admirable respect for local sensibilities by emphasizing that he was not in Ecuador to make changes, but to study the situation and to advise the government. He also prudently refrained from commenting on specifics before he could consult with the president and become familiar with local conditions. Financial writers warned, however, that unless the government supported the foreign adviser, enacted appropriate legislation, and implemented the recommended reforms, the mission would accomplish nothing. Some feared that a single expert could not reform so many structures and procedures; others feared that regionalists in congress would oppose meaningful change; but most informed Ecuadorians seemed optimistic that Hord could accomplish much with the support of the authorities.[17]

Despite the initial widespread public backing, Hord received only partial support from the government. Congress approved his first recommendation, enacting a 1 percent sales tax to increase government revenue. But President Tamayo failed to appoint the Technical Advisory Financial

Committee to assist Hord in drawing up measures to reform the country's economic and financial structures. The president, who was more concerned with negotiating a loan and construction contracts with Italian companies, instead revived the Permanent Legislative Committee and appointed three civilian attaches of the Italian legation as voting members. He justified this action on the ground that the Italian government paid for the services of these experts in finance, engineering, and agriculture. Although congress had originally formed the committee to study a reform program submitted by a group of Italian advisers and to draft laws based upon its evaluation of the experts' recommendations, it eventually rejected the proposed legislation and the committee resigned. The Permanent Legislative Committee revived by Tamayo included Gómez Jaramillo, minister of finance, Abelardo Moncayo, the former president of the committee, and Víctor Manuel Peñaherrera, all respected Ecuadorian financial experts. Hord criticized the committee's composition, believing it unwise to grant foreigners with official ties to their own governments a major role in Ecuador's national planning. To make matters worse the North American expert lacked a formal role on the committee. Despite strenuous lobbying, Hord failed to change its membership. Instead he had to establish an informal working group in the Ministry of Finance, which included members of the Permanent Legislative Committee, to participate in the planning process. The ad hoc arrangement worked, but Hord's official exclusion from the committee lessened his stature and thus diminished his ability to influence a society acutely concerned with status.[18]

The ad hoc group's major achievement was to prepare and submit a centralized budget for fiscal 1925 to the 1924 congress. Although amendments to protect regional projects forced the adoption of an unbalanced and only partially centralized budget, the budget bill was a significant victory for advocates of centralized fiscal control. Even more important, as originally presented, the 1925 budget provided Ecuador's first realistic projections of income and expenditure based on an analysis of actual collections and disbursements in previous years.[19] In addition the ad hoc working group adopted a program with six principal objectives: a balanced budget, resumed debt service, increased production and exports, reestablishment of the gold standard, and consolidation of the public debt.

Although hampered by inadequate statistics, Hord and the Permanent Legislative Commission found their work primarily disrupted by government instability. Between the time of Hord's arrival in August 1923 and the end of July 1925, Ecuador had two constitutional presidents, an acting president, a plural executive, and five ministers of finance. Rapid turnover of personnel in the executive branch made it impossible to establish clear priorities because each new administrator had different goals.

Hord's role as a reformer and planner miscarried as he became involved in the day-to-day decision making through requests for information and advice on specific issues. His recommendations were ignored when they conflicted with the desires and interests of those soliciting his opinion, but his advice was used to justify unpopular political decisions when it suited those in power. Hord rapidly lost his status as an apolitical expert because his "politicization" progressively diminished his usefulness as a consensus builder. The First Provisional Governing Junta sought to anull his contract, charging that the Tamayo government had signed an agreement inimical to the country's interests and that Hord had failed to fulfill the terms of the contract. The national press joined in criticizing Hord's performance conveniently overlooking what it had emphasized when he arrived: no individual could introduce reforms without support from the government. Hord ably defended his record in a report to Dillon and informed the new minister of finance that he would fight to retain his position. The new government retained the American to avoid the embarrassment of a public confrontation at a time when it hoped for prompt diplomatic recognition by the United States. Dillon reassigned Hord to the Oficina Consultiva Técnica, a new dependency of the Ministry of Finance, a transfer that signaled the end of Hord's role as a comprehensive planner. Thereafter he would be employed primarily in auditing various government offices and government-controlled agencies. The press attacked Hord viciously after his contract expired in June 1927; characterizing his hiring a complete mistake in contrast to the Kemmerer Mission, which the papers hailed as an unqualified success.[20]

The Kemmerer Mission

Guayaquil bankers and businessmen launched a campaign to invite Edwin W. Kemmerer to propose financial reforms long before July 9, 1925. Víctor E. Estrada, of the Banco de Descuento of Guayaquil, had been corresponding with Kemmerer about Ecuadorian problems before negotiations for the mission began. Their letters indicate that Ecuadorians were familiar with Kemmerer's work in Guatemala and Colombia. The coastal bankers understood that a Kemmerer advisory mission would recommend currency stabilization as well as devaluation, tax reform, the modernization of the banking system, and the creation of a central bank. Their efforts to secure his expert advice continued after the military coup, particularly at the government-sponsored conference on the economy in February and March of 1926. The bankers believed that Kemmerer had the necessary economic and financial expertise and the prestige to silence critics and to introduce the needed reforms.[21]

Edwin W. Kemmerer enjoyed an international reputation as a foreign financial adviser when the Ecuadorian government contacted him. The Princeton professor of economics, who obtained his first experience as financial adviser in 1903 when he worked as a member of the United States Philippines Commission, specialized in currency reform and central banking. During that three-year assignment he drafted the organizing statutes for the postal saving system and the agricultural bank of the islands, placed its monetary system on the gold standard, and served as chief of the division of currency. In subsequent years he advised, either alone or more frequently as the head of a commission, Egypt, India, the Straits Settlements, Puerto Rico, Germany, Mexico, Guatemala, Colombia, Poland, the Union of South Africa, and Chile. Each mission enhanced his reputation and increased the demand for his services. Convinced that currency reform could not be achieved in isolation, Kemmerer preferred to work with a group of experts who examined banking, budgeting, taxation, the public debt, and foreign exchange problems of the countries he agreed to advise. Thus, when the Ecuadorian government approached him, he proposed forming an advisory commission.

The government authorized Kemmerer to form a five-member commission to spend four months, beginning in October 1926, evaluating Ecuador's financial problems. The government agreed to pay seventy thousand dollars, plus the advisory group's travel, living, office, and incidental expenses and to provide legal advisers, translators, clerks, stenographers, and draftsmen. Kemmerer, who chaired the group, would examine currency and banking problems as well as public credit and government borrowing policies. The other members of the mission included a specialist on practical banking to study bank organization and operations; a tax expert to examine government revenue, expenditures, and budgeting; an accountant to investigate accounting and fiscal control; and a customs specialist to recommend changes in aduana administration. The government subsequently amended the contract to include a railroad expert, agreeing to pay an additional ten thousand dollars. The mission also included a general secretary, Kemmerer's secretary, and an assistant for the general secretary.[22]

To form the advisory mission Kemmerer sought individuals with experience in Latin America, a good command of Spanish, a thorough knowledge of economic and financial principles, and the ability to frame innovative approaches for unusual problems. If he did not know the individuals, Kemmerer carefully checked their references to ensure that those accepted had the highest credentials. The group that traveled to Ecuador possessed expertise and much experience. Howard M. Jefferson, the expert on practical banking, had worked for the Federal Reserve Bank of New York and had earlier participated in Kemmerer's advisory missions to Chile and Colombia. Joseph T. Byrne, an expert on accounting and fiscal control, had previously assisted in the reorganization of the Santo Domingo customs, had served as collector general of Peruvian customs, and had participated in the Kemmerer mission to Chile. Robert Vorfeld, an expert in customs administration, worked with the Tariff Commission in Washington and had earlier organized the customs of Paraguay. Only Oliver C. Lockhart, the tax expert, and B. B. Milner, the railroad specialist, lacked a knowledge of Spanish and had to take intensive courses to prepare for the mission. Lockhart, professor of economics at the University of Buffalo, had directed the tax department of the National Bank of Commerce in New York. Milner, a graduate of Purdue, was the assistant to the president of the New York Central Lines and had served as an advisor on tariffs and traffic to the Imperial government of Japan. Edward Feely, the secretary of the mission who worked closely with Kemmerer to coordinate the group's activities, was a former United States commercial attaché in Buenos Aires. F. W. Fetter, a Princeton graduate student, acted as Kemmerer's private secretary. Two Ecuadorians accompanied the mission—Alejandro Campana of the Ecuadorian consulate in New York and Francisco Banda, a doctoral student at the School of Foreign Service at Georgetown University, who was attached to the Ecuadorian legation in Washington.[23]

Kemmerer asked the Ecuadorian government, as well as his colleagues, to prepare carefully for the group's arrival in Quito. He requested that the government prepare translations of the laws, reports, and documents pertinent to the mission. He also asked Banda to translate those laws needed by the group before its departure. In Ecuador, the government appointed Ernesto Moncayo A. to oversee preparations for the Kemmerer Mission, which received offices in the new post office building in the center of Quito as well as office equipment and supplies ordered from the United States. John Hord was assigned the task of preparing a statement for Kemmerer concerning the fiscal reforms proposed in previous years with an indication of the actions taken in each case. The director general de estadística, who was charged with providing the mission with statistical information, sent circulars to public and private groups and individuals throughout the country soliciting data and opinions about the country's problems and their possible solutions. These requests resulted in a flood of reports and analyses of Ecuador's problems. Newspapers, filled with statistical information, discussed issues on the basis of data rather than conjecture. Perhaps the most important long-term result of the scramble to gather material for the mission was the realization that much information was either fragmentary or from questionable sources, leading public officials and the general public to demand better provisions for gathering and retaining statistical information.

The requests for information served a dual purpose for the Kemmerer Mission; they provided the advisers with data that would have been unavailable if the foreign experts had relied only on existing government statistics, and it brought individuals and groups into the reform process by giving them an opportunity to share their views with the mission. These activities helped build support for the reforms even before the advisers arrived. They also alerted the experts to the special interests that had to be considered. The group read information on public finances, which arrived at Princeton before the departure of the mission, and discussed it, often by letter. The process, which continued while Kemmerer was in Poland on another advisory mission, frequently resulted in requests for additional information. When the Kemmerer Mission arrived in Ecuador, it was familiar with local conditions and prepared to begin work immediately.[24]

On October 16, 1926, Ecuadorians greeted the arrival of the Kemmerer Mission with great hope and enthusiasm. The press reiterated the accomplishments of the Princeton economist, noting that he was also the author of many books and articles on currency reform, banking and public credit, as well as president of the American Economic Association. Similar articles appeared about the other members of the mission and about the Ecuadorians appointed to assist them. Editorials welcoming the advisers informed them that the entire country expected the group to salvage Ecuador's finances. After the first surge of excitement the press began to offer advice and to urge Ecuadorians to inform the mission about the country's needs. The press was filled with suggestions and information for the experts throughout the group's stay in Ecuador. Editorials exhorted the government and the people to accept the mission's recommendations as if it were medicine prescribed by a doctor, noting that Poland had profited from the Kemmerer Mission by enacting the proposals into law. Highland newspapers repeatedly stressed that the interests of the entire nation should be the only consideration in judging the recommendations; the concerns of special groups, they argued, could not always be protected. Generally, regionalist sentiments were muffled during the mission's stay in the country.[25]

The Kemmerer Mission followed a strict work schedule and avoided premature disclosures of its findings. It warned the public not to expect news releases and that it would not publish its recommendations until February. Kemmerer's determination to maintain confidentiality brought him into conflict with the United States ambassador in Quito who believed he should receive advance copies of the mission's proposals. Kemmerer, however, insisted that he was employed by the Ecuadorian government and both the United States embassy and the Ecuadorian public would have to wait until the government released the projects. The mission welcomed the advice and opinions of interested parties, but only granted access to the advisers through the Ministry of Finance in order to avoid unnecessary interruptions. During the first weeks the experts analyzed the material available on their special areas, occasionally conferring with local specialists or requesting additional information. Then they met in Quito and in Guayaquil with numerous government officials, bankers, businessmen, industrialists, labor groups, and agriculturalists to obtain their advice and opinions.

The Guayaquil meeting was the better organized and illustrates the manner in which the mission functioned. The governor of Guayas Province formed a series of committees composed of leaders from the banking, business, commercial, and agricultural sectors of the coastal economy who reviewed one or more issues and framed recommendations for the Kemmerer Mission. The committee on agricultural and industrial development, for example, examined Ecuador's position as a cacao producer and determined that it would never regain its former prominence in the world market. The committee indicated that the country's political situation and its tax system discouraged investment in agriculture by both domestic and foreign entrepreneurs. Only a stable constitutional government and a tax code that provided exemptions or reduced levies during the critical early years of a new enterprise would attract capital and investment. The committee also reported that local industry, still in its infancy, required government support and encouragement through protective tariffs and through efforts to ensure that government entities purchased national products whenever possible. Other committees examined banking, commerce, tariffs, record keeping, public finances, government monopolies, commercial and fiscal legislation, and currency stabilization. Their careful and detailed reports prompted Kemmerer to request that the committees continue to function so that the foreign advisers might call on them, either individually or collectively, for information. After explaining the responsibilities of the members of the mission, he requested that information to be sent to the specialist concerning the issue.

As a result of his long experience, Kemmerer had a carefully planned structure for the mission. He formed teams of two individuals; one member took the primary responsibility for an area, assisted by a second adviser with expertise in the field. Robert Vorfeld, for example, who had the primary responsibility for customs administration, was assisted by Joseph Byrne, the mission's expert on accounting and fiscal control. During the research and drafting stages of the project, each two-man committee presented daily progress reports to the entire mission. During the formative stages of a project, there were wide-ranging discussions in which mission members frequently offered differing opinions on both the problems and the proper solutions. The project committee then prepared a preliminary draft based on their analysis of the existing data for the rest of the mission to criticize, including the two secretaries who were also economists. After incorporating these criticisms, the project committee rewrote the proposal and presented it to the mission for final approval. It then submitted the authorized version to the appropriate government authorities for comment and considered their responses in framing the final official project. The procedure was efficient, but the mission could not complete its work in the time allotted by the contract because the government asked the advisers for studies that had not been part of the original agreement. The Kemmerer Mission required a twenty-day extension to finish its work. Before extending his stay in Ecuador, Kemmerer received permission from the Bolivian government to delay the start of a mission scheduled to begin immediately upon the completion of the Ecuadorian project.[26]

The Kemmerer Mission's final recommendations, submitted to the government in February and March of 1927, consisted of two thousand pages of proposed laws, with attached explanatory statements, and a series of reports on special topics. It was Kemmerer's practice not to present a single comprehensive report. He considered it more effective to submit memoranda on specific subjects either in the form of drafts of laws ready to present to congress, or as administrative orders to be issued by the executive. This format also allowed the advisory group to control the

The fluvial network in the coast facilitated commercial agricultural development

River transportation on the coast

Coastal shipping

Preparing dried cacao for shipment

Inauguration of the Guayaquil and Quito Railway. Seated left to right are Archer Harman, builder of the rail line and President Eloy Alfaro. Standing from right to left are Minister Amalio Puga, William H. Fox, General Francisco Hipolito Moncayo, Ministers César Borja, Belisario V. Torres and Alfredo Monje.

Human, animal and rail transport in the sierra

Railway construction in the sierra

Clearing a landslide on the Guayaquil and Quito rail line

President Leonidas Plaza G.

President Gonzalo Cordova with aides

Check for the Ecuadorian Government account at the Banco Comercial y Agrícola

Luis N. Dillon

The Plural Government in July 1925. Seated from right to left: Julio E. Moreno, Francisco Arízaga Luque, Modesto Larrea Jijón, Luis N. Dillon, José Rafael Bustamante, Francisco J. Bolona, Pedro Pablo Garaicoa and General Francisco Gómez de la Torre

New provisional government appointed early in 1926 with military officers

President Isidro Ayora and
Edwin W. Kemmerer

Edwin W. Kemmerer and
Minister of Finance Pedro Nuñez

Members of the Kemmerer Mission with the Minister of Finance. Seated
right to left: Oliver C. Lockhart, Edwin W. Kemmerer, Minister of Finance Pedro Nuñez, Howard M. Jefferson, Joseph T. Byrne; standing
right to left: Edward Feely, F. W. Fetter, Robert Vorfeld, and B. B. Milner

exact wording of the law, thus eliminating the possibility that vague or poorly worded laws might be written by less knowledgeable individuals. An explanatory report outlining the underlying principles supporting the proposals and providing interpretative commentary on individual articles, which supporters of the project could use in congressional debates or for explanations to the public, accompanied the mission's recommendations. In his recommendations to create new institutions or to adopt new and sophisticated procedures, Kemmerer urged the government to appoint thoroughly qualified individuals to administer the new entities and policies. This recommendation generally meant hiring experienced foreigners until local personnel could be trained.

The laws proposed by the Kemmerer Mission sought to meet two objectives: to modernize and strengthen Ecuadorian institutions and procedures and to eliminate budget deficits. To accomplish the first objective, the mission recommended a new system for managing public funds and for regulating the fiscal and banking system. It proposed to achieve the second goal through the centralization of government income, a revision of the tax system, and the allocation of government funds through a national budget. The Kemmerer Mission submitted the following drafts of laws to the Ecuadorian government: a central bank law, a monetary law, a general banking law, a law regulating loan contracts secured by land, a budget law, a law restructuring government accounting and creating a comptroller's office, a law revising rural property taxes, a law revising income tax, a law regulating customs administration, a law revising export duties on tagua, a new tariff law, a law amending the penal code to make the forging and passing of fraudulent checks a serious crime, amendments to articles of the constitution in conflict with the projected laws, and amendments to the Code of Civil Procedures and the Organic Law of the Judiciary.[27]

Kemmerer also submitted a series of special reports on public credit, public works, the alcohol monopoly, municipal finances, the monetary law, the organization and activities of the executive branch, the stamp law, and the proposed Quito-to-Esmeraldas railroad. In their reports on public credit and public works, the most important ones for the country's financial rehabilitation, the advisers examined public policy and the long series of deficits during the liberal era. They argued that while any country at Ecuador's stage of development needed good credit as a prerequisite to an extended public works program, the country's public works policy had undermined its credit rating.

Between 1914 and 1926 Ecuador had spent about twenty million dollars with few concrete results. On the contrary, the expenditure had harmed the country because funds, which should have amortized the foreign debt, were diverted instead to public works projects, and taxes mortgaged to service the foreign debt were reassigned by congress to public works projects. Since local banks provided additional funds for public works programs, these projects also deprived Ecuadorian entrepreneurs of access to capital. The advisers recommended that in the future public works projects be funded by foreign loans or direct foreign investment. To accomplish this Ecuador would have to change its attitude toward foreign investment as well as rehabilitate its credit rating. Private foreign investors, declared the advisers, had contributed significantly to the development of the United States and many Latin American countries. Ecuador, in contrast, had attracted little foreign investment because it refused to grant foreign entrepreneurs a level of profit commensurate with their risks. Ecuadorians needed to accept the fact that foreign investors expected profits and consider them a necessary cost of development. The government could protect the national interest by refusing to grant permanent concessions to foreigners and by insisting that the country receive a substantial share of the profits. For the present, Ecuador could not expect to obtain large foreign loans for public works, or for any other purpose, given its long history of defaults. Therefore, the country had to consolidate its obligations and renew prompt and uninterrupted debt service.

The mission also indicated that Ecuador could not develop a sound public works program without comprehensive national planning, which heretofore the government had sacrificed to sectional interest. Congress' practice of indiscriminately appropriating funds for almost any program proposed had left the country with many projects that remained unfinished. To resolve this problem the advisers urged the government to formulate a long-term coordinated program of construction in which the state would initiate public works projects in order of their national priority. Despite the political difficulties such a policy faced, the Kemmerer Mission believed that a determined administration could convince the congress to pursue the national interest. It recommended the creation of a Public Works Advisory Committee to study proposals and assist the director of public works in selecting those to be included in the national public works program. The foreign advisers realized that the suggestions they offered were not new, but they believed that the public would now accept these recommendations.[28]

The press gave extensive coverage to the reports of the Kemmerer Mission which began to appear in February 1927. Journalists emphasized that the recommendations were based on a careful analysis of Ecuadorian conditions and were not partisan political proposals. They hailed the advisers as "scientists" who had refused to become involved in national politics. They also supported the suggestion that the country hire foreign experts to implement the reform laws since it was critical that the new institutions and procedures be established properly. When the government asked Kemmerer to nominate Americans to the position of superintendent of banks, comptroller general, adviser to the Guayaquil-Quito Railroad, adviser to the Central Bank, and adviser to the collector of customs, only a few papers mentioned the "negative" experience with John Hord. The Ayora regime acted with dispatch: all but one of the American administrators were appointed and working in Ecuador by the time the Kemmerer Mission departed for Bolivia in mid-March 1927.[29]

Many Ecuadorians and foreigners believed that regionalist politics might prevent the approval of the reforms if the country returned to constitutional government before the recommendations were implemented. Nevertheless, various groups, both in the highlands and on the coast, insisted upon a return to constitutionality. The Ayora government and the military preferred to approve the Kemmerer reforms with a minimum of debate, but the state of public opinion still concerned them. Ayora's political position was strengthened on March 4, 1927, when an attempt to overthrow his government and install General Gómez de la Torre as *jefe supremo* until a constituent assembly could be elected, failed. The government charged that disgruntled bankers, conservatives, and old-style politicians, who opposed the Kemmerer reforms, planned the rebellion. The regime rapidly arrested and exiled a number of people before anyone could challenge its explanation. The government's decisive action discredited and silenced its critics, gained public support, and permitted the administration to enact into law most of the Kemmerer reforms.[30]

The enactment of the Kemmerer reforms and the experiences of the four experts retained to implement them demonstrates the resilience of old patterns and the manner in which Ecuadorians used new structures to further traditional interests. As Kemmerer's farewell speech indicated, the adoption of the mission's recommendations only began the process of financial reorganization and recovery. Passing laws would prove much easier than implementing them. In Ecuador, a national psychology, which placed a higher value on status and reputation than on expertise and achievement, aggravated the problems of administration. The Americans charged with inaugurating the new system were professionals, most of them with experience in Latin America. Harry L. Tompkins, superintendent of banks, had worked for twenty-seven years in banking, including years at the Mercantile Bank of America in Lima, Peru. James Edward, comptroller general, had served in the Philippines, Cuba, Santo Domingo, Bolivia, and Puerto Rico. William F. Roddy, director of customs, who had previously worked in the Philippines, came to Ecuador from Nicaragua where he had directed customs administration from 1918 to 1927. Earl B. Schwulst, adviser to the Central Bank, had been with the Federal Reserve Bank in Dallas, Texas. B. B. Milner, who originally traveled to Ecuador as a member of the Kemmerer Mission and who spent most of his time working directly with the Guayaquil and Quito Railway, chose to remain after the other advisers departed. From February through May 1927, he increased the railway's earning by 400,000 sucres without raising fares. Milner left Ecuador in the summer of 1927 after his contract expired. The other long-term advisers would terminate their relationships with the Ecuadorian government under less auspicious circumstances.[31]

The Central Bank

The first two major reform laws promulgated by the Ayora regime established a new value for the sucre and founded the Central Bank. The government considered these measures basic to the nation's financial reorganization and recovery. It established the value of the currency at five sucres per dollar, a 41 percent reduction from its former legal value. Ecuadorians calmly accepted the stabilization of the sucre at its free market value. Prices and salaries, particularly in the private sector, had been adjusted to reflect the sucre's declining value since 1921. The devaluation did not produce severe internal dislocations (see table 35). The government also decreed a return to the gold standard. Ayora repealed the 1914 Ley Moratoria effective the date the new Central Bank officially opened.

The Kemmerer Mission considered the Caja Central incapable of meeting the long-term needs of Ecuador because that institution operated in a mechanical manner and, thus, could not aid commercial banks in times of emergency by discounting their commercial paper. Also, the Caja could not influence operations in the open market through changes

TABLE 35

VALUE OF THE SUCRE IN NEW YORK 1920–1926

Year	Value of the sucre[1]
Official parity	48.66
1920	44.20
1921	28.20
1922	26.00
1923	20.60
1924	19.50
1925	23.00
1926	19.80

Source: Ecuador, Misión de Consejeros Financieros, "Suplemento a la exposición de motivos de la ley de monedas presentada al Presidente de la República y al Ministro de Hacienda el 3 de Marzo de 1927," KP.

[1]Value in U.S. cents.

in the discount rate and therefore, could not prevent either speculation or the abnormal outflows of gold often associated with an overexpansion of credit. Kemmerer's Central Bank project, which Ayora enacted without modification, created an institution authorized to engage in business with member banks and with the public. It received the exclusive right to issue currency with 50 percent metallic backing, to discount eligible paper, and to manipulate the discount rate. The type of paper eligible for discount or for use as collateral limited the bank's lending power to member banks and to the public. The law strictly defined the origin, maturity, and number of required signatures for such paper. Because acceptable commercial paper was relatively scarce in Ecuador, the Central Bank's ability to influence the money supply through changes in the rediscount rate was largely illusory. Indeed, these money management tools proved unequal to the task of protecting Ecuadorian reserves or stemming the sharp contraction of private banking credit during the Great Depression.

The Central Bank received a fifty-year charter to ensure that it could operate free of the pressure of national politics. The bank, which served as the depository of national government funds as well as its fiscal agent, established its headquarters in Quito. Recognizing that Guayaquil was the nation's most important commercial city, the Kemmerer Mission formed a major branch of the bank in the port city and endowed it with virtual autonomy since the advisers expected the coastal branch to handle more business than the main office in Quito. The Central Bank board set policy for all the branches, but the Guayaquil branch did not have to clear its actions with the main office in Quito. This autonomy was reemphasized in the requirement that the Central Bank board hold half its meetings in Guayaquil and the other half in Quito. To satisfy highland sensibilities, the law provided that any city with over 80,000 people could have a major branch of the Central Bank; only Guayaquil qualified at the time. If two-thirds of the board of directors agreed, smaller cities also could obtain a branch.

The Central Bank had a complex organization. A nine-member board of directors controlled the bank chosen as follows: two each by the government and the class A stockholders, one each by class B stockholders, the Quito Chamber of Commerce, the Guayaquil Chamber of Commerce, the National Society of Agriculture, and Ecuadorian labor organizations. The board elected the president and vice-president for one-year terms, both of whom could be board members, as well as a general manager who served at the discretion of two-thirds of the board. The law fixed the Central Bank's maximum initial capital at ten million sucres, with 3,750,000 sucres coming from the required subscriptions of member banks. Central Bank shares were divided into two categories: class A, which commercial banks in Ecuador were required to subscribe in amounts equal to 15 percent of their capital and surplus, and class B shares, which could be held by individuals, the government, and corporations. Member banks could hold class B stock within certain limits, but they could not participate in the election of the representatives of class B stockholders.

The bank began operations with a substantial gold reserve because it absorbed the gold held by the Caja Central. The government received the profit resulting from the revaluation of the gold reserves in the monetary law of March 4, 1927. This money, however, had to be used to pay five million sucres of government indebtedness to the former banks of issue, excluding debt secured by mortgages and the debt of the Banco Comercial y Agrícola. The fate of that institution was sealed when the government refused to include it in the repayment plan on the grounds that the regime and the bank had reached a mutually satisfactory agreement on May 1, 1926, and that the accord should not be modified.[32]

On Kemmerer's recommendation, the government hired Earl B. Schwulst, who arrived in Quito early in April 1927 and participated in the meetings of the organizing committee of the Central Bank. Harry L. Tompkins, who was hired as superintendent of banks, also attended these meetings and worked on projects related to the Central Bank until September 1927, when the government promulgated the general banking law that specified the functions of the superintendent of banks. The first board of directors of the Central Bank included only one man with practical banking experience, Enrique Cueva. Luis A. Carbo, who had some theoretical knowledge of currency and finance, resigned from the board within a short time to accept the position of deputy superintendent of banks in Guayaquil. The other board members consisted of Federico Malo, Augustín Rendon, Luis A. Dillon, Luis N. Dillon, N. Clemente Ponce, Neptalí Bonifaz and the representative of the class-B stockholders to be elected shortly. Schwulst prepared a draft of the by-laws for the bank and an agenda prior to the board's first meeting in May. As a first item of business, and over the adviser's objections, the board voted itself salary and travel allowances much higher than those of directors of comparable institutions. Then they chose Neptalí Bonifaz, one of the two government representatives, president of the Central Bank, and his friend and personal lawyer, N. Clemente Ponce, vice-president. The board also selected Alberto Bustamante, the former manager of the Caja Central, manager.

Neptalí Bonifaz was a wealthy landowner, who had spent thirty years in France and who only recently had returned to Ecuador. The Ayora administration appointed him to the board believing that Bonifaz's long absence had insulated him from local political conflicts. The new bank president had neither business experience nor understanding of the difference between a central bank and commercial banks. His exaggerated sense of personal and family pride made it difficult for him to get along with others. He frequently became embroiled in bitter disputes with rivals or with those who had injured his sensibilities. He balanced these negative qualities with a firm commitment to the Central Bank, considerable personal energy, a willingness to work, and an instinctive belief that the bank should pursue a conservative loan policy during its early years.[33]

President Bonifaz clashed with the American adviser almost immediately. Bonifaz wanted to purchase the Banco del Pichincha building to house the new institution. In June 1927 the new bank possessed approximately one-and-a-half million sucres of capital in cash; the Banco del Pichincha building was selling for seven hundred thousand sucres, and local architects estimated that it would require an additional one hundred thousand sucres to refurbish and equip the structure. Schwulst opposed the purchase. In his view, it was a bad policy to invest such a large proportion of the Central Bank's working capital in a building. He advised the board that the Guayaquil branch, which would be busier, needed larger facilities than the Quito headquarters, which would handle a smaller volume of business. The American recommended that the Central Bank in Quito rent space. President Bonifaz considered the proposal an affront to the bank's dignity and angrily threatened to cancel Schwulst's contract unless he changed his opinion. The foreign adviser refused to capitulate. He managed to block the purchase, as well as to retain his position by prevailing upon President Ayora to modify his contract to clearly state his independence from the Central Bank president and board. The incident not only created ill will between the bank president and the adviser but also caused Bonifaz to withdraw his support from President Ayora. The Central Bank opened for business in rented quarters on August 10, 1927. The bank began operations without incident since Ecuadorians believed that the new institution would solve the country's problems.[34]

Relations between the Central Bank board and Schwulst continued to worsen. The adviser became involved in a series of disputes with the board and, particularly, with Bonifaz over correct procedures. The class-B stockholders elected Juan Barberis their representative shortly after the bank's inauguration. But Bonifaz and some other board members objected. They planned to annul Barberis's election and hold a new referendum in which the board would use the regional offices of the finance ministry to campaign for a candidate of its choice. Schwulst argued against annulling the election because it would create bad publicity and destroy public confidence in a supposedly apolitical institution. The board relented and permitted Barberis to join its ranks only after the representative of the class-B stockholders threatened to expose its activities.

Shortly after this incident, Bonifaz threatened to resign because Harry Tompkins, the superintendent of banks, appointed Luis A. Carbo deputy superintendent in Guayaquil. Bonifaz, who had informed President Ayora of his objections to Carbo, considered the appointment a personal affront. Tompkins, however, maintained that the superintendent of banks, who had supervisory authority over the Central Bank, should not permit that institution or any other bank to influence his decisions. He named Carbo to the post because of his qualifications, not because of personal politics. Nevertheless, Bonifaz remained adamant. He convinced three other bank board members, Luis A. Dillon, Enrique Cueva, and N. Clemente Ponce to resign collectively if Carbo remained deputy superintendent of banks. Since the threat carried serious political consequences for the beleaguered Ayora regime and the Central Bank, Schwulst attempted to mediate. He convinced President Ayora, the minister of finance, and Carbo that Bonifaz's exaggerated sense of pride would prevent him from modifying his position and that his resignation, only a short time after the bank's opening, would imperil the whole financial reform program. Carbo, who was related to President Ayora through marriage, agreed to resign rather than provoke a public confrontation with Bonifaz.[35]

Despite Schwulst's belated attempts to cooperate with Bonifaz and the board, relations deteriorated. The board of directors continued to base its actions on political considerations rather than the technical reasoning of the adviser. The directors were also disturbed because Superintendent of Banks Tompkins often supported Schwulst's recommendations. In an effort to resolve these disputes, the Ecuadorians asked Kemmerer to arbitrate. Tensions only increased when Kemmerer supported Schwulst's views. Since highlanders dominated the board, some of its actions can be traced to regionalist sentiment. Bonifaz, for example, wanted to modify the bank's statutes to permit the granting of loans with maturity dates of 180 days, instead of the current maximum of 90 days, as well as to liberalize the definition of discountable paper. Schwulst opposed the change as too liberal for a recently founded central bank attempting to promote conservative banking practices. Guayaquil bankers also opposed the change, which would place the Central Bank in direct competition with private commercial banks. Bonifaz, who failed in his efforts to revise the statute, concluded that Schwulst was not only a meddlesome foreigner but also a defender of coastal interests.

The final confrontation between the Central Bank board and the American adviser began in November 1927, when the board decided to ignore his objections and purchase the Banco del Pichincha building for 700,000 sucres. Bonifaz believed that the edifice would enhance the stature of the institution and would obscure the fact that the Guayaquil branch had more activity than the Quito headquarters. As expected, Schwulst opposed the purchase. This time Bonifaz charged that the adviser had leaked the purchase price to the press, thereby compromising the Central Bank. Although the charge was never substantiated, Bonifaz formally demanded that the Ecuadorian government cancel Schwulst's contract. He also withheld the adviser's salary and locked him out of his office. The American protested directly to President Ayora and filed a suit against Bonifaz and the board in the Ecuadorian courts. Bonifaz, determined to be rid of Schwulst, denounced him to the newspapers, threatening to resign and overthrow the Ayora government if the president did not abrogate the American adviser's contract. The press rallied to Bonifaz's support against the American "imperialist conspiracy" to control the Central Bank. In the United States, Edwin Kemmerer advised the State Department against becoming embroiled in the dispute, believing that

Ecuadorian courts should settle the matter. The State Department agreed with the Princeton economist that the proposed reforms were too important to be jeopardized by defending the rights of a single American citizen.

Ecuadorians, however, had a different perspective on the matter. The press became convinced of the "conspiracy" when the Ecuadorian courts decided that the government had to pay Schwulst and when Harry Tompkins, in his capacity as superintendent of banks, ordered the payment. After prolonged negotiations, President Ayora obtained Schwulst's agreement to the cancellation of his contract. The controversy did not end when Schwulst left the country in March 1928. Superintendent of Banks Tompkins wrote a letter to the board of directors of the Central Bank criticizing them for their unjust treatment of Schwulst. He also suggested that Bonifaz's resignation both as bank president and as a member of the board of directors would best serve the Central Bank. As might be expected, the board reacted angrily to Tompkins's letter. Upon learning of the incident, the press published violently anti-American editorials, attacking not only Tompkins, but all the American experts and recommending that they depart immediately.[36]

The Superintendent of Banks

The Kemmerer Mission proposed that Ecuador establish a banking department in the Ministry of Finance, headed by a superintendent of banks to regulate Ecuadorian banking. In an attempt to shield the superintendent, a presidential appointee, from political pressures, the law stipulated that he could be removed from office only for a crime or for proven incompetence. The Supreme Court would adjudicate any charge leveled against the superintendent. The duties of the office included a yearly report, whose contents were specified by law, to the minister of finance. The Kemmerer Mission intended that the superintendent prevent poor banking practices and only secondarily prevent crime. The office, based on practice in the United States, had been established successfully in Colombia and Chile. Kemmerer also recommended that the first superintendent be a foreign expert and that he receive only a three-year appointment, the time necessary to organize the office and to prepare an Ecuadorian national to assume the post.

Ecuadorian bankers supported the new office for regulating banking activities. During the March 1926 economic conference the bankers, already familiar with Kemmerer's proposals to other countries, agreed that a superintendency of banks could be established in Ecuador with only minor modifications. But before creating such an office, the legislature had to reorganize Ecuadorian banking law. When Kemmerer arrived, the current banking law only applied to banks of issue. Other banks operated as corporations under the commercial code. No legislation regulated commercial banks or agricultural credit and few restrictions limited mortgage banks, which essentially operated under a law enacted in 1869. The Kemmerer Mission's general banking law addressed these needs. It required that banks and corporations engaged in banking or credit activity reincorporate under the new law and receive bank charters of limited duration. The new law prescribed strict accounting and disclosure procedures and required regular published reports that revealed the true condition of the financial institutions. It defined the powers of commercial banks, established limits on amounts they could loan, and the maximum maturity dates for loans. The new legislation also attempted to strike a balance between a bank's need for liquidity and the country's need for agricultural credit.

The Kemmerer Mission opposed the creation of specialized banks in Ecuador. Although the country required diversified banking services, such as long-term agricultural loans and short-term credits for entrepreneurs, the mission believed Ecuador too small to sustain a variety of credit institutions. The financial advisers, instead, favored general service banks with specialized departments. The new law also provided for the eventual formation of the Mortgage Bank of Ecuador, a private institution, owned principally by mortgage banks and mortgage sections of commercial banks. The mortgage bank would provide a mechanism for consolidating the indebtedness of the smaller institutions and issuing bonds large enough in value to attract buyers in foreign markets.[37]

Tompkins's tenure as superintendent of banks did not begin until the government enacted the general banking law in September 1927. The delay occurred, in part, because the Ayora government believed it necessary to revise the organic law of the Ministry of Finance in order to facilitate the changes recommended by the Kemmerer Mission before formally creating the superintendency of banks. During the several months Tompkins did not possess legal status as superintendent of banks he assisted the Central Bank by preparing a consolidated balance sheet for Ecuadorian banks as of April 1927 and organizing a credit file for the Central Bank. From the outset he clashed with the bank's board of directors by supporting Schwulst's technical recommendations that did not agree with the board's views. His relations with the board of directors deteriorated further when he began to organize the superintendency of banks; as indicated earlier, his appointment of Luis A. Carbo as deputy superintendent of Guayaquil infuriated Bonifaz. Disregarding the sensibilities of the Central Bank's board, Tompkins insisted on his authority to appoint qualified personnel. Although Carbo's resignation settled the question, within a few weeks Tompkins again clashed with the Central Bank board when he sided with Schwulst in that adviser's confrontation with the board. Tompkins's correct, but impolitic, letter criticizing the board's actions toward Schwulst and his suggestion that Bonifaz resign inflamed not only the board but also the press and the public. His popularity on the coast, which might have supported him against the highland faction on the Central Bank board, diminished because in his official capacity Tompkins had to liquidate the Banco Comercial y Agrícola. Although regionalists, who triumphed in the 1925 coup, ordained the destruction of the coastal bank, a large segment of the public held Tompkins responsible for the act because he technically ended the bank's existence.[38]

Tompkins's difficulties in Ecuador also stemmed from his interpretation of the responsibilities and prerogatives of the office of the superintendent of banks. The Minister of Finance Alberto Gómez Jaramillo considered the American to be his subordinate whereas Tompkins believed he had independent authority. These misunderstandings led to acrimony and conflict. Late in 1928 Tompkins submitted his first annual report that strongly criticized the minister of finance, alleging that he had attempted to obstruct the work of the superintendent of banks. Gómez Jaramillo angrily refused to allow his ministry to publish the report as required by law and called Tompkins to Quito to insist that he resign. When the American refused, the minister requested that the Supreme Court revoke his contract. The Court informed the government that it must press formal charges if it wished the justices to act. Any hope of an amicable settlement ended when the press published a copy of Tompkins's report with extended commentaries. They also printed numerous polemics in which the two parties accused one another of incompetence and possible criminal activity.

The minister of finance took formal action against Tompkins in January 1929. Gómez Jaramillo pressed charges before the Supreme Court and he also fined Tompkins two-months' pay for failing to keep him adequately informed. The American refused to pay the fine, arguing that as head of his department he could not be considered subordinate to the minister of finance, and that he was justified in not submitting confidential information from the banks because he believed the ministry could not maintain confidentiality. Gómez Jaramillo charged that Tompkins had failed to fulfill the obligations of his contract that required monthly reports; that he administered his department incompetently; that he had alienated the public; and that he had committed financial irregularities. When the Supreme Court heard the case in February 1929, Tompkins's Ecuadorian lawyer demonstrated that the twenty-two count indictment was baseless, except for the charge accusing him of failing to submit monthly reports to the minister of finance. Since the case had evoked a strong emotional reaction in Ecuador, the Court treated it gingerly. In November 1929 the Supreme Court ruled in favor of Tompkins, but based its ruling on technical grounds. Thus the American was not completely exonerated in the eyes of the public. Tompkins's victory proved pyrrhic: when the Court handed down its decision, Tompkins had lost his job.

While the Supreme Court considered the case, a constituent assembly had promulgated Ecuador's thirteenth constitution, which prohibited foreigners from discharging administrative or executive functions in the national government. Under this constitutional provision, the three Americans working as comptroller, director general of customs, and superintendent of banks were demoted to the rank of advisers to those offices. The legal changes effective March 31, 1929, however, failed to include proper budgetary provisions for the advisers. The salaries of the Americans were halted until August when the budget was revised. The situation complicated the dispute between Tompkins and the Ecuadorian government. Although he continued to work as superintendent of banks until August 1929, Tompkins refused to accept his salary as long as the government upheld the fines imposed by the minister of finance. In addition, he persisted in his attacks on Ecuadorian politicians. Tompkins submitted a report to the congress on the state of Ecuador's economy in which he declared that the nation failed to develop not because it lacked resources or capital but because its public and private leaders did not possess morality and civic consciousness. This analysis and the violent public and private attacks he continued to make against Ayora and other government officials ensured their animosity. Tompkins refused to report to work in Quito at the end of August; he notified the authorities that they had violated his contract by failing to pay his salary every month. He demanded that Ecuador pay at once his entire salary through February 12, 1930, the date his contract expired. When the government refused, Tompkins asked the United States government to intervene in his behalf.

The State Department declined on the grounds that he had not exhausted remedies in the Ecuadorian courts.

After attempts to resolve the issue informally failed, Tompkins filed suit against the Ecuadorian government in mid-1930. The original suit, the appeals, and ancillary litigation remained unsettled until 1936. The American won some of his claims against the government of Ecuador, but the Court upheld the fines imposed by Minister of Finance Gómez Jaramillo and ruled that Tompkins had no valid claims against Ecuador for the period following the expiration of his contract. As ordered by the Court, the government paid Tompkins 72,000 sucres. Ecuadorian creditors attached more than half the settlement, 40,450 sucres. Although unemployed, the American had refused to leave the country while his case was in litigation. He subsisted on loans and other forms of credit, as well as on the largess of some guayaquileños. Unlike the other two Americans affected by the 1929 constitution, who reached a quiet settlement with the Ecuadorian government, Tompkins pursued a policy of confrontation. In the end, he obtained less than the government offered in 1929 as a pretrial settlement. The court award was neither a vindication nor a meaningful victory over the government. Tompkins's erratic behavior and his recalcitrance suggest a nervous breakdown that made him incapable of acting in his own best interest. He died in Guayaquil on March 12, 1937. The Tompkins episode was a *cause célèbre* which prompted anti-American and antiforeign sentiment. It obscured the fact that the other American experts continued to operate in a professional manner during Tompkins's well-publicized conflict and that the United States government did not interfere, considering the matter an internal Ecuadorian question.[39]

The Comptroller General

The Kemmerer Mission also recommended the creation of a comptroller's office, the Contraloría, as an independent department of the executive branch. The comptroller was to be appointed by the president, receive ministerial rank, and serve a six-year term. He had final decision on all accounting and auditing matters and was responsible to congress for his actions. To insulate him from political pressures, the law provided that the comptroller could only be removed or suspended from office for neglect of his duties or for criminal cause through a Supreme Court decision or impeachment by the congress. The comptroller was responsible for collecting information and statistical data on government income and expenditure for the budget. Thus the comptroller played a key role in the preparation of the budget, which, by law, had to be balanced. In addition, the Contraloría centralized in one office duties that had been divided among the provincial and central offices of the Ministry of Finance and the Tribunal of Accounts. Ecuadorian officials considered the comptroller's office so important that the Ayora government believed it necessary to change the general statute of the Ministry of Finance before creating the new office. The press even speculated that the Contraloría abolished the need for a finance ministry.

When James H. Edwards arrived in Ecuador in March 1927 to assume the duties of comptroller general, he discovered that his first major task consisted of drafting a new general statute for the Ministry of Finance. This proved difficult because Ecuadorian officials, including Minister of Finance Pedro L. Núñez, were unclear about the proper roles and relationship between the Contraloría and the Ministry of Finance. In the past, ministers of finance dedicated most of their time to the mechanical aspects of the office, such as signing all payment orders. As a result, they tended to have little time for more important administrative and policy functions. Officials, whose jobs were threatened or who were concerned with the diminution of their authority and status, also tended to oppose the new office. The Tribunals of Accounts, for example, previously responsible for auditing government accounts, would be abolished by the establishment of the comptroller's office. Edwards completed the new general statute (*ley orgánica*) in August 1927. The new law assigned administrative and policy authority to the minister of finance. It also created new departments—Treasury, Revenue, General Purchasing, General Accounting, and Bureau of the Budget—to modernize the administration of national finances, and it abolished many small offices with limited jurisdiction. After careful review, the Ayora government promulgated the law on November 16, 1927.

During its first year the Contraloría faced the normal problems resulting from the inauguration of a new fiscal agency. There were errors and confusion at first while the staff learned new accounting and auditing procedures. Edwards's hard work, determination, and optimism were largely responsible for the eventual success of the office. Despite all his efforts Edwards endured considerable criticism; some directed at the difficulties in the Contraloría's operation, others at its level of effectiveness. The displaced personnel of the Tribunal of Accounts became a source of discontent. While the old tribunals had frequently been in arrears for years, the Contraloría rapidly brought the government's accounts up to date, collecting one million sucres in fines in the process. The office's efficiency naturally alienated those fined. Discontent in Quito also focused on the inequities which foreign advisers introduced into government salaries. Highlanders, for example, criticized the cost of the advisers' services as well as the power granted to foreigners by the government. They joined the displaced employees in undermining Edwards's position.

By the end of 1928 rumors began circulating in Quito that Edwards would be demoted. Given the experience of other American advisers, the gossip did not seem farfetched. The public criticism concerned Edwards who sought assurances from Ayora that his status would remain unchanged. Having received the president's support, Edwards declined an offer to join a new Kemmerer mission to China. Opponents of foreign advisers succeeded in convincing the constituent assembly to diminish the authority of foreign experts in the new Constitution of 1929. They used Harry Tompkins's intemperate actions and statements to discredit all American advisers. Minister of Finance Alberto Gómez Jaramillo notified Edwards on March 27, 1929 that while the new constitution prevented him from remaining in the post of comptroller general, the government intended to honor his contract and would appoint him adviser to the Ministry of Finance. James Edwards, however, left Ecuador for New York in September 1929, after agreeing to the cancellation of his contract. The Ecuadorian government paid his salary through November 1929, as well as travel expenses to the United States.[40]

The Director General of Customs

William F. Roddy, the director general of customs, remained in office longer than any other foreign expert, even though his job brought him into conflict with an important segment of the Guayaquil business community. Roddy retained his position as well as the confidence of the government because he significantly increased customs revenues. His support waned when receipts declined as a result of the world depression.

The Kemmerer Mission's customs administration law, approved April 26, 1927, created the office of Director General of Customs to centralize customs administration. The director received full authority to organize, staff, and administer all Ecuadorian customs facilities, a great change from past practice when he had to share that responsibility with the administrator of customs, the ministro de hacienda, and the governor of Guayas province. The new centralized authority allowed the director to improve administration and reduce impediments that had burdened customs collection. Roddy introduced prompt and thorough audit procedures, standardized and numbered documents to expedite auditing, and decreased the number of operations necessary to complete customs clearance. Under the old system importers had to complete as many as eighty procedures to clear their merchandise. He also introduced methods to increase efficiency. For example, he encouraged the prompt removal of goods from government controls by imposing a storage charge for items not claimed within fifteen days. Once articles cleared customs, owners had forty-eight hours to remove the items without incurring graduated warehousing fees; the government publicly auctioned goods left over forty days.

Roddy not only perfected procedures but also improved the quality of the staff. Whereas the aduana had previously hired many low paid and poorly trained employees, the new director reduced the number of workers, but increased their salaries. All potential employees had to pass examinations and undergo a probationary period. They were trained before being assigned to duty and retained and promoted on the basis of achievement and merit. Roddy also acted to enforce the new customs administration law that attempted to reduce contraband by stationing patrols offshore, by instituting surprise inspections of vessels, by using undercover customs agents, and by rewarding customs officials who apprehended smugglers. These programs generally increased revenue collections; they also precipitated widespread discontent.

The new director general of customs endured substantial criticism when he enforced the reformed aduana law because it radically transformed customs procedures. Importers and brokers, as well as customs employees, had considerable difficulty adjusting to the new practices. Accustomed to leaving their goods in government warehouses for long periods, importers opposed the imposition of charges, fines, or even the loss of their property if they failed to remove them expeditiously. The customs employees dismissed for incompetence or inefficiency joined in the protest against Roddy. In some cases, political pressure delayed government approval of top-ranking customs appointments, forcing the aduana to operate without the necessary supervisory personnel. The most significant reason for the growing anti-Roddy sentiment was that customs regulations were actually being enforced, perhaps for the first time in Ecuador's history. The highly paid director general did not succumb to bribes and was not influenced by local ties when making customs decisions. No Ecuadorian official could have resisted the political and regional pressures exerted on Roddy. The businesslike attitude of the director improved the morale and confidence of the customs service. Old practices, such as tipping customs personnel in return for lax aduana enforcement, quickly decreased as customs employees began to exhibit a new sense of purpose.

A reformed tariff law also contributed to increased customs revenues. Since tariff revision had not been part of the original Kemmerer agreement, the mission was not prepared to draft a complete new aduana code when the Minister of Finance Pedro Núñez requested it. Kemmerer agreed to revise the code on the understanding that he could model it on the reformed tariffs of Paraguay and the Dominican Republic as well as the Ecuadorian customs law of 1926. The Paraguayan and Dominican tariffs, designed primarily to raise revenue, contained few provisions to shield local industry. The 1926 Ecuadorian tariff had abolished the old surtax system of additional levies and readjusted rates to achieve comparability with the rates in force before World War I. The 1926 code failed to address the problem of revenue collections. Some high rates promoted smuggling, while other duties, on commodities with relatively inelastic demand, were set too low to produce the maximum revenue. The Kemmerer Mission remedied these flaws by increasing the tax on a few imported items of general consumption, including cotton textiles, lard, kerosene, gasoline, and wheat flour, commodities that accounted for 35 to 45 percent of Ecuador's imports. In 1926 these items paid an average ad valorem tax equivalent of 19.5 percent. The Kemmerer Mission indicated that other countries taxed these commodities at a rate between 25 and 45 percent without significantly lowering consumption. Furthermore, their bulk and weight reduced the likelihood that higher duties would unleash a wave of smuggling. Considering Ecuadorian conditions, the mission recommended raising the duty on flour from ten to fifteen centavos per kilo, equivalent to a 37 percent ad valorem rate. Although a significant increase, it was still well below the tax burden of other wheat importing countries in Latin America (the Dominican Republic [.225 sucres per kilo], Peru [.20 sucres per kilo], and Colombia [.40 sucres per kilo]). The advisers also recommended raising the duty on the other items in this group to produce revenues equivalent to 20 to 40 percent of their value.

While sympathizing with the idea of taxing luxury goods at extremely high rates, the mission noted that this laudable goal did not increase customs revenues. Luxury items generally possessed high values in relation to size and weight and, therefore, were more likely to be smuggled into the country if the duties were excessive. The new tariff law reduced the duty on luxury goods to facilitate tax collection, while basic necessities were burdened with higher levies in the belief that increased duties would neither create enforcement problems nor adversely affect the public.

Since the director of customs had to enforce significantly higher aduana levies on items of general consumption, he became a natural target for public dissatisfaction. The government backed Roddy because customs collections rose. The American remained director general of customs even after the Constitution of 1929 prohibited foreigners from holding such positions. The government justified this violation of its constitution on the grounds that the deputy director, who was an Ecuadorian, technically administered the aduana with Roddy's advice.

In November 1929 the Ayora regime negotiated a new contract with Roddy appointing him technical adviser to customs, thus legalizing his status. Many Ecuadorians severely criticized the new contract. The press complained about paying foreigners for work which Ecuadorians could perform. It described the new director general of customs as an honorable man who did not require surveillance by a foreigner. Some papers accused Roddy of having acted arbitrarily and illegally to increase customs collections by levying unjustified fines. The Council of State also questioned the contract's constitutionality when it reviewed the national budget. Although the council had only objected to certain provisions of the contract, and not President's Ayora's decision to retain Roddy, the press used the disagreement to turn public opinion against the accord. But the president remained adamant. Customs revenues provided Quito with over 40 percent of ordinary government revenues in 1929 and he did not want collections to decline.

To neutralize the widespread discontent, President Ayora rewrote the contract to accommodate the council's objections. The new agreement, effective February 23, 1930 through December 31, 1932, could be terminated by either party with three months' notice. Roddy received a salary of $16,000 per year and was permitted to return to the United States on a leave of absence. The worsening economic situation upon his return to Ecuador in August 1930 placed Roddy in an increasingly difficult position. The worldwide economic crisis had affected Ecuador's exports and, therefore, its imports. The business community and the press blamed the efficient customs service for exacerbating the crisis. In September the congress recommended that the government terminate Roddy's contract. When President Ayora refused, congress sought other methods: on November 20, 1930, while debating the national budget, it voted to grant

Roddy only three months' salary and a sum to cover his return travel expenses to the United States. The Ayora administration tried to defend Roddy. Minister of Finance Francisco Sexto Durán declared that those who criticized the American were generally those who violated customs regulations. He personally vouched for Roddy's integrity; earlier, as a subordinate in the customs administration, the minister had come to know the American well.

These arguments did not sway Roddy's opponents who dominated the congress. The minister of finance had to notify the American that his contract would end February 28, 1931. Roddy, in turn, requested that the government release him from his contract in January because he wanted to join Kemmerer in a mission to Peru. The American adviser remained on cordial terms with President Ayora when he left Ecuador. Indeed, the Ecuadorian chief executive regretted Roddy's departure because he feared that without the American's influence, customs officials would return to their former practices.[41]

Although the Kemmerer Mission provided Ecuador with new institutions and modern procedures, the country's political, economic, and social realities remained unchanged. Even before the foreign advisers departed, Ecuadorians had begun to adapt the new structures to conform to their interests.

6. The Aftermath of Reform

During the 1930s severe economic dislocations exacerbated Ecuador's perennial problems: insufficient government revenues and chronic political instability. Many of the institutional and procedural changes adopted in 1927 at the recommendation of the Kemmerer Financial Mission proved incapable of maintaining fiscal integrity in these years of extraordinary economic, social, and political stress. The new structures were modified rapidly to conform to traditional Ecuadorian patterns and practices. The Kemmerer reforms would have been modified in any event, but the Great Depression accelerated the process.[1] Ironically, it was the improved accounting and auditing procedures of the new Contraloría and directory of the treasury that provided the government with timely economic and financial data that hastened the cooptation of the Central Bank, the customs service, the private banking system, and other like institutions.[2] When the rapid and ill-conceived modifications adopted by governments after 1929 worsened the financial crisis, Ecuadorians again sought to bring law into agreement with national reality by relying on the advice of an "impartial" expert sympathetic to their current predilections. Ecuador obtained the services of another foreign adviser, the Mexican economist Manuel Gómez Morín, who possessed a different conception of the role of banking in a developing nation.

The Politics of Instability

After 1929 the Ayora government suffered increasing public criticism for its policies, many of them based on the recommendations of the Kemmerer Mission. Ecuador's new centralized budget appeared bloated to those accustomed to seeing it reflect only a portion of total revenues and expenditures. The strict control of public works expenditures alienated regionalists. Opponents of the administration insisted that tax reforms—the 1927 tariff and the revised income tax—enriched the government at the expense of a poor nation. Critics damned the 1928 agreement between the Swedish Match Company and the Ayora regime to obtain funds for the Banco Hipotecario—the national mortgage bank—as inimical to Ecuadorian interests. Public dissatisfaction mounted as internal conditions deteriorated in concert with the disruptions in the world economy. Critics accused the Central Bank of causing an economic depression by contracting the size of the money supply. They blamed the Ayora government for exacerbating the nation's problems.[3] Popular discontent erupted in mass demonstrations in Quito, prompting some military units to demand the president's resignation. Exhausted after four years of attempting to introduce a new order in Ecuador, Ayora resigned on August 24, 1931.

Ayora's ouster ushered in the most turbulent decade in Ecuador's long history of political instability. Although there were many reasons for the extraordinary number of presidents, acting presidents, and military and civilian dictators who ruled the country in the 1930s, perhaps the most important was the public's growing belief in the active state. As the economy worsened, more Ecuadorians turned to the government for immediate solutions to the nation's economic and social problems. Along with the heightened expectation of the government's role, there was a parallel growth of political participation in a country that had yet to develop institutions and mechanisms for mass politics. When their hopes were not realized, the increasingly active urban masses poured into the streets demanding changes in government leadership. Ironically, a neoconservative, José María Velasco Ibarra, emerged as the champion of the masses.[4]

Regionalism also contributed significantly to the instability of the 1930s. The Constitution of 1929 granted the congress, the traditional exponent of regional interests, power to veto or to control the activities of the executive branch. Critics of President Ayora had prevented him from governing by forcing his ministers to resign through votes of no confidence. None of the presidents who succeeded him could govern while the congress was in session. Those like the Guayaquil businessman Juan de Díos Martínez Mera, who respected the constitution, were driven out of office by the congress. Others, like Velasco Ibarra, attempted to resolve the stalemate between the legislature and executive branches by abolishing the congress and ruling as "dictators." They in turn were ousted by the defenders of the "constitutional order."[5]

Ideological as well as regional antagonism emerged in the single honest presidential election held during the decade. The election of 1931, like that of 1875, was free because it occurred immediately after an extralegal change in government and before the new administration could take control over the electoral machinery. Former President Alfredo Baquerizo Moreno, as president of the senate, assumed executive authority only a week before the election. The conservative candidate Neptalí Bonifaz, former president of the Central Bank, won because he received over-whelming support from the highlands even though he received only a few hundred votes in the coastal provinces. Two candidates, Modesto Larrea Jijón and Ildefonso Mendoza, divided the liberal vote (see table 36).

TABLE 36
1931 ELECTION

Candidate	Votes	Percent of votes
Neptalí Bonifaz	26,062	48.0
Modesto Larrea Jijón	15,630	28.8
Ildefonso Mendoza	12,628	23.2
Total	54,320	100.0

Source: *El Telégrafo*, no. 16,780 (January 2, 1932).

The president-elect never served because of widespread discontent, including several abortive revolts. The country became divided as liberals and conservatives, highlanders and costeños, virulently criticized each other. Congress met in these strained circumstances to ratify elections. Dominated by liberals, socialists, and anti-Quito factions, congress an-nulled the election on the grounds that Bonifaz was technically a Peruvian citizen and, therefore, ineligible to serve as president of Ecuador. The decision sparked a bloody four-day civil war in August 1932 in which conservatives, with support of the Quito garrison, drove the congress from the capital. Congress retook Quito behind the guns of the provincial regiments. This sorry episode briefly chastened Ecuadorians of all political persuasions, but their pledges of future cooperation vanished rapidly and political instability continued.[6] Nineteen men served in succession as chief executive between 1931 and 1948; none completed their term of office (see Appendix J).

The Economic Crisis

Although Ecuador suffered during the Great Depression, its citizens did not experience the same level of deprivation as did the populations of more developed countries. Since most Ecuadorians lived in rural areas, they had access to food and shelter and could avoid the full impact of the economic decline. National trade declined substantially, but no more than in other countries. Argentina, Bolivia, Chile, Paraguay, and Uruguay, for example, experienced a larger percentage decline in exports than Ecuador, while Brazil, Colombia, and Peru were only slightly better off.[7] Ecuadorians, however, were more concerned with their own experiences; they did not look upon their situation with the detachment of a historian writing in the 1980s. The assurances of government officials and foreign experts that the country was weathering the depression with relative ease did not convince them. They continued to demand that the government provide relief from the nation's worst economic disaster. As the situation worsened, Ecuadorians insisted that the government introduce agriculture, trade, and tariff measures that would foster agricultural and industrial production.[8]

During the 1930s Ecuadorian governments experimented with a variety of measures to improve economic conditions and to make national products more competitive in world markets. Ecuador attempted to control trade through exchange controls, protectionist tariffs, restrictions on imports, and special bilateral agreements involving barter, payment in nonconvertible currencies, and preferential tariffs. In its rush to confront the extraordinary world situation, the government burdened the 1927 tariff with additional charges that complicated customs transactions, abandoning the concept of the aduana as a source of revenue for an ill-conceived protectionist policy.[9]

Most of the measures to protect the national economy from world depression failed; some hurt Ecuador. The protectionist duties generally failed to stimulate import substitution and also cut deeply into government revenues. Exchange controls designed to reduce imports also hindered exporters, thus reducing the level of exports (see tables 37 and 38).[10] Perhaps the worst aspect of government experimentation with economic policy was that it caused uncertainty among the economically active community. Entrepreneurs could not be certain that a new policy would remain in effect because governments rose and fell within months and ministers often lasted only a few weeks. Without political stability, no government could formulate a national economic policy. Thus govern-

ment efforts hindered rather than aided the country's economic recovery
in the 1930s. As long as the world economy remained crippled, Ecuador,
as an exporter of primary materials, could do little to overcome its own
economic crisis.[11]

TABLE 37
GOVERNMENT INCOME 1927–1938

Year	Amount in sucres	Amount in dollars
1927	65,150,080	13,030,016
1928	61,576,032	12,315,206
1929	64,479,711	12,785,983
1930	60,821,471	12,043,856
1931	45,270,377	8,946,715
1932	42,162,183	7,109,980
1933	41,842,329	6,973,721
1934	48,282,197	4,470,574
1935	66,486,114	6,302,001
1936	77,463,606	7,391,565
1937	87,137,818	7,650,379
1938	120,833,271	8,551,541

Source: Ecuador, Dirección de Ingresos, *Informe al Ministro de Hacienda, 1939, Anexo 31.*

TABLE 38
BUDGETED AND ACTUAL ORDINARY GOVERNMENT INCOME 1927–1938

Year	Budgeted income	Actual income
1927	41,988,00	65,150,080
1928	59,893,068	61,576,032
1929	64,694,827	64,479,711
1930	64,037,200	60,821,471
1931	61,476,500	45,270,377
1932	49,115,440	42,162,183
1933	49,220,000	41,842,329
1934	50,762,400	48,282,197
1935	63,950,000	66,486,114
1936	80,100,000	77,463,606
1937	83,578,000	87,137,818
1938	137,028,750	120,833,271

Source: Ecuador, Dirección de Ingresos, *Informe al Ministro de Hacienda, 1939, Anexo 31.*

Inflation and Banking Politics

Central Bank loans to the government during the 1930s fueled one of the worst inflations experienced by any American nation. Only Chile suffered greater decline in the value of its currency. The inflation erupted after four-and-a-half years of monetary stability inaugurated in August 1927 by the Banco Central. The bank's conservative policies could neither stem the loss of the nation's gold reserves nor blunt the sharp contraction of the money supply resulting from the growing financial crisis (see tables 39 and 40). Ecuador possessed 44,085,490 sucres in metallic reserves when the bank opened in 1927. During the next few years, until Ecuador returned to inconvertibility in February 1932, the bank sold more gold every year than it purchased. The gold drain increased sharply after 1929. When Ecuador went off the gold standard, the nation possessed 14,253,041 sucres in gold reserves.[12] Although bankers and government officials wished to protect the country's gold reserves, the public feared the contraction of the money supply. The amount of money in circulation in 1931 was less than half the sum available in 1927. The public perceived

TABLE 39

GOLD RESERVES OF THE CENTRAL BANK OF ECUADOR 1927–1939

Year	Sucres	Grams of gold
1927	44,085,490	13,266,779
1928	38,029,255	11,449,990
1929	35,063,646	10,557,440
1930	28,639,062	8,618,439
1931	15,492,532	4,662,214
1932	17,408,986	5,088,230
1933	18,340,216	5,327,337
1934	27,156,303	5,846,330
1935	38,830,834[a]	3,862,192[a]
1936	42,525,686[b]	3,643,202[b]
1937	39,890,498	3,386,173
1938	39,798,376	3,216,639
1939	40,857,151	3,271,275

Source: Ecuador, Banco Central, *Boletín*, año 13, no. 150–151 (January-February 1940), 27.

[a]December 18, 1935, the gold reserves were revalued; the old price was 3.3229 sucres per gram of gold and the new price was 9.968331 sucres per gram of gold.

[b]June 13, 1936, the gold reserves were revalued a second time. The new price of gold was fixed at 11.6466 sucres per gram of gold.

TABLE 40

MONETARY CIRCULATION 1927–1946[a]

Year[1]	Amount[2]	Year[1]	Amount[2]
1927	38.7	1937	68.1
1928	36.5	1938	73.1
1929	30.0	1939	77.9
1930	23.5	1940	80.2
1931	19.1	1941	120.2
1932	30.3	1942	169.3
1933	43.1	1943	232.2
1934	56.7	1944	294.6
1935	59.9	1945	321.2
1936	67.1	1946	349.7

Source: Calculated from data in Ecuador, Banco Central, *Boletín*, año 12, no. 137–138 (December 1938-January 1939), n.p.; año 21, no. 242–244 (September-October 1937), 76.
[a]In millions of sucres.
[1]As of December 31.
[2]From 1932 to 1946 notes and coins; prior to 1932 notes only.

this as the cause, not the result, of the economic crisis. There was, therefore, widespread support for increased currency emissions as well as for allocating funds earmarked for debt service to meet domestic needs.[13]

The economic crisis, as well as public pressure, induced the government to return to a policy of deficit spending financed by bank loans. This time, however, the loans were from the Central Bank. On the same day the president approved the suspension of the gold standard, he signed a decree requiring the Central Bank to lend the government fifteen million sucres for public works projects, agricultural credit, and to pay the internal debt. The bank reluctantly agreed to loan the government twelve million sucres.[14] This loan was only the first of many. Between March 11, 1932, and August 19, 1937, the government borrowed 47 million sucres from the Central Bank to cover budget deficits, to fund public works projects, to finance military expenditures, and to pay the government's debt to the Banco Hipotecario to permit the mortgage bank to expand agricultural credit (see table 29). The unprecedented currency expansion unleashed raging inflation. The cost of living soared (see tables 41 and 42). The government profited from two currency devaluations during these years, reducing its debt to the Central Bank by 22,178,012 sucres. In August 1937 it signed a new contract consolidating its remaining 26 million sucre debt to the Central Bank. The consolidation set the stage for subsequent loans and renewed inflation in the 1940s.[15]

TABLE 41

EXCHANGE RATE 1927–1940

Year	Exchange rate[1]	Year	Exchange rate[1]
1927	5.00	1934	10.80
1928	5.00	1935	10.55
1929	5.04	1936	10.48
1930	5.05	1937	11.39
1931	5.06	1938	14.13
1932	5.93	1949	14.83
1933	6.00		

Sources: Calculated from data in Ecuador, Dirección de Ingresos, *Informe al Ministro de Hacienda, 1939, Anexo 30*; Ecuador, Banco Central, *Boletín*, año 13, no. 150–151 (January-February 1940), 36.

[1]Sucres per dollar.

The rampant inflation and growing national debt to the Central Bank prompted the government in November 1937 to ask the noted Mexican economist Manuel Gómez Morín to form an advisory commission to reform the Central Bank statute and other banking and currency laws. One of the founders of central banking in Mexico, Gómez Morín's vision of such institutions contrasted sharply with that of Edwin Kemmerer. The Mexican economist considered central banks a key link in the capital formation process of developing nations which functioned best when supported by a system of national development banks. In his view, the central bank's primary function, was to funnel credit to those sectors of the economy which the government believed critical to the development process. In Ecuador, as in Mexico in the 1930s, the vital sector was agriculture.

The Gómez Morín Committee, which included the Guayaquil banker Víctor Emilio Estrada, revised the Central Bank statute and the private banking law; it also proposed founding an agricultural development bank. The Central Bank received a pivotal role in determining the types of loans private banks could provide their customers through its authority to vary the discount rate for different types of paper. The Central Bank, together with the proposed agricultural bank, would provide the government a significant tool to direct economic growth. The shortage of international risk capital, which persisted until the late 1940s, as well as Ecuador's continuing default of its foreign debt, hampered the implementation of the development banking concept. Nevertheless, the Gómez Morín

TABLE 42
PRICE INDEX 1921–1943[a]

Year	Index	Year	Index
1921	100.0	1933	134.5
1922	113.1	1934	185.6
1923	123.7	1935	180.5
1924	139.7	1936	220.3
1925	145.4	1937	264.1
1926	182.3	1938	255.7
1927	169.7	1939	256.9
1928	138.9	1940	262.4
1929	144.3	1941	284.8
1930	143.3	1942	370.8
1931	106.4	1943[b]	427.6
1932	100.09		

Source: List compiled by the Junta Central de Asistencia Pública as reported in Howard H. Tewksbury to secretary of state, Quito, June 17, 1943, NA, 822.5017/5.
[a]Index based on the following commodities: rice, sugar, meat, coffee, coal, wheat flour, barley flour, bean flour, corn flour, eggs, milk, corn, lard, and potatoes.
[b]January-April 1943.

Committee irrevocably changed Ecuador's structure and concept of government-bank relations.[16]

During the decade from 1915 to 1925 Ecuador financed its economic development through credit expansion provided by private banks of issue as well as by deficit spending by the national government. The country had no other source of capital because its poor credit rating and limited resources failed to attract foreign loans or investment. In 1925 as a result of an economic and political crisis, highlanders gained control of the government. The new rulers believed that Ecuador's traditional methods of financing economic growth were not only unorthodox but also harmful.

Following the advice of the Kemmerer Mission, they returned Ecuador to the gold standard, balanced its budgets, and financed government activities through increased taxes and small loans. The country's new orthodoxy proved short-lived. As a result of the world depression, the government suspended convertibility in 1932 and returned to its traditional policy of deficit spending and bank loans, this time from the Central Bank. By that time, however, world economic thought had changed. Powerful industrial nations embarked on programs similar to

Ecuador's to overcome the worldwide depression. Influential economists, like John M. Keynes, justified such policies with bold new economic theories. By an irony of history, traditional Ecuadorian policies of deficit spending and monetary expansion became popular and acceptable economic policies in the 1930s, shortly after the country officially had repudiated them. It was easy, therefore, for Ecuadorians to return to the comfortable patterns of the past under the guise of advanced economic principles.

Conclusion

Throughout its history Ecuador has faced two fundamental obstacles to development: geographic fragmentation and limited natural resources. Geography, which had been a major barrier to national integration, fostered political, social, and economic division. The twin cordilleras of the Andes divide the country into three main regions: the Oriente, the Sierra, and the Costa. The thinly populated Oriente remained marginal until the 1970s. The coast was the nation's only economically dynamic area because fluvial networks united the region, and its soil and climatic conditions made commercial tropical agriculture possible. In contrast, the highlands, which historically contained the majority of Ecuador's population and the nation's capital, were not only separated from the two other regions by high mountain ranges but were also divided internally into a series of isolated mountain valleys. Poor soils and inhospitable climatic conditions that limited opportunities to develop commercial agriculture characterized the area. Since the country possessed no precious minerals or other valuable resources that could attract sufficient capital investment to overcome the area's geographic barriers, Ecuador remained a poor country, deeply divided by sectionalism.

Regionalism, the political expression of the division and isolation imposed by geography, has been a significant and enduring factor in Ecuadorian politics. Although the country's political history is punctuated by violent political change, that instability is misleading because it masks fundamental continuities in fiscal practices and public policy. Ecuadorian historical statistics demonstrate that evolutionary, not revolutionary, change characterizes the nation's history. Control of the state and its resources were important in a country with limited opportunities in other sectors of national life. Ecuador's political history becomes intelligible when one recognizes that regional desires to control the government lay behind much of the country's instability. The expansion of the coastal economy coincided with the rise of the Liberal party. Although liberals attempted to form a truly national political movement by incorporating into the party "progressive" groups from all areas of the country, they could not overcome regionalism. The growing antagonism between highland and coastal liberals resulted in the 1925 coup that drove the coastal liberals from office.

Regionalism affected government finances as it did other aspects of national life. The coast, and its chief city Guayaquil, earned most of the nation's income because the area produced nearly all the country's exports and received most of its imports. Since Ecuadorians refused to pay direct taxes and the state did not have the power to enforce compliance with the law, governments tended to rely on easily collected indirect taxes, principally customs duties. Thus national revenues were directly linked to the performance of Ecuadorian exports, particularly cacao. The ascendancy of the Liberal party in the late nineteenth century was directly related to the growth of cacao exports. Expenditures increased throughout the nineteenth and early twentieth century as the scope of government activity gradually broadened. Regionalists, however, had more success using the state's new resources for their own purposes than did the national government in fashioning a consensus for expenditures based on national priorities.

Although the Liberal party stressed the concept of an active state to promote national development, regionalists quickly realized that the expansion of state activities could benefit their provinces. They insisted that all areas simultaneously receive a share of the public projects. Since they distrusted the national government, particularly the executive branch, regionalist legislators, who dominated the congress, froze appropriations by law and created innumerable autonomous agencies to supervise individual projects. As a result, the national government lost control of the majority of national revenue. While Ecuadorian governments, especially during the liberal period, attempted to regain control of national income, none managed to overcome the entrenched regionalists in the congress. The demands of the military, in the face of political and regional upheavals, further disrupted government finances. Faced with massive deficits, Ecuadorian governments found it necessary to obtain loans. Because Ecuador historically had defaulted on its loans and rarely serviced its debts, foreign banks would not lend to the government except on very stringent terms. In such circumstances the government was forced to turn to local banks for loans.

Budget deficits forged a close bond between the government and the banks, especially Guayaquil banks. This relationship was neither the creation of the liberals nor a conspiracy by coastal bankers to control the state; rather it had been a central feature of Ecuador's political economy since banks were established in the 1860s. Bank loans, supplied mainly by the Banco del Ecuador and the Banco Comercial y Agrícola, contributed significantly to government revenue from 1895 to 1926. As long as cacao exports remained high, Ecuador's unorthodox fiscal arrangements worked well. Disruptions in world trade during World War I coincided with a sharp drop in productivity. Together they precipitated a major economic and political crisis in Ecuador. To protect the nation's monetary system the government enacted the Ley Moratoria. This act convinced the serranos that Guayaquil bankers dominated national politics to the detriment of the highlands. Because the Banco Comercial y Agrícola was the government's principal banker, the serranos concentrated their criticism against that institution. On July 9, 1925, a group of lieutenants overthrew the Córdova government and introduced a reform program to wrest national power from the "corrupt coastal banking oligarchy."

The military first entrusted national renovation to a plural executive and when that proved ineffective they installed a "progressive dictator," Isidro Ayora. The new regime invited a team of American advisers led by Edwin W. Kemmerer to suggest reforms. Since independence Ecuadorians had relied on foreign experts to legitimize the views held by a group or faction within the country, not to impose alien reforms on a reluctant nation. Ecuadorians employed advisers in a conscious effort to direct their own future; advisory missions were not an example of foreign imperialism. The Kemmerer Mission fits this pattern. Since 1920 Ecuadorian financiers, including Guayaquil bankers, had discussed the need to create a central bank and to centralize and modernize government finances. Indeed, Guayaquil bankers had even offered to pay for the Kemmerer Mission if the government were unable to pay. The highlanders, who gained control of the government in 1925, used the need for reforms to oust coastal liberals from power and to destroy the Banco Comercial y Agrícola, the only truly national financial institution in the country.

Ecuadorians agreed on the need to restructure the nation's banking and fiscal systems. They disagreed on how to accomplish this reform. The Ayora regime established the Central Bank by confiscating the gold reserves of the coastal banks. Highlanders expected that with the new

Central Bank headquartered in Quito, financial power would come to the sierra. Acting on the advice of the Kemmerer Mission, the Ayora administration returned to the gold standard, established a comptroller's office and created an effective national government structure through new fiscal, judicial, and administrative legislation. Although costeños were unhappy about the damage inflicted on the Guayaquil banks, they did not blame the Kemmerer Mission since Ecuadorians from all parts of the country agreed on the need for reform. But they were less supportive of the American experts who remained to implement the reforms. As the new procedures and institutions began to function and came into conflict with different national interests, Ecuadorians criticized the foreign advisers. In a few months most were driven from the country, charged with abusing their authority and misunderstanding Ecuador's needs.

The structures and institutions established by the Kemmerer reforms proved unable to withstand the extraordinary economic and political stresses of the Great Depression. Ecuador abandoned the gold standard in 1932, but not before the country had lost most of its reserves. Because of massive government deficits funded by Central Bank loans, the country endured one of the worst inflations in its history. Confronted with an extraordinary economic situation, Ecuadorians returned to older patterns of government financing. They also opted for a more direct government role in stimulating recovery and development. In 1937 the government invited Manuel Gómez Morín to recommend reforms, knowing that the noted Mexican economist's views were in sharp contrast to those advocated earlier by Kemmerer. As expected, Gómez Morín sanctioned the new Ecuadorian concept of the active state.

Ecuadorian history underscores the resiliency and vitality of traditional patterns and structures. These traditions persist because they represent time-tested ways of dealing with fundamental realities that in Ecuador have included the isolation and divisions imposed by geography. They also represent realistic, workable accommodations Ecuadorians made to their circumstances. Reformers who seek to influence development cannot simply depend on abstract rational analysis. They must also learn to understand a nation's local traditions and adopt its accustomed methods if they are to succeed in directing change and resolving local problems.[1]

Appendixes

APPENDIX A

Selected Exports by Percent of Value 1847–1972

Year	Cacao	Coffee	Bananas	Rice	Sugar	Fish
1847	57.4	.1	---	---	---	---
1853	42.9	.2	---	---	---	---
1855	27.6	.4	---	---	---	---
1857	64.0	.2	---	.8	---	---
1864	58.5	1.8	---	...	.4	---
1879	53.5	.9	...	...	...	---
1884	63.4	2.8	---	---	...	---
1889	74.7[a]	6.5	---	---	...	---
1890	67.3[a]	5.9	---	---	1.3	---
1891	77.5[a]	9.0	---	---	2.1	---
1892	72.7[a]	7.6	---	---	2.3	---
1893	73.7[a]	7.8	---	---	1.1	---
1897	66.2	7.5	---	---	.1	---
1898	69.8	4.4	---	---	3.4	---
1899	61.8	2.0	---	---	.1	---
1900	70.7	5.4	---	---	1.6	---
1901	74.6	4.0	---	---	...	---
1902	73.1	5.0	---	---	...	---
1903	65.5	3.6	---	...	1.0	---
1904	65.5	4.4	---	---	.3	---
1905	58.7	4.3	---	---	.5	---
1906	55.5	4.3	---	---	---	---
1907	58.8	1.7	---	---	---	---
1908	66.8	3.9	---	---	---	---
1909	58.4	4.3	---	...	...	---
1910	57.8	5.4	.2	...	...	---
1911	61.3	8.8	.3	---	---	---
1912	55.8	9.3	.2	...	...	---
1913	63.2	5.3	.3	...	.1	---
1914	77.3[a]	4.5	.3	...	...	---
1915	75.2	3.6	.3	...	...	---
1916	72.6	3.6	.1	...	...	---
1917	65.4	3.9	.2	...	...	---
1918	62.2	6.3	.2	---	...	---
1919	68.2	2.9	.1	...	...	---
1920	71.3	1.8	.2	---	.1	...
1921	60.0	1.8	.3	2.7	.1	...

APPENDIX A (Continued)

Selected Exports by Percent of Value 1847–1972

Year	Tagua	Panama Hats	Crude Oil	Balsa	Rubber	Gold
1847	---	15.8	---	---	...	15.3
1853	---	30.8	---	---	---	12.5
1855	---	50.1	---	---	.8	6.2
1857	---	13.2	---	---	.4	.9
1864	---	17.8	---	---	4.9	---
1879	5.1	.2	---	---	1.0	.1
1884	1.4	4.7	---	---	4.1	14.0
1889	6.7	—	---	---	3.3	---
1890	2.8	3.1	---	---	3.9	.9
1891	3.1	—	---	---	5.7	---
1892	8.0	—	---	---	1.8	---
1893	6.4	—	---	---	1.4	---
1897	6.8	3.5	---	---	9.6	---
1898	5.3	1.0	---	---	5.1	.6
1899	4.3	1.1	---	---	6.2	.3
1900	10.4	2.1	---	---	7.0	.2
1901	9.9	2.3	---	---	3.5	1.5
1902	5.4	3.8	---	---	3.8	4.6
1903	6.6	3.8	---	---	5.8	3.8
1904	9.5	3.8	---	---	4.8	1.8
1905	10.5	6.9	---	---	8.1	2.7
1906	11.9	10.2	---	---	7.0	2.8
1907	11.9	10.2	---	---	5.7	2.6
1908	3.7	6.0	---	---	3.2	2.8
1909	12.3	9.3	---	...	6.2	5.6
1910	12.2	9.2	...	...	7.4	4.4
1911	6.9	11.1	---	---	5.5	---
1912	6.8	10.0	---	---	5.1	2.5
1913	15.6	7.2	---	---	1.1	2.1
1914	3.5	7.4	...	---	.7	2.8
1915	4.1	6.5	...	---	1.5	4.1
1916	7.2	5.7	---	...	1.9	2.8
1917	5.3	5.7	---	...	2.2	5.4
1918	7.5	6.7	---	---	.5	5.2
1919	10.0	7.9	---	...	1.0	2.4
1920	11.8	7.3	---	...	.3	2.7
1921	12.8	3.8	---	...	.1	4.7

APPENDIX A (Continued)

Selected Exports by Percent of Value 1847–1972

Year	Cacao	Coffee	Bananas	Rice	Sugar	Fish
1922	65.6	7.8	.3	.7	.1	...
1923	49.2	14.1	.6	.9	2.0	...
1924	49.4	15.2	.4	1.4	.7	...
1925	46.7	10.5	.6	.2	...	...
1926	41.6	18.1	...	.5	.3	...
1927	38.5	10.0	.8	1.1	.4	...
1928	30.1	17.6	...	2.9	.3	...
1929	24.7	13.6	...	4.9	.9	...
1930	29.0	9.4	...	4.6	1.1	...
1931	21.6	10.5	...	3.3	.2	...
1932	22.9	16.3	...	1.9	3.3	...
1933	19.7	12.6	.1	3.4	1.3	...
1934	25.0	19.0	2.0	1.6	...	...
1935	21.0	12.8	2.7	5.9	...	...
1936	21.6	13.6	6.4	2.3	...	...
1937	30.5	15.0	4.6	.4	...	...
1938	36.6	15.6	7.0	8.1	.1	---
1939	22.1	9.1	4.2	4.0	.1	---
1940	17.5	9.8	3.8	8.7	.1	---
1941	17.2	11.9	2.3	11.6	.1	---
1942	13.5	5.8	1.0	17.2	.1	---
1943	13.2	11.0	.5	24.1	...	---
1944	9.0	9.3	.4	27.5	...	---
1945	14.2	11.3	.7	16.0	...	---
1946	15.8	7.3	1.6	38.2	...	---
1947	32.8	8.9	4.0	29.0	...	---
1948	30.0	16.1	6.9	24.2	...	---
1949	28.3	17.6	16.7	12.0	...	---
1950	29.1	27.6	12.8	10.7	.5	.1
1951	31.5	27.7	20.0	1.5	---	.1
1952	21.6	25.2	26.7	11.0	---	.1
1953	20.8	24.9	31.3	6.4	.1	.1
1954	34.1	27.6	27.4	2.6	...	.2
1955	20.8	25.8	41.4	2.3	...	1.4
1956	18.5	31.9	39.3	1.3	...	2.4
1957	19.4	30.0	35.0	3.5	.9	2.3
1958	15.2	27.4	50.9	2.6	.8	3.0

APPENDIX A (Continued)

Selected Exports by Percent of Value 1847–1972

Year	Tagua	Panama Hats	Crude Oil	Balsa	Rubber	Gold
1922	8.1	6.7	- - -	...[b]	.4	3.9
1923	9.1	6.4	- - -	...[b]	1.7	5.4
1924	13.9	3.7	...	...[b]	.9	4.4
1925	17.9	4.4	.6	...[b]	6.8	4.8
1926	9.6	8.7	3.5	...[b]	4.2	4.1
1927	6.0	6.1	5.6	.1	2.1	5.0
1928	6.5	4.6	12.3	...[b]	...	7.7
1929	7.1	7.9	17.7	...[b]	.1	8.3
1930	4.5	10.4	21.4	.4	- - -	9.2
1931	5.9	11.4	27.9	.2	...	11.2
1932	2.4	5.5	29.4	.4	...	13.8
1933	6.7	5.5	27.6	.4	.2	17.0
1934	4.5	5.4	11.9	.8	.2	...
1935	3.8	5.0	13.1	.4	1.1	...
1936	7.4	4.6	9.2	.7	2.9	11.3
1937	11.1	4.9	13.4	.8	2.5	11.4
1938	4.1	4.6	25.7	1.4	2.4	12.7
1939	5.7	3.0	14.4	1.7	2.6	16.0
1940	5.1	3.9	14.8	1.9	2.3	17.1
1941	3.0	8.1	6.7	4.2	3.5	14.7
1942	2.4	7.4	8.3	8.6	11.9	8.5
1943	1.6	6.4	6.1	11.0	5.9	7.0
1944	1.3	14.8	6.2	6.8	8.2	5.7
1945	1.9	18.4	7.4	4.9	6.2	4.1
1946	2.1	15.4	3.4	1.3	2.8	4.7
1947	2.0	7.3	2.4	.4	.1	3.9
1948	1.3	7.0	3.5	.6	- - -	4.6
1949	1.6	8.6	2.8	.9	- - -	7.3
1950	1.0	4.9	1.8	.9	.1	4.2
1951	1.0	4.6	2.0	1.7	.5	.4
1952	.5	2.7	1.0	1.0	.1	.7
1953	.7	3.4	1.7	1.1	- - -	.9
1954	.4	1.3	1.2	.7	- - -	.5
1955	.3	.9	1.4	.9	- - -	.4
1956	.4	1.2	.7	.9	- - -	.5
1957	.3	.8	.9	1.4	- - -	.4
1958	.3	.6	.6	1.1	- - -	.5

APPENDIX A (Continued)

Selected Exports by Percent of Value 1847–1972

Year	Cacao	Coffee	Bananas	Rice	Sugar	Fish
1959	12.8	16.1	63.0	1.6	1.5	2.7
1960	13.3	18.4	60.8	2.5	.6	2.4
1961	12.0	14.5	63.4	2.0	1.9	4.1
1962	11.0	17.7	58.0	.4	4.0	2.9
1963	12.6	14.2	53.0	2.4	3.7	3.5
1964	11.9	16.2	52.8	.8	4.4	3.7
1965	14.3	28.5	38.5	---	5.5	2.8
1966	11.7	21.8	46.6	2.0	4.4	2.8
1967	15.0	24.0	44.0	---	4.5	2.3
1968	22.0	19.4	41.7	---	4.5	2.0
1969	16.1	17.5	43.8	---	7.1	3.5
1970	11.0	25.1	46.8	---	4.7	2.6
1971[c]	11.7	16.8	46.6	---	6.2	5.0
1972[d]	7.6	14.2	36.2	...	5.7	...

APPENDIX A (Continued)

Selected Exports by Percent of Value 1847–1972

Year	Tagua	Panama Hats	Crude Oil	Balsa	Rubber	Gold
1959	.2	.5	.2	1.1	- - -	.5
1960	.1	.7	- - -	.9	- - -	.4
1961	- - -	.4	- - -	.9	- - -	.4
1962	- - -	.3	.1	.8	- - -	.5
1963	- - -	.3	.1	1.0	- - -	.4
1964	- - -	.4	.4	.9	- - -	.4
1965	- - -	.7	.4	1.2	. . .	- - -
1966	- - -	.3	1.0	1.4	. . .	- - -
1967	- - -	.4	.7	1.9	. . .	- - -
1968	- - -	.5	.5	1.9	. . .	- - -
1969	- - -	.5	.7	2.2	. . .	- - -
1970	- - -	.3	.4	1.4	. . .	- - -
1971[c]	—	.9	.5	1.5	. . .	- - -
1972[d]	—	. . .	19.9	. .	. . .	- - -

Sources: Calculated from data in Ecuador, Dirección de Estadística, *Ecuador en Cifras, 1938–1942*, p. 408–419; Ecuador, Banco Central, *Boletín* (1944–1972); Ecuador, Banco Central, *Memoria* (1950–1970); Ecuador, Banco Central, *Comercio exterior Ecuatoriano*, (1948–1964); Ecuador, Dirección General de Estadística, *Comercio exterior de la República del Ecuador* 1913–1915, 1916–1925, 1925–1926; Ecuador, Ministro de Hacienda, *Boletín de estadística fiscal y comercial*, III (1912); Ecuador, Ministerio de Hacienda, *Informe* 1847, 1853, 1880, 1885, 1888, 1890, 1892, 1902, 1904, 1913; Ecuador, Ministerio de Hacienda, *Boletín*, no. 2 (1928), no. 22 (1930); Ecuador, Dirección de Ingresos, *Informe* (1938), 7 of annex; Ecuador, Ministerio del Tesoro, *Boletín* (June, 1928); Ecuador, Ministerio del Tesoro, *Informe*, 1946 (Anexos).

[a]Author used weight of cacao exports and a value of 0.52 sucres/kilo to arrive at value of cacao exports for this year.

[b]Percentages for 1971 are figured from preliminary data that is subject to revision.

[c]Percentages for 1972 are figured from estimates based on the data for January-November 1972.

[d]In these years balsa exports not listed as a separate category.

- - - none

. . . less than .05

—— no data

APPENDIX B

Source of Customs Revenue by Province for Selected Years 1830–1944

Year	Guayas[2] Absolute amount[1]	%	Manabí[3] Absolute amount[1]	%	Esmeraldas[4] Absolute amount[1]	%	Other Provinces[5] Absolute amount[1]	%	Total Collections Absolute amount[1]	%
1830	311,500[a]	100.0	--	--	--	--	--	--	311,500	100.0
1832	200,000[a]	100.0	--	--	--	--	--	--	200,000	100.0
1846	347,714	93.8	23,092	6.2	--	--	--	--	370,806	100.0
1854	471,902	93.7	31,481	6.3	--	--	--	--	503,384	100.0
1857	602,758	96.7	19,677	3.2	--	--	561	.1	622,997	100.0
1861	878,997	94.8	46,218	5.0	--	--	1,423	.2	926,638	100.0
1862	508,429	91.0	48,979	8.8	268	...	1,031	.2	558,708	100.0
1863	495,191	91.3	45,388	8.4	1,103	.2	743	.1	542,425	100.0
1864	490,752	89.3	56,964	10.4	588	.1	1,054	.2	549,358	100.0
1865	521,796	92.3	41,448	7.3	951	.2	959	.2	565,154	100.0
1866	701,712	94.2	39,414	5.3	1,283	.2	2,447	.3	744,856	100.0
1867	703,943	93.7	44,254	5.9	1,500	.2	1,866	.2	751,563	100.0
1872	1,591,680	94.7	55,067	3.3	32,305	1.9	1,768	.1	1,680,819	100.0
1877	1,243,288	97.3	--	--	--	--	34,724	2.7	1,278,012	100.0
1879	1,738,387	94.9	60,309	3.3	28,567	1.6	2,962	.2	1,830,224	100.0
1884	2,088,408	96.7	45,947	2.1	25,048	1.2	996	...	2,160,399	100.0
1886	1,681,892	94.7	66,892	3.8	25,237[b]	1.4	1,174	.1	1,775,196	100.0
1887	3,270,919	96.6	83,925	2.5	29,879	.9	688	...	3,385,411	100.0
1888	2,708,029	96.2	74,947	2.7	27,599	1.0	10,866	.1	2,816,689	100.0

APPENDIX B (Continued)

Source of Customs Revenue by Province for Selected Years 1830–1944

Year	Guayas[2]		Manabí[3]		Esmeraldas[4]		Other Provinces[5]		Total Collections	
	Absolute amount[1]	%	Absolute amount[1]	%	Absolute amount[1]	%	Absolute amount[1]	%	Absolute amount[1]	%
1889	2,378,415	96.0	60,535	2.5	25,256	1.0	13,348	.5	2,477,554	100.0
1890	3,056,353	96.2	89,653	2.8	17,081	.5	17,488	.5	3,180,575	100.0
1891	2,231,522	95.6	71,428	3.1	15,980	.7	14,251	.6	2,333,181	100.0
1896/97	3,854,774	97.0	113,847	2.9	---	---	5,965	.1	3,974,586	100.0
1900	6,696,551	90.5	455,650	6.2	103,394	1.4	140,697[c]	1.9	7,396,292	100.0
1901	6,406,130	88.0	566,681	7.8	120,556	1.7	179,066[c]	2.5	7,272,433	100.0
1902	6,413,046	88.4	551,417	7.6	147,300	2.0	145,102[c]	2.0	7,256,865	100.0
1903	7,298,495	90.1	520,505	6.4	111,407	1.4	169,215[c]	2.1	8,099,622	100.0
1910	8,547,704	81.1	1,583,507	15.0	375,213	3.6	26,945	.3	10,533,369	100.0
1914	9,990,607	88.5	1,187,749	5.5	79,283	.7	53,252	.5	11,285,230	100.0
1917[c]	9,189,960[d]	86.4	906,610[d]	8.5	239,515[d]	2.3	302,993[d]	2.8	10,639,078[d]	100.0
1928[c]	22,425,046	83.9	2,944,626[d]	11.0	468,775[d]	1.8	889,279[d]	3.3	26,727,726[d]	100.0
1944	90,698,569	95.2	1,956,132	2.1	203,218	.2	2,378,780	2.5	95,236,699	100.0

Sources: Calculated from data in Ecuador, Ministerio de Hacienda, *Informe* 1833, 1847, 1855, 1858, 1863, 1865, 1867, 1873, 1880, 1885, 1887, 1888, 1890, 1892, 1896–97, 1902, 1903, 1904; Ecuador, Ministerio de Hacienda *Boletín de estadística fiscal y comercio* III (1912), VII (1917); Ecuador, Ministerio del Tesoro, *Boletín* 7 (1946); *El Nacional* (Quito), 127 (1868); Ecuador, Ministro Secretario de Estado, *Exposición* 1831; Ecuador, Ministro de Hacienda, *Boletín* 9 (1929).

[1]Current pesos 1830–1884; current sucres 1886–1944; the sucre was officially devalued in 1927.

[2]Includes Guayaquil for all years and Ballenita, Mangearalto, and Salinas when applicable.

APPENDIX B (Continued)

Source of Customs Revenue by Province for Selected Years 1830–1944

[3]Included Manta for all years and Cayo, Machalilla, Bahía de Caraques when applicable.

[4]Includes Esmeraldas and Vargas Torres.

[5]Includes Tulcán in province of Carchi, Puerto Bolívar, Charcas, and Santa Rosa in province of El Oro, Macara in province of Loja when applicable. After 1914 includes duties on postal packages from Quito, Cuenca, and Loja.

[a]District of Guayaquil.

[b]Incomplete due to revolutionary activity.

[c]Includes the following amounts from Puerto Bolívar: 135,251 in 1900; 170,883 in 1901; 125,898 in 1902; and 137,664 in 1903.

[d]Includes duties on postal packages.

- - - none

. . . less than .05

APPENDIX C

*Customs Revenue as a Percentage of National
Government Income for Selected Years 1830–1972*

Year	Absolute amount[1] in 1000s	% of Ordinary national government income[2]
1830	312	44
1832	200	36
1839	321	39
1846	371	34
1852[a]	310	41
1853	546	53
1854	503	51
1855	498	47
1856	559	53
1857	623	49
1861	927	64
1862	559	50
1863	542	40
1864	549	38
1865	565	36
1866	745	54
1867	752	47
1868	765	53
1869	880	53
1870	1,346	60
18/1	1,463	59
1872	1,681	58
1873	1,768	57
1874	1,525	49
1875	1,127	40
1876	1,329	56
1877	1,278	59
1878	1,438	59
1879	1,830	60
1880	981	40
1885	1,155	46
1886	1,775	56
1887	3,385	76
1888	2,817	70
1889	2,473	80
1890	3,181	76

APPENDIX C (Continued)

Customs Revenue as a Percentage of National Government Income for Selected Years 1830–1972

Year	Absolute amount[1] in 1000s	% of Ordinary national government income[2]
1891	2,333	65
1892	2,860	75
1893	3,509	81
1895	3,236[b]	- - -[b]
1896	3,678[b]	- - -[b]
1897	5,373	78
1898	6,129	79
1899	6,008	79
1900	7,396	91
1901	7,272	68
1902	7,257	78
1903	8,100	81
1905	8,133	70
1906	10,205	79
1907	9,204	73
1908	9,637	75
1909	12,349	78
1910	10,533	78
1911	8,135	60
1912	12,777	64
1913	13,398	68
1914	11,285	67
1915	9,092	61
1916	10,533	66
1917	10,639	64
1918	7,306	53
1919	9,571	63
1920	13,384	78
1921	12,343	79
1922	10,004	54
1923	10,008	54
1924	11,634	55
1925	20,284	55
1926	19,005	42
1927	23,277	36[c]
1928	26,728	43

APPENDIX C (Continued)

Customs Revenue as a Percentage of National
Government Income for Selected Years 1830–1972

Year	Absolute amount[1] in 1000s	% of Ordinary national government income[2]
1929	27,806	43
1930	23,309	38
1931	17,496	39
1932	12,702	30
1933	12,582	30
1934	20,201	42
1935	29,118	44
1936	31,011	40
1937	30,161	34
1938	45,303	37
1939	35,571	30
1940	43,518	40
1941	38,709	36
1942	53,398	41
1943	67,501	40
1944	95,237	45
1945	90,203	36
1946	99,615	33
1947	152,626	39
1948	125,539	34
1949	130,121	33
1950	171,882	44
1951	204,570	47
1952	228,881	50
1953	308,000	55
1954	536,029	50
1955	567,697	56
1956	491,721	43
1957	575,937	43
1958	578,603	42
1959	587,692	44
1960	651,347	46
1961	750,996	48
1962	772,557	48
1963	938,397	51

APPENDIX C (Continued)

Customs Revenue as a Percentage of National Government Income for Selected Years 1830–1972

Year	Absolute amount[1] in 1000s	% of Ordinary national government income[2]
1964	1,048,000	50
1965	958,000	48
1966	1,092,000	50
1967	1,442,832	55
1968	1,513,479	59
1969	1,545,000	52
1970	2,034,000	55
1971	2,225,000	50
1972	2,417,000	44

Sources: Calculated from data in Ecuador, Ministro Secretario de Estado, *Exposición* 1831; Ecuador, Ministerio de Hacienda, *Informe* 1833, 1847, 1853, 1857, 1863, 1867, 1873, 1880, 1885, 1887, 1888, 1890, 1892, 1894, 1902, 1903, 1904, 1906, 1913, 1915, 1921, 1939; Ecuador, Ministerio de Hacienda, *Boletín de estadística fiscal y comercial*, III (1912); VII (1917); Ecuador, Ministerio de Hacienda, *Boletín* 1–4 (1928); 9 (1929); 23 (1930); Ecuador, Ministerio del Tesoro, *Boletín* 7 (1946); 49–50 (1957); Ecuador, Banco Central, *Boletín* 426–427 (1963); 438–442 (1964); 453–458 (1965); Ecuador, Banco Central, *Memoria* 1954, 1957, 1958, 1959, 1963, 1964, 1965, 1966, 1968, 1969, 1972.

[1]Current pesos 1830–1880; current sucres 1885–1972.

[2]Calculated from absolute figures in this table and from data in Appendix K, except for 1954–1960. In those years the percentage was calculated using data on total national government income because customs revenue for 1954–1960 included amounts not in the operational budget that was used in Appendix K.

[a]Includes only income from November 1, 1852 to June 30, 1853.

[b]Incomplete data on government revenue for this year made it impossible to calculate percentage.

[c]Government income from revaluation of currency caused customs percentage to fall. If government revenue from this source is excluded, customs is 45% of income.

APPENDIX D

Cacao Exports 1847–1970

Year	Kilos 1000s	Value in 1000s sucres	% of total exports
1847	6,036	814	57.4
1853	6,621	759	42.9
1855	7,544	639	27.6
1857	7,358	1,873	64.0
1864	5,725	1,824	58.5
1879	15,762	6,194	53.5
1884	8,848	3,975	63.4
1890	17,699	6,570	67.3
1897	15,781	5,962	66.2
1898	20,895	10,539	69.8
1899	25,723	13,237	61.8
1900	18,791	10,908	70.7
1901	23,179	12,255	74.8
1902	24,398	13,231	73.1
1903	23,005	12,195	65.5
1904	28,564	15,249	65.5
1905	21,127	10,916	58.7
1906	23,426	12,198	55.5
1907	19,703	13,478	58.8
1908	32,119	17,737	66.8
1909	31,570	14,523	58.4
1910	36,305	16,214	57.8
1911	38,803	16,095	61.3
1912	38,225	15,716	55.8
1913	41,869	20,524	63.2
1914	47,210	20,769	77.3
1915	37,019	19,938	75.1
1916	42,667	26,236	72.6
1917	45,193	21,947	65.4
1918	38,416	17,116	62.2
1919	44,680	29,491	68.2
1920	39,790	35,573	71.3
1921	40,709	20,363	60.0
1922	40,361	30,241	65.6
1923	29,564	18,890	49.2
1924	30,505	30,249	49.4
1925	32,281	33,986	46.7

APPENDIX D (Continued)

Cacao Exports 1847–1970

Year	Kilos 1000s	Value in 1000s sucres	% of total exports
1926	20,567	26,436	41.6
1927	22,238	36,908	38.5
1928	23,737	29,653	30.1
1929	16,386	21,256	24.7
1930	19,184	23,403	29.0
1931	13,839	12,254	21.6
1932	14,419	11,267	22.9
1933	11,004	8,720	19.7
1934	16,143	27,165	25.0
1935	19,701	23,828	21.0
1936	17,114	31,472	21.6
1937	20,652	49,985	30.5
1938	16,882	39,276	36.6
1939	13,276	37,033	22.1
1940	11,208	29,354	17.5
1941	14,433	34,364	17.2
1942	13,761	40,326	13.5
1943	16,827	51,793	13.2
1944	15,750	41,985	9.0
1945	16,827	53,547	14.2
1946	16,526	74,934	15.8
1947	19,757	189,038	32.8
1948	16,660	178,583	30.0
1949	19,168	118,339	28.3
1950	26,778	248,984	29.1
1951	24,069	267,429	31.5
1952	23,276	255,642	21.6
1953	22,580	233,360	20.8
1954	29,735	512,050	34.1
1955	24,409	284,950	20.8
1956	29,229	266,435	18.5
1957	26,856	279,832	19.4
1958	22,456	327,621	15.2
1959	28,540	210,999	12.8
1960	36,320	324,611	13.3
1961	29,278	249,931	12.0
1962	31,598	283,811	11.0

APPENDIX D (Continued)
Cacao Exports 1847–1970

Year	Kilos 1000s	Value in 1000s sucres	% of total exports
1963	35,393	353,260	12.6
1964	26,853	301,046	11.9
1965	39,280	357,768	14.3
1966	32,208	343,259	11.7
1967	45,023	501,762	15.0
1968	65,072	863,109	22.0
1969	32,400	535,097	16.1
1970	36,098	510,897	11.0

Sources: Calculated from data in Ecuador, Dirección de Ingresos, *Informe* (1938), 7 of annex; Ecuador, Banco Central, *Comercio exterior Ecuatoriano* (1948–1964); Ecuador, Banco Central, *Boletín* (1944–1972); Ecuador, Banco Central, *Memoria* (1950–1970); Ecuador, Ministerio de Hacienda, *Informe* 1847, 1853, 1880, 1885, 1890, 1902; Compañía Guía del Ecuador, *El Ecuador: Guía comercial agrícola e industrial de la República* (Guayaquil, 1909); Ecuador, Ministerio de Hacienda, *Boletín de estadística fiscal y comercial* III (1912); Ecuador, Dirección General de Estadística, *Comercio exterior de la República del Ecuador*, 1916–1925; Ecuador, Ministerio de Tesoro, *Boletín* (June 1928).

APPENDIX E

Coffee Exports 1847–1970

Year	Kilos 1000s	Value in 1000s sucres	% of total exports
1847	14	2	.1
1853	19	3	.2
1855	46	10	.4
1857	16	6	.2
1864	127	55	1.8
1884[a]	608[a]	177[a]	2.8[a]
1897	1,676	672	7.5
1898	2,531	657	4.4
1899	1,769	421	2.0
1900	2,814	838	5.4
1901	2,154	649	4.0
1902	3,453	901	5.0
1903	2,642	673	3.6
1904	—	1,015	4.4
1905	—	792	4.3
1906	—	931	4.2
1907	—	391	1.7
1908	—	1,042	3.9
1909	3,380	1,057	4.3
1910	3,961	1,511	5.4
1911	4,659	2,291	8.8
1912	2,774	2,609	9.3
1913	3,689	1,719	5.3
1914	2,980	1,212	4.5
1915	2,321	952	3.6
1916	3,229	1,297	3.6
1917	2,669	1,301	3.9
1918	3,487	1,736	6.3
1919	1,692	1,262	2.9
1920	1,588	1,349	2.7
1921	6,152	3,224	9.5
1922	4,073	3,589	7.8
1923	5,602	5,392	14.1
1924	5,794	9,317	15.2
1925	4,114	7,621	10.5
1926	6,073	11,519	18.1
1927	5,869	9,581	10.0

APPENDIX E (Continued)
Coffee Exports 1847–1970

Year	Kilos 1000s	Value in 1000s sucres	% of total exports
1928	9,150	17,275	17.6
1929	7,312	11,672	13.6
1930	9,450	7,602	9.4
1931	8,337	5,930	10.5
1932	8,027	8,048	16.3
1933	7,007	5,580	12.6
1934	14,356	20,656	19.0
1935	12,510	14,515	12.8
1936	13,274	19,803	13.6
1937	13,734	24,613	15.0
1938	13,708	16,704	15.6
1939	12,906	15,227	9.1
1940	14,571	16,384	9.8
1941	11,047	23,827	11.9
1942	6,140	17,280	5.8
1943	12,340	33,176	11.0
1944	14,458	35,626	9.3
1945	10,737	33,863	11.3
1946	7,636	34,840	7.3
1947	10,394	51,325	8.9
1948	19,492	95,651	16.1
1949	10,345	72,877	17.6
1950	20,249	254,358	27.6
1951	16,619	237,154	27.7
1952	19,964	302,796	25.2
1953	18,074	282,923	24.9
1954	21,037	413,570	27.6
1955	23,090	342,989	25.8
1956	24,888	444,000	31.9
1957	29,237	444,828	30.0
1958	30,231	390,749	27.4
1959	23,766	263,438	16.1
1960	32,369	336,231	18.4
1961	22,924	243,540	14.5
1962	32,964	375,169	17.7
1963	29,951	331,441	14.2
1964	25,148	380,974	16.2

APPENDIX E (Continued)
Coffee Exports 1847–1970

Year	Kilos 1000s	Value in 1000s sucres	% of total exports
1965	47,564	628,230	28.5
1966	43,131	585,702	21.8
1967	57,910	717,676	24.0
1968	49,518	624,007	19.4
1969	38,161	468,804	17.5
1970	52,575	1,169,445	25.1

Sources: Ecuador, Banco Central, *Memoria* (1955), XXXII of annex; 85 of annex; Ecuador, Banco Central, *Comercio exterior Ecuatoriano*, 1948–1964; Ecuador, Departamento Central de Estadística, *Comercio exterior*, 1911–1920, 1916–1925; Ecuador, Banco Central, *Boletín* 45:531–533 (1971) 245; Ecuador, Dirección General de Estadística, Registro Civil y Censo. *Informe* May 31, 1934, p. 13; Ecuador, Ministerio de Hacienda, *Informe* 1847, 1855, 1857, 1867, 1885, 1902, 1904, 1906; Ecuador, Ministerio de Hacienda, *Boletín de estadística fiscal y comercial* III (1912); Compañía Guía del Ecuador, *El Ecuador: Guía comercial, agrícola e industrial de la República* (Guayaquil, 1909).

[a]Includes exports from Guayaquil and Bahía.

—— no data

APPENDIX F

Tagua Exports 1870–1960

Year	Kilos 1000s	Value in 1000s sucres	% of total exports
1870	1,117	50	1.2[a]
1871	739	41	1.0[a]
1872	2,406	119	2.7[a]
1873	2,911	146	4.6[a]
1874	3,249	146	3.6[a]
1875	2,684	150	5.5[a]
1876	3,552	159	4.5[a]
1877	391	26	.6[a]
1878	4,755	426	12.2[a]
1879	5,568	585	5.1
1880	3,154	212	2.5[a]
1881	1,977	89	1.7[a]
1882	1,750	127	2.2[a]
1883	779	70	1.4[a]
1884	—	88	1.4
1885	612	30	.5[a]
1886	2,389	154	1.4
1887	3,914[b]	319[b]	3.1[b]
1889	12,976	530	6.7
1890	8,639	270	2.8
1891	6,311	225	3.1
1892	15,282	965	8.0
1893	19,606	918	6.4
1897	10,456	612	6.8
1898	15,215	805	5.3
1899	14,654	920	4.3
1900	22,132	1,600	10.4
1901	24,190	1,618	9.9
1902	18,241	983	5.4
1903	18,130	1,235	6.6
1904	21,085	2,208	9.5
1905	19,036	1,954	10.5
1906	21,797	2,615	11.9
1907	21,423	2,716	11.9
1908	10,363	985	3.7
1909	18,399	3,062	12.3
1910	16,734	3,428	12.2

APPENDIX F (Continued)
Tagua Exports 1870–1960

Year	Kilos 1000s	Value in 1000s sucres	% of total exports
1911	13,429	1,804	6.9
1912	18,247	1,923	6.8
1913	31,684	4,399	15.6
1914	8,583	944	3.5
1915	9,115	1,081	4.1
1916	20,199	2,610	7.2
1917	16,303	1,777	5.3
1918	15,829	2,068	7.5
1919	25,510	4,319	10.0
1920	23,099	5,879	11.9
1921	23,864	4,339	12.8
1922	27,994	3,713	8.1
1923	22,981	3,494	9.1
1924	22,972	8,544	13.9
1925	22,430	12,975	17.9
1926	17,537	6,107	9.6
1927	24,896	5,767	6.0
1928	23,826	6,380	6.5
1929	25,792	6,076	7.1
1930	19,987	3,648	4.5
1931	20,082	3,360	5.9
1932	11,987	1,185	2.4
1933	24,497	2,963	6.7
1934	25,289	4,872	4.5
1935	22,924	4,262	3.8
1936	31,251	10,743	7.4
1937	34,506	18,242	11.1
1938	18,303	6,943	4.1
1939	24,610	9,482	5.7
1940	18,218	8,585	5.1
1941	14,000	6,018	3.0
1942	13,035	7,113	2.4
1943	11,171	6,274	1.6
1944	10,787	7,341	1.3
1945	11,085	7,368	1.9
1946	12,531	11,095	2.1
1947	11,755	12,605	2.0

APPENDIX F (Continued)
Tagua Exports 1870–1960

Year	Kilos 1000s	Value in 1000s sucres	% of total exports
1948	8,946	8,214	1.3
1949	8,202	7,807	1.6
1950	9,721	9,051	1.0
1951	8,267	8,807	1.0
1952	5,779	5,584	.5
1953	7,747	7,654	.7
1954	7,219	6,991	.5
1955	6,428	5,752	.4
1956	6,018	4,110	.3
1957	5,961	4,455	.3
1958	3,832	2,323	.2
1959	2,651	1,404	.1
1960	2,643	1,361	.1

Sources: Calculated from data in Ecuador, Ministerio de Hacienda, *Informe* 1885, 1888, 1892; Ecuador, Ministerio de Hacienda, *Boletín,* 22 (1930); Compañía Guía del Ecuador, *El Ecuador: guía comercial, agrícola e industrial de la República* (Guayaquil, 1909); Ecuador, Ministerio de Hacienda, *Boletín de estadística fiscal y comercial* III (1912); Ecuador, Dirección Nacional de Estadística, *Ecuador en cifras* 1938–1942 (Quito, 1944); Great Britain, Department of Overseas Trade, *Economic and Commercial Conditions in Ecuador* 1928, 1932, 1934, 1936, 1938, Ecuador, Dirección General de Estadística, *Comercio exterior de la República del Ecuador 1925–1926*; Ecuador, Ministerio del Tesoro, *Informe* 1946, *Anexos*; Ecuador, Banco Central, *Boletín* 400–401 (1960).

[a]Percentage of product exports excluding minerals and currency.

[b]Includes only exports from port of Esmeraldas.

—— no data

APPENDIX G
Banana Exports 1934–1970

Year	Metric tons	Sucres[1]	Percent exports
1934	35,987	2,150	2.0
1935	47,603	3,075	2.7
1936	56,978	6,027	6.4
1937	47,713	5,691	4.6
1938	55,503	7,558	7.0
1939	51,662	7,005	4.2
1940	47,206	6,448	3.8
1941	34,224	4,658	2.3
1942	22,592	3,107	1.0
1943	15,799	2,159	.5
1944	13,881	1,898	.4
1945	17,799	2,872	.7
1946	33,394	7,382	1.6
1947	68,944	23,179	4.0
1948	99,634	37,000	6.9
1949	137,988	66,253	16.7
1950	169,625	112,163	12.8
1951	246,454	170,275	20.0
1952	429,820	320,692	26.7
1953	406,363	354,960	31.3
1954	492,151	415,066	27.4
1955	612,615	551,407	41.1
1956	578,915	547,579	39.3
1957	669,063	517,803	35.0
1958	742,743	532,066	50.9
1959	885,571	665,591	63.0
1960	895,053	695,374	60.8
1961	842,342	839,746	63.4
1962	897,832	1,117,514	58.0
1963	1,014,340	1,293,137	53.0
1964	1,172,474	1,281,799	52.8
1965	874,580	962,171	38.5
1966	1,070,665	1,370,585	46.6
1967	1,145,699	1,476,878	44.0

APPENDIX G (Continued)
Banana Exports 1934–1970

Year	Metric tons	Sucres[1]	Percent exports
1968	1,259,151	1,638,470	41.7
1969	1,173,884	1,463,033	43.8
1970	1,335,055	2,182,513	46.8

Sources: Calculated from data in Ecuador, Banco Central, *Memoria 1955,* xxix of annex; *1964,* 84 of annex; Ecuador, Banco Central, *Comercio Exterior Ecuatoriano,* 1948–1964; Ecuador, Banco Central, *Boletín* 45: 531–533 (1971), 245.

[1]Thousands of sucres.

APPENDIX H
Population of Ecuador 1779–1974

Provinces[1]	1779/1780		1825	
	Population	%	Population	%
Coast	31,995	7.18	81,217	16.35
Esmeraldas	2,497	.56	2,352	.47
Manabí	7,699	1.73	17,444	3.51
Los Ríos	3,518	.79	10,367	2.09
Guayas	18,281	4.10	42,807	8.62
El Oro	—	—	8,247	1.66
Sierra	400,949	89.87	404,210	81.36
Carchi	---[a]	---[a]	---[a]	---[a]
Imbabura	48,645[b]	10.90	58,725[b]	11.82
Pichincha	59,291[c]	13.31	65,605[c]	13.20
Cotopaxi	49,919	11.19	55,814	11.23
Tungurahua	43,372	9.72	37,495	7.55
Chimborazo	78,736[d]	17.65	61,475[d]	12.37
Bolívar	14,368	3.22	15,006	3.02
Cañar	---[e]	---[e]	---[e]	---[e]
Azuay	82,708[f]	18.54	75,785[f]	15.25
Loja	23,810	5.34	34,305	6.90
Oriente	13,177[g]	2.95	11,419[g]	2.30
Galápagos Islands	—	—	—	—
Total	446,121		496,846	

APPENDIX H (Continued)
Population of Ecuador 1779–1974

Provinces[1]	1838/1840 Population	%	1857/1858 Population	%
Coast	90,352	14.66	128,257	17.14
Esmeraldas	5,229	.85	6,429	.86
Manabí	23,641	3.84	30,208	4.04
Los Ríos	10,045	1.63	- - -[i]	- - -[i]
Guayas	51,437	8.35	91,620[j]	12.24[i]
El Oro	—	—	- - -[i]	- - -[i]
Sierra	525,857	85.34	620,040	82.86
Carchi	- - -[a]	- - -[a]	- - -[a]	- - -[a]
Imbabura	84,741[b]	13.75[b]	75,285[b]	10.06[b]
Pichincha	72,712	11.80	85,915	11.48
Cotopaxi	74,505	12.09	77,498	10.36
Tungurahua	66,155	10.74	69,539	9.29
Chimborazo	83,965[h]	13.63[h]	120,314	16.08
Bolívar	- - -[i]	- - -[i]	- - -[i]	- - -[i]
Cañar	- - -[e]	- - -[e]	- - -[e]	- - -[e]
Azuay	102,689[f]	16.66[f]	120,407[f]	16.09[f]
Loja	41,090	6.67	71,082	9.50
Oriente	—	—	—	—
Galápagos Islands	—	—	—	—
Total	616,209		748,297	

APPENDIX H (Continued)

Population of Ecuador 1779–1974

Provinces[1]	1889 Population	%	1909 Population	%
Coast	242,118	19.04	481,200	29.29
Esmeraldas	14,553	1.14	25,000	1.52
Manabí	64,123	5.04	120,000	7.30
Los Ríos	32,800	2.58	60,000	3.65
Guayas	98,042	7.71	231,200	14.07
El Oro	32,600	2.56	45,000	2.74
Sierra	949,643	74.67	1,081,406	65.82
Carchi	36,000	2.83	45,800	2.79
Imbabura	67,940	5.34	80,000	4.87
Pichincha	205,000	16.12	230,860	14.05
Cotopaxi	109,600[k]	8.62	105,000[k]	6.39
Tungurahua	103,033	8.10	90,000	5.48
Chimborazo	122,200	9.61	146,246	8.90
Bolívar	43,000	3.38	53,000	3.23
Cañar	64,014	5.03	57,500	3.50
Azuay	132,400	10.41	200,000	12.17
Loja	66,456	5.23	73,000	4.44
Oriente	80,000	6.29	80,000	4.87
Galápagos Islands	—	—	250	.02
Total	1,271,761		1,642,856	

APPENDIX H (Continued)
Population of Ecuador 1779–1974

Provinces[1]	1926 Population	%	1933 Population	%
Coast	1,115,264	38.07	799,914	30.76
Esmeraldas	54,593	1.86	43,883	1.69
Manabí	347,847	11.87	235,077	9.04
Los Ríos	161,800	5.52	104,547	4.02
Guayas	483,508	16.51	351,438	13.51
El Oro	67,516	2.30	64,969	2.50
Sierra	1,814,050	61.93	1,611,899	61.99
Carchi	78,125	2.67	64,836	2.49
Imbabura	161,223	5.50	129,872	5.00
Pichincha	304,794	10.40	261,902	10.07
Cotopaxi	193,017[k]	6.59	176,831[k]	6.80
Tungurahua	227,181	7.76	184,752	7.11
Chimborazo	288,713	9.86	223,938	8.61
Bolívar	88,657	3.03	82,513	3.17
Cañar	94,743	3.23	107,691	4.14
Azuay	201,911	6.89	222,717	8.56
Loja	175,686	6.00	156,847	6.03
Oriente	—	—	186,272	7.16
Galápagos Islands	—	—	2,031	.08
Total	2,929,314		2,600,116	

APPENDIX H (Continued)
Population of Ecuador 1779–1974

Provinces[1]	1942 Population	%	1950 Population	%
Coast	1,007,018	32.64	1,298,495	40.54
Esmeraldas	57,496	1.86	75,407	2.35
Manabí	321,041	10.41	401,378	12.53
Los Ríos	131,276	4.26	150,260	4.69
Guayas	415,734	13.48	582,144	18.18
El Oro	81,471	2.64	89,306	2.79
Sierra	1,886,748	61.16	1,856,445	57.96
Carchi	77,755	2.52	76,595	2.39
Imbabura	146,360	4.74	146,893	4.59
Pichincha	305,175	9.88	386,520	12.07
Cotopaxi	199,190	6.45	165,602	5.17
Tungurahua	207,138	6.71	187,942	5.87
Chimborazo	261,963	8.48	218,130	6.81
Bolívar	102,825	3.33	109,305	3.41
Cañar	122,809	3.98	97,681	3.05
Azuay	258,447	8.37	250,975	7.84
Loja	205,086	6.64	216,802	6.77
Oriente	189,005	6.12	46,471	1.45
Galápagos Islands	2,192	.07	1,346	.04
Total	3,084,963		3,202,757	

APPENDIX H (Continued)
Population of Ecuador 1779–1974

Provinces[1]	1962 Population	%	1974 Population	%
Coast	2,127,358	47.53	3,169,190	48.75
Esmeraldas	124,881	2.79	203,406	3.13
Manabí	612,542	13.69	808,615	12.44
Los Ríos	250,062	5.59	384,113	5.91
Guayas	979,223	21.88	1,512,838	23.27
El Oro	160,650	3.59	260,218	4.00
Sierra	2,271,345	50.75	3,139,693	48.30
Carchi	94,649	2.11	120,263	1.85
Imbabura	174,039	3.89	217,813	3.35
Pichincha	587,835	13.13	981,053	15.09
Cotopaxi	154,971	3.46	235,615	3.63
Tungurahua	178,709	3.99	276,114	4.25
Chimborazo	276,668	6.18	306,138	4.71
Bolívar	131,651	2.94	146,424	2.25
Cañar	112,733	2.52	147,463	2.27
Azuay	274,642	6.14	365,657	5.62
Loja	285,448	6.38	343,153	5.28
Oriente	74,913	1.67	187,904	2.89
Galápagos Islands	2,391	.05	4,058	.06
Total	4,476,007		6,500,845	

APPENDIX H (Continued)
Population of Ecuador 1779–1974

Sources: Data for 1779/1780, 1825, 1838/1840, 1857/1858 from Michael T. Hamerly, *Historia social y económica de la antigua provincia de Guayaquil 1763–1842* (Guayaquil, 1973), tablas 1 and 2, pp. 80 and 83; data for 1887 from Pedro Fermín Cevallos, calculations cited in United States Senate, Bureau of the American Republics, *Handbook of Ecuador* (Washington, 1894), p. 16; data for 1909 from Compañía Guía del Ecuador, *El Ecuador: Guía comercial, agrícola e industrial de la república* (Guayaquil, 1909); data for 1926 from Luis T. Paz y Miño's calculations published in *El Telégrafo* (March, 1926); data for 1933 from Ecuador, Dirección General de Estadística, Registro Civil y Censo, *Informe* (May 31, 1934), pp. 7–8; data for 1942 from Ecuador, Dirección Nacional de Estadística, *Ecuador en Cifras 1938–1942* (Quito, 1944), p. 56; data for 1950 from Ecuador. Dirección General de Estadística y Censos, *Primer censo de población del Ecuador*. 4 vols. (Quito, 1954), I, p. 6; data for 1962 from Ecuador, Junta Nacional de Planificación y Coordinación Económica, *Segundo censo de población y primer censo de vivienda* (Quito, 1964); Ecuador, Junta Nacional de Planificación, *III Censo de población, I de vivienda* (Quito, 1974).

¹The provinces listed for the coast and the sierra are the modern political divisions. Data for the years 1779 through 1858 was adapted from the calculations of Michael T. Hamerly; in some cases it was impossible to reconstruct the population for certain modern provinces.

ªIncluded in Imbabura.

ᵇHamerly's Ibarra, and Otavalo; includes Carchi.

ᶜHamerly's Quito.

ᵈHamerly's Riobamba and Alausí.

ᵉIncluded in Azuay.

ᶠHamerly's Cuenca; includes Cañar.

ᵍHamerly's Quijos, Macas, and Maynas; some of this territory later became part of Perú.

ʰIncludes Hamerly's Riobamba, Guaranda, and Alausí.

ⁱIncluded in Guayas.

ʲIncludes Guayas, Los Ríos, and El Oro.

ᵏLeón.

—— no data.

Note: Population data for Ecuador varies in quality. Data in this appendix is presented to give readers a sense of gross demographic trends. Figures for the years 1779/1780, 1825, 1838/1840, and 1857/1858 are adapted from Hamerly's calculations that are based on partial census that remain in manuscript form. Therefore, figures for these years are relatively reliable. Figures for 1889 were calculated by Cevallos from a variety of official sources. Since many of these sources provided only estimates, Cevallos's figures are not as reliable. The figures for 1909 were adapted from population estimates made by various provincial officials and should be considered gross estimates. Paz y Mino's figures for 1926 are too high. However, they appear to be an accurate reflection of the proportional distribution of population by provinces. The 1933 and 1942 figures were calculated by the official statistical agency of Ecuador; it analyzed the number of births and deaths to arrive at population growth. This method determined the rate of population change rather accurately but fails to reflect the actual size of the population since there was no census carried out to determine the population base. Figures for 1950, 1962, and 1974 are the result of national census and are the most accurate presently available. As a result of the rounding off of

APPENDIX I
Population Density 1779–1974[a]

	Persons Per Square Kilometer			
Provinces	1779/1780	1825	1838/1840	1889
Coast	.48	1.23	1.37	3.67
Esmeraldas	.17	.16	.35	.97
Manabí	.42	.96	1.30	3.51
Los Ríos	.59	1.75	1.70	5.55
Guayas	.87	2.03	2.44	4.65
El Oro	—	1.42	—	5.60
Sierra	5.78	5.83	7.58	13.70
Carchi[1]	4.38	5.29	7.63	9.72
Imbabura[2]	6.73	8.13	11.73	14.10
Pichincha	3.04	3.36	3.72	10.49
Cotopoxi	9.93	11.10	14.82	21.80
Tungurahua	13.50	11.67	20.60	32.08
Chimborazo	14.17	11.07	15.12	22.00
Bolívar	3.36	3.51	—	10.07
Cañar[3]	8.16	7.48	10.13	18.95
Azuay[4]	7.07	6.47	8.77	16.97
Loja	1.98	2.85	3.41	5.52
Oriente	.28	.25	—	1.72
Galápagos Islands	—	—	—	

figures, the percentages in the subcategories do not always equal the category percentage nor does the total of all categories always equal 100%.

APPENDIX I (Continued)
Population Density 1779–1974[a]

Provinces	Persons Per Square Kilometer			
	1909	1933	1942	1950
Coast	7.29	12.11	15.25	19.66
Esmeraldas	1.67	2.93	3.84	5.03
Manabí	6.57	12.88	17.59	21.99
Los Ríos	10.15	17.68	22.20	25.41
Guayas	10.97	16.67	19.72	27.62
El Oro	7.72	11.15	13.98	15.33
Sierra	15.60	26.16	27.21	26.77
Carchi[1]	12.38	17.52	21.00	20.70
Imbabura[2]	16.61	26.96	30.38	30.50
Pichincha	11.81	13.40	15.62	19.78
Cotopoxi	20.88	35.17	39.62	32.94
Tungurahua	28.02	57.52	64.49	58.51
Chimborazo	26.33	40.31	47.16	39.27
Bolívar	12.41	19.32	24.08	25.59
Cañar[3]	17.02	31.88	36.36	28.92
Azuay[4]	25.63	28.54	33.12	32.16
Loja	6.07	13.03	17.04	18.02
Oriente	1.72	4.01	4.07	1.00
Galápagos Islands	.03	.26	.28	.17

APPENDIX I (Continued)
Population Density 1779–1974[a]

Provinces	Persons Per Square Kilometer	
	1962	1974
Coast	32.21	47.98
Esmeraldas	8.34	13.58
Manabí	33.55	44.30
Los Ríos	42.29	64.96
Guayas	46.46	71.78
El Oro	27.57	44.66
Sierra	32.76	45.28
Carchi[1]	25.57	32.49
Imbabura[2]	36.13	45.22
Pichincha	30.08	50.20
Cotopoxi	30.82	46.86
Tungurahua	55.64	85.96
Chimborazo	49.81	55.11
Bolívar	30.82	34.28
Cañar[3]	33.37	43.65
Azuay[4]	35.19	46.86
Loja	23.72	28.52
Oriente	1.61	1.55
Galápagos Islands	.31	.52

Sources: Calculated from data in table 1 and Appendix H.

[a]Calculated from data in Appendix H and table 1.

[1]To calculate population density for 1779/1780, 1825, and 1838/1840, one-third of the population of Imbabura in table 1 was used as the population of Carchi for those years.

[2]Calculations for Imbabura in the years 1779/1780, 1825, and 1838/1840 are based on a population equal to two-thirds of figure listed in table 1. See note 1.

[3]To calculate population density for 1779/1780, 1825, and 1838/1840, one-third of the population of Azuay in table 1 was used as population of Cañar for those years.

[4]Calculations for Azuay in the years 1779/1780, 1825, and 1836/1840 are based on a population equal to two-thirds of figure listed in table 1. See note 3.

—— no data

APPENDIX J
Presidential Terms in Ecuador

Classified by Stable (S) or Nonstable (NS) Change[1]

	Took office	Left office
Juan José Flores[2]	13 May 1830 (NS)	21 Sept. 1830 (S)
	22 Sept. 1830 (S)	10 Sept. 1834 (NS)
Vicente Rocafuerte[2,3]	10 Sept. 1834 (NS)	8 Aug. 1835 (S)
	9 Aug. 1835 (S)	30 Jan. 1839 (S)
Juan José Flores[2,3]	31 Jan. 1839 (S)	15 Jan. 1843 (S)
	16 Jan. 1843 (NS)	31 March 1834 (S)
	1 Feb. 1843 (S)	6 March 1845 (NS)
Provisional Junta (3 men)	6 March 1845 (NS)	7 Dec. 1845 (S)
Vicente Ramón Roca[3]	8 Dec. 1845 (S)	15 Oct. 1849 (S)
Manuel de Ascásubi	15 Oct. 1849 (NS)	20 Feb. 1850 (NS)
Diego Noboa[2]	20 Feb. 1850 (NS)	25 Feb. 1851 (S)
	26 Feb. 1851 (S)	17 July 1851 (NS)
José María Urvina[2,3]	17 July 1851 (NS)	6 Sept. 1852 (S)
	7 Sept. 1852 (S)	31 Aug. 1856 (S)
Francisco Robles	1 Sept. 1856 (S)	1 May 1859 (NS)
Provisional Junta (3 men)	1 May 1859 (NS)	17 Jan. 1860 (NS)
Gabriel García Moreno[2,3]	17 Jan. 1860 (NS)	1 April 1861 (S)
	2 April 1861 (S)	6 Sept. 1865 (S)
Jerónimo Carrión	7 Sept. 1865 (S)	5 Nov. 1867 (NS)
Pedro José de Arteta	5 Nov. 1867 (NS)	19 Jan. 1868 (S)
Javier Espinosa	20 Jan. 1868 (S)	18 Jan. 1869 (NS)
Gabriel García Moreno[2]	18 Jan. 1869 (NS)	31 July 1869 (S)
	1 Aug. 1869 (S)	6 Aug. 1875 (NS)
Francisco Javier León	6 Aug. 1875 (NS)	19 Aug. 1875 (NS)
Manuel de Ascásubi	19 Aug. 1875 (NS)	8 Dec. 1875 (S)
Antonio Borrero	9 Dec. 1875 (S)	18 Dec. 1876 (NS)
Ignacio Veintimilla[2]	18 Dec. 1876 (NS)	20 April 1878 (S)
	21 April 1878 (S)	26 March 1882 (NS)
	26 March 1882 (NS)	9 July 1883 (NS)
Provisional Junta (5 men)	9 July 1883 (NS)	9 Feb. 1884 (S)

APPENDIX J (Continued)
Presidential Terms in Ecuador

	Took office	Left office
José María Plácido Caamaño[3]	10 Feb. 1884 (S)	30 June 1888 (S)
Antonio Flores Jijón	1 July 1888 (S)	31 Aug. 1892 (S)
Luis Cordero	1 Sept. 1892 (S)	15 April 1895 (NS)
Vicente Lucio Salazar	15 April 1895 (NS)	5 June 1895 (NS)
Eloy Alfaro[2,3]	5 June 1895 (NS) 17 Jan. 1897 (S)	16 Jan. 1897 (S) 31 Aug. 1901 (S)
Leonidas Plaza Gutiérrez[3]	1 Sept. 1901 (S)	31 Aug. 1905 (S)
Lizardo García	1 Sept. 1905 (S)	16 Jan. 1906 (NS)
Eloy Alfaro[1]	16 Jan. 1906 (NS) 1 Jan. 1908 (S)	31 Dec. 1907 (S) 11 Aug. 1911 (NS)
Carlos Freile Zaldumbide	11 Aug. 1911 (NS)	31 Aug. 1911 (S)
Emilio Estrada	1 Sept. 1911 (S)	21 Dec. 1911 (NS)
Carlos Freile Zaldumbide	21 Dec. 1911 (NS)	5 March 1912 (NS)
Francisco Andrade Marín	5 March 1912 (NS)	31 Aug. 1912 (S)
Leonidas Plaza Gutiérrez[3]	1 Sept. 1912 (S)	31 Aug. 1916 (S)
Alfredo Baquerizo Moreno[3]	1 Sept. 1916 (S)	31 Aug. 1920 (S)
José Luis Tamayo[3]	1 Sept. 1920 (S)	31 Aug. 1924 (S)
Gonzalo Córdova	1 Sept. 1924 (S)	9 July 1925 (NS)
Provisional Junta (7 men)	9 July 1925 (NS)	10 Jan. 1926 (NS)
Provisional Junta (6 men)	10 Jan. 1926 (NS)	31 March 1926 (NS)
Isidro Ayora[2]	31 March 1926 (NS) 17 April 1929 (S)	16 April 1929 (S) 24 Aug. 1931 (NS)
Luis Larrea Alba	24 Aug. 1931 (NS)	15 Oct. 1931 (NS)
Alfredo Baquerizo Moreno	15 Oct. 1931 (NS)	28 Aug. 1932 (NS)
Carlos Freile Larrea	28 Aug. 1932 (NS)	2 Sept. 1932 (NS)
Alberto Guerrero Martínez	2 Sept. 1932 (NS)	4 Dec. 1932 (S)
Juan de Diós Martínez Mera	5 Dec. 1932 (S)	17 Oct. 1933 (NS)
Abelardo Moncayo	17 Oct. 1933 (NS)	31 Aug. 1934 (S)
José María Velasco Ibarra	1 Sept. 1934 (S)	20 Aug. 1935 (NS)

APPENDIX J (Continued)
Presidential Terms in Ecuador

	Took office	Left office
Antonio Pons	20 Aug. 1935 (NS)	26 Sept. 1935 (NS)
Federico Páez	26 Sept. 1935 (NS)	22 Oct. 1937 (NS)
Alberto Enríquez Gallo	22 Oct. 1937 (NS)	10 Aug. 1938 (NS)
Manuel María Borrero	10 Aug. 1938 (NS)	2 Dec. 1938 (NS)
Aurelio Mosquera Narváez	2 Dec. 1938 (S)	17 Nov. 1939 (NS)
Carlos Alberto Arroyo del Río	17 Nov. 1939 (NS)	10 Dec. 1939 (NS)
Andrés F. Córdova Nieto	10 Dec. 1939 (NS)	10 Aug. 1940 (NS)
Julio E. Moreno	10 Aug. 1940 (NS)	31 Aug. 1940 (S)
Carlos Alberto Arroyo del Río	1 Sept. 1940 (S)	28 May 1944 (NS)
Provisional Junta	28 May 1944 (NS)	31 May 1944 (NS)
José María Velasco Ibarra[2]	31 May 1944 (NS)	9 Aug. 1944 (S)
	10 Aug. 1944 (S)	30 March 1946 (NS)
	30 March 1946 (NS)	23 Aug. 1947 (NS)
Carlos Mancheno Cajas	23 Aug. 1947 (NS)	2 Sept. 1947 (NS)
Mariano Suárez Veintimilla	2 Sept. 1947 (NS)	17 Sept. 1947 (S)
Carlos Julio Arosemena Tola[4]	18 Sept. 1947 (S)	31 Aug. 1948 (S)

Source: Georg Maier, "Presidential Succession in Ecuador:1860–1968," *Journal of Inter-American Studies and World Affairs,* vol 13, no. 3–4 (July-October 1971), 475–509.

[1]This table does not include regional rulers nor vice-presidents who assumed office temporarily because the incumbent was either out of the country or physically handicapped.

[2]These individuals either assumed office as nonelected presidents and were later elected with no interruption in office, or they proclaimed a dictatorship after having been constitutionally elected, or both.

[3]These individuals completed their constitutional term of office.

[4]This individual was elected for an interim period by the congress until elections could be held.

APPENDIX K

National Government Income for Selected Years 1830–1970

Year	Absolute amount[1] in 1000s	Income from national property[2]	Income from national services[3]	Sources of National Government Income in Percentage Terms				Other income
				Income from Taxes				
				Direct taxes[4]	Indirect taxes[5]	Taxes on transfers[6]	Total taxes	
1830	708	--[a]	--[a]	39.1	51.3	9.6	100.0	--[a]
1832	554	.1	--[a]	49.2	42.8	7.4	99.4	.5
1834	677	.1	--[a]	38.7	50.9	9.6	99.2	.7
1836	750	.4	.2	33.3	56.8	7.3	97.4	2.0
1837	770	.4	.2	33.3	56.8	7.3	97.4	2.0
1839	824	.4	.2	33.3	56.8	7.3	97.4	2.0
1840	838	.4	.2	33.3	56.8	7.3	97.4	2.0
1846	1,105	.5	2.2	16.7	54.0	17.2	87.9	9.4
1847	993	.7	1.7	23.2	60.3	5.3	88.8	8.8
1848	892	1.2	2.3	23.3	61.8	3.2	88.3	7.7
1852[b]	762	.3	2.4	25.7	60.0	10.5	96.2	1.1
1853	1,037	.3	4.7	24.7	59.3	6.4	90.4	4.6
1854	991	.4	6.2	24.0	58.9	3.8	86.7	6.7
1855	1,049	.4	7.3	23.8	59.2	3.5	86.5	6.8
1856	1,060	.5	7.2	20.9	61.2	4.3	86.4	5.9
1857[c]	1,276	.5	9.2	19.1	60.9	4.2	84.2	6.1
1858	1,288	1.0	9.0	14.8	65.4	5.1	85.3	4.7

APPENDIX K (Continued)
National Government Income for Selected Years 1830–1970

Year	Absolute amount[1] in 1000s	Income from national property[2]	Income from national services[3]	Sources of National Government Income in Percentage Terms — Income from Taxes — Direct taxes[4]	Indirect taxes[5]	Taxes on transfers[6]	Total taxes	Other income
1861	1,448	1.5	8.8	10.5	69.7	6.0	86.2	3.5
1862	1,128	.9	6.7	11.7	59.3	10.3	81.3	11.1
1863	1,350	3.6	5.4	14.2	51.6	18.4	84.2	6.8
1864	1,444	1.4	5.2	12.3	50.0	12.7	75.0	18.4
1865	1,587	.6	5.0	29.2	49.8	11.9	90.9	3.5
1866	1,369	1.6	7.0	8.0	63.5	14.9	86.4	5.0
1867	1,610	1.3	7.0	23.0	61.7	6.2	90.9	.8
1868	1,442	1.6	8.6	6.8	76.5	5.8	89.1	.7
1869	1,664	2.1	7.7	9.9	72.7	7.4	90.0	.2
1870	2,248	2.5	8.0	8.3	72.5	7.6	88.4	1.1
1871	2,483	.7	7.2	12.1	64.0	10.7	86.8	5.3
1872	2,909	1.4	5.9	10.4	52.5	9.4	72.3	20.4
1873	3,099	1.2	7.5	5.6	66.2	12.9	84.7	6.6
1874	3,092	.4	6.3	16.6	60.9	8.4	85.9	7.4
1875	2,849	.9	6.7	17.4	48.3	7.7	73.4	19.0
1876	2,387	---[a]	7.2	13.8	66.7	2.0	82.5	10.3
1877	2,154	.4	5.2	25.6	53.0	6.9	85.5	8.9
1878	2,455	2.1	4.8	13.9	63.7	8.0	85.6	7.5

APPENDIX K (Continued)

National Government Income for Selected Years 1830–1970

Year	Absolute amount[1] in 1000s	Income from national property[2]	Income from national services[3]	Sources of National Government Income in Percentage Terms				Other income
				Income from Taxes				
				Direct taxes[4]	Indirect taxes[5]	Taxes on transfers[6]	Total taxes	
1879	3,043	.8	3.0	27.0	48.9	17.3	93.2	3.0
1880	2,442	.9	6.9	17.2	71.9	.8	89.9	2.3
1882	2,212	.2	7.3	10.7	75.4	5.8	91.9	.6
1883	2,683	1.0	4.7	12.5	69.8	11.6	93.9	.4
1884	3,164	.3	6.6	15.5	68.2	6.3	90.1	3.0
1885	2,524	.4	6.2	21.4	57.1	6.6	85.1	8.3
1886	3,176	.3	5.4	20.7	61.8	5.0	87.5	6.8
1887	4,479	.7	6.8	12.6	74.4	4.6	91.6	.9
1888	4,047	.6	6.6	13.8	67.5	5.6	86.9	5.9
1889	3,111	1.1	6.7	20.0	61.3	8.1	89.4	2.8
1890	4,183	.7	7.1	2.7	80.0	5.5	88.2	4.0
1891	3,584	.6	6.9	4.1	81.7	5.8	91.6	.9
1892	3,799	.4	7.2	4.3	79.7	5.8	89.8	2.6
1893	4,326	.7	7.7	3.0	81.2	5.9	90.1	1.5
1895	5,128	.6	5.7	10.2	70.7	6.8	87.7	6.0
1897	6,860	.4	4.0	5.6	79.1	4.9	89.6	6.0
1898	7,805	.3	4.5	3.8	77.6	4.1	85.5	9.7
1899	7,626	.4	5.1	3.2	79.5	5.2	87.9	6.6

APPENDIX K (Continued)
National Government Income for Selected Years 1830–1970

Year	Absolute amount[1] in 1000s	Income from national property[2]	Income from national services[3]	Sources of National Government Income in Percentage Terms				Other income
				Income from Taxes				
				Direct taxes[4]	Indirect taxes[5]	Taxes on transfers[6]	Total taxes	
1900	8,137	.3	3.2	4.2	86.9	4.2	95.3	1.2
1901	10,703	.2	6.4	3.1	77.8	4.0	84.9	8.5
1902	9,281	.3	6.5	2.8	77.2	4.4	84.4	8.8
1903	10,059	.3	17.7	3.5	73.3	4.2	81.0	1.0
1904	8,559	.3	7.5	4.6	78.7	4.7	88.0	4.2
1905	11,538	.3	6.3	4.0	81.5	4.5	90.0	3.4
1906	12,922	.2	10.3	1.3	81.4	3.7	86.4	3.1
1907	12,571	.3	6.1	3.9	82.9	3.1	89.9	3.7
1908	12,807	.3	8.7	3.0	78.8	3.0	84.8	6.2
1909	15,895	.3	6.5	2.4	83.1	3.8	89.3	3.9
1910	13,454	.5	6.2	3.8	74.2	3.8	81.8	11.5
1911	13,536	.4	5.6	1.7	70.8	4.0	76.5	17.5
1912	19,973	.4	3.0	2.0	72.1	3.0	77.1	19.5
1913	19,845	1.6	5.2	1.2	73.7	4.8	82.6	10.6
1914	16,914	.2	6.9	2.8	75.7	3.8	85.6	7.3
1915	14,885	.2	6.4	3.5	68.9	4.9	83.7	9.7
1916	16,053	.4	7.2	3.2	79.2	5.4	89.2	3.2
1917	16,572	.6	7.4	3.2	75.9	6.5	87.6	4.4

APPENDIX K (Continued)
National Government Income for Selected Years 1830–1970

| Year | Absolute amount[1] in 1000s | Income from national property[2] | Income from national services[3] | Sources of National Government Income in Percentage Terms — Income from Taxes | | | | Other income |
				Direct taxes[4]	Indirect taxes[5]	Taxes on transfers[6]	Total taxes	
1918	13,826	.5	5.8	5.4	71.6	7.0	86.3	7.4
1919	15,178	.5	7.0	3.9	71.7	7.6	85.2	7.3
1920	17,214	.8	7.2	4.3	79.9	7.1	91.3	.7
1921	15,654	1.0	.2	2.7	78.4	7.2	89.0	4.8
1922	18,677	.9	5.0	4.9	72.7	11.6	91.5	2.6
1923	18,532	1.0	4.9	3.5	76.3	7.4	88.5	5.6
1924	21,132	.8	6.6	3.8	73.7	6.3	85.9	6.7
1925	36,816	1.1	6.7	4.0	78.4	5.6	89.8	2.4
1926	44,856	1.0	5.7	3.0	74.2	5.0	85.8	7.5
1927	65,150	1.2	4.7	3.2	61.1	4.0	68.3	25.8
1928	61,576	2.2	4.7	6.4	75.2	4.1	85.7	7.4
1929	64,480	3.3	4.9	6.3	71.7	4.5	82.5	9.3
1930	60,821	5.5	4.9	7.6	74.0	4.2	85.8	3.8
1931	45,270	4.4	6.0	7.4	72.6	2.0	82.0	7.6
1932	42,162	4.1	5.1	5.4	62.3	2.2	69.3	20.9
1933	41,842	6.6	5.5	7.4	67.8	2.8	78.0	9.9
1934	48,242	4.4	6.5	5.7	75.6	2.0	83.3	5.8
1935	66,486	4.4	5.5	8.0	77.2	2.0	87.2	2.9

APPENDIX K (Continued)
National Government Income for Selected Years 1830–1970

| Year | Absolute amount[1] in 1000s | Income from national property[2] | Income from national services[3] | Sources of National Government Income in Percentage Terms — Income from Taxes | | | | Other income |
				Direct taxes[4]	Indirect taxes[5]	Taxes on transfers[6]	Total taxes	
1936	77,464	2.5	5.8	8.7	68.0	2.9	79.6	12.1
1937	86,585	3.3	6.3	9.9	65.5	2.9	78.3	12.1
1938	120,833	7.3	6.0	9.7	62.0	4.6	76.3	10.4
1939	117,187	6.0	6.4	8.2	65.8	4.9	78.9	8.7
1940	108,533	6.3	6.4	10.3	68.1	5.2	83.6	3.7
1941	109,001	5.2	6.9	13.6	65.3	5.8	84.8	3.2
1942	128,985	5.2	7.3	14.4	63.5	7.5	85.3	2.1
1943	168,284	4.5	6.1	16.7	60.5	7.6	84.8	4.6
1944	211,958	4.2	7.9	16.4	60.9	6.3	83.6	4.3
1945	252,717	3.8	6.7	16.3	60.8	6.8	83.9	5.6
1946	298,813	- -d	5.9	17.2	71.2	- -e	88.4	5.7
1948	373,403	- -d	5.6	21.9	68.0	- -e	89.9	4.5
1949	390,648	- -d	5.1	20.9	67.6	- -e	88.5	6.4
1950	388,685	- -d	5.5	15.2	74.4	- -e	89.6	4.9
1951	438,207	1.4	2.9	- -f	- -f	- -e	82.0	13.7
1952	454,639	1.2	3.0	12.0	72.2	- -e	85.1	10.7
1953	561,176	1.9	2.6	11.0	69.9	- -e	80.9	14.6
1954	616,844	1.2	3.3	9.1	72.9	- -e	82.0	13.5

APPENDIX K (Continued)

National Government Income for Selected Years 1830–1970

| Year | Absolute amount[1] in 1000s | Income from national property[2] | Income from national services[3] | Sources of National Government Income in Percentage Terms | | | | Other income |
| | | | | Income from Taxes | | | | |
				Direct taxes[4]	Indirect taxes[5]	Taxes on transfers[6]	Total taxes	
1955	739,202	1.6	3.0	10.9	65.4	---e	76.3	19.1
1956	768,793	1.9	3.8	12.1	60.4	---e	72.5	21.8
1957	802,454	1.8	6.1	12.8	72.5	---e	85.3	6.8
1958	851,215	1.8	3.9	15.1	73.1	---e	88.2	6.1
1959	858,975	1.4	2.9	12.2	63.9	---e	76.1	19.6
1960	916,678	1.0	2.6	9.3	47.1	---e	56.4	40.0
1961	1,564,505	1.2	4.3	10.1	50.1	---e	60.2	34.3
1962	1,622,727	1.4	5.7	12.1	55.5	---e	67.6	25.3
1963	1,843,786	1.3	7.4	9.7	58.6	---e	68.3	23.0
1964	2,460,628	.8	5.8	12.0	54.0	---e	66.0	27.4
1965	2,535,712	1.2	5.7	11.5	45.8	---e	57.3	35.8
1966	2,146,946	1.0	5.9	11.1	45.6	---e	56.7	36.4
1967	2,632,223	1.0	6.2	11.0	54.3	---e	65.3	27.5
1968	2,922,649	1.5	5.3	8.5	44.6	---e	53.1	40.1
1969	3,356,000	5.2	4.7	9.8	43.0	---e	52.8	37.3
1970	3,716,000	1.8	5.7	10.6	46.5	---e	57.1	35.4

APPENDIX K (Continued)

National Government Income for Selected Years 1830–1970

Sources: Calculated from data in Ecuador, Ministerio de Hacienda, *Informe* 1833, 1841, 1847, 1853, 1854, 1855, 1857, 1858, 1867, 1871, 1873, 1878, 1880, 1883, 1885, 1887, 1888, 1890, 1892, 1894, 1896–97, 1899, 1901, 1902, 1903, 1904, 1905, 1906, 1908, 1909, 1913, 1915, 1918, 1919, 1921, 1922 *Anexos*, 1931; Ecuador, Ministerio de Hacienda, *Boletín* 11 (1929), 61 (1933); Ecuador, Ministro Secretario de Estado, *Exposición 1831*; Ecuador, Ministerio del Tesoro, *Boletín* 5 (1946), 7 (1946), 19–20 (1949), 49–50 (1957); Ecuador, Director del Tesoro, *Informe* 1933; Ecuador, Ministerio de Hacienda, *Balances* 1922–1925; Ecuador, Banco Central, *Boletín* 396–397 (1960); Ecuador, Banco Central, *Memoria* 1954, 1957, 1958, 1959, 1962, 1964, 1966, 1969, 1970, 1972; Ecuador, Ministerio de Hacienda, *Boletín de estadística comercial y de la hacienda pública* VII (1917).

aNot listed as a source of income.

bIncome from November 1, 1852 through June 30, 1853.

cFiscal year and calendar year coincide from 1857.

dIncluded in other income.

eIncluded in indirect taxes.

fIncluded in total taxes.

1Current pesos 1830–1884; current sucres 1885–1970.

2Includes income from mines, state immovable property, and state industries.

3Includes income from postal service, telecommunications, and port charges.

4Includes property taxes and income taxes. In the nineteenth century, it also included the diezmos and Indian tribute until they were abolished in 1889 and 1857 respectively.

5Includes customs revenue, consular fees, and taxes on salt, tobacco, alcohol, and matches. Also includes revenue from salt, tobacco, alcohol, and matches for years in which they were state monopolies.

6Includes taxes on property transfers, fiscal stamps, and taxes on various transactions.

Appendix L / 223

APPENDIX L

National Government Expenditure for Selected Years 1830–1975

Year	Absolute Amount[1] in 1000s	National Government Expenditure in Percentage Terms								
		Executive	Legislature	Education	Military	Public works	Welfare	Police	Public debt	Other expenditures
1830	692	--[a]	--[a]	--[a]	73.9	--[a]	--[a]	--[a]	--[a]	26.1[b]
1832	550	--[a]	--[a]	--[a]	57.1	--[a]	--[a]	--[a]	--[a]	42.9[b]
1839	650	1.8	3.4	1.7	57.7	.2	--[c]	--[d]	--[c]	35.2
1846	1,339	.8	1.6	.2	34.1	.6	.3	--[d]	43.3	19.1
1852	744	1.3	.4	.7	49.5	.1	.1	--[d]	24.0	23.9
1853	1,278	1.4	1.4	1.1	36.1	--[c]	.1	--[d]	23.8	36.1
1854	1,284	1.0	1.7	.5	39.0	.9	.1	--[d]	22.7	34.1
1855	1,423	.9	1.5	1.1	34.2	.7	.1	--[d]	26.3	35.2
1856	1,558	1.1	1.3	.7	32.6	.3	.2	--[d]	29.0	34.8
1857	1,712	.9	1.5	.9	28.5	1.3	.2	--[d]	31.9	34.8
1861	2,141	.9	.8	.2	39.0	.7	.3	--[d]	40.7	17.4
1862	2,388	.5	...	.9	28.3	5.9	.3	--[d]	33.3	30.8
1863	2,447	.5	...	1.4	29.0	4.6	.3	--[d]	40.1	24.1
1864	2,084	.6	.4	1.3	34.4	3.9	.4	--[d]	27.7	31.3
1865	2,627	.6	.6	1.9	26.5	5.3	.2	--[d]	30.7	34.2
1866	2,223	.4	.1	1.8	25.7	2.6	.6	--[d]	39.9	38.9
1867	2,146	.8	1.2	2.2	19.9	3.9	.7	.2	37.9	33.2
1869	2,424	.2	.6	3.5	24.6	8.1	.7	--[c]	29.5	32.8
1870	3,003	.4	--[c]	2.6	23.9	9.1	1.3	.2	13.6	48.9

APPENDIX L (Continued)

National Government Expenditure for Selected Years 1830–1975

National Government Expenditure in Percentage Terms

Year	Absolute Amount[1] in 1000s	Executive	Legislature	Education	Military	Public works	Welfare	Police	Public debt	Other expenditures
1872	3,312	.4	--c	6.6	22.6	12.9	3.4	2.0	28.6	23.5
1875	2,776	.6	.9	11.6	31.7	16.0	3.2	--c	29.1	6.9
1878	3,272	.7	1.2	5.4	28.3	6.6	2.8	.9	--c	54.1
1884	4,854	.4	1.3	5.1	22.0	5.2	2.3	3.9	20.9	38.9
1885	3,930	.7	1.0	4.6	24.8	2.3	1.6	--c	--c	65.0
1886	4,674	.3	1.0	4.0	28.5	2.6	2.9	2.9	12.3	45.4
1887	4,429	.3	.9	6.4	27.0	11.6	2.1	3.9	22.7	25.1
1888	3,629	.4	1.7	8.8	34.8	14.0	3.9	3.6	12.5	20.3
1889	3,075	.5	.1	10.9	35.4	11.1	4.4	7.1	--c	30.5
1890	3,936	.3	1.5	11.7	25.2	12.5	5.9	6.3	14.5	22.1
1891	3,946	.5	.1	12.5	29.2	16.2	6.3	7.0	10.3	17.9
1892	4,081	.4	1.4	12.6	26.3	12.0	6.5	7.8	7.3	25.7
1893	4,433	.4	...	12.5	24.9	8.9	5.4	7.0	8.0	32.9
1895	8,780	1.3	...	3.0	30.0	2.3	7.1	4.4	34.9	17.0
1897	5,690	.6	1.6	6.8	32.8	6.1	3.1	7.3	31.9	9.8
1898	5,408	1.2	1.2	6.5	37.9	4.8	2.3	8.0	14.7	23.4
1899	6,663	.6	1.0	6.6	42.0	4.9	2.4	8.2	24.8	9.5
1900	7,375	.5	.8	7.1	42.9	5.2	2.7	7.8	18.7	14.3
1902	9,343	.5	.6	9.0	25.5	4.3	3.6	8.2	30.9	17.4

APPENDIX L (Continued)

National Government Expenditure for Selected Years 1830–1975

Year	Absolute Amount¹ in 1000s	National Government Expenditure in Percentage Terms								
		Executive	Legislature	Education	Military	Public works	Welfare	Police	Public debt	Other expenditures
1903	7,819	.6	1.0	11.2	31.9	7.7	5.0	9.5	25.0	8.1
1904	10,526	.7	.5	9.3	22.6	7.8	3.6	7.3	26.1	22.1
1905	10,156	.8	.5	9.1	23.0	10.2	3.6	7.3	18.7	26.8
1907	12,219	.3	.4	6.8	26.2	5.9	2.1	6.2	25.7	26.4
1908	12,675	.4	.8	9.8	30.1	7.6	3.6	8.1	8.7	30.9
1909	15,564	.4	1.2	9.5	23.1	5.4	2.7	6.5	16.6	34.6
1910	25,810	.2	.6	5.9	22.6	3.8	1.8	4.3	45.3	15.5
1911	22,437	.2	.6	5.0	19.7	2.0	3.0	3.7	37.8	28.0
1912	20,614	.3	.7	9.4	18.7	5.0	1.9	5.8	38.0	20.2
1913	21,665	.4	.7	10.6	18.9	18.2	2.0	6.1	25.3	17.8
1914	20,221	.2	.7	8.4	37.6	12.2	2.9	10.3	7.7	20.0
1915	18,995	.3	.7	7.8	34.7	13.6	2.0	10.7	17.5	12.7
1916	15,907	.4	.9	12.2	32.8	12.6	2.2	11.4	19.3	8.2
1917	16,545	.3	1.0	11.2	28.7	8.4	9.5	9.3	--ᶜ	31.6
1918	17,666	.1	1.0	14.3	25.4	9.6	2.7	8.1	21.9	16.9
1919	20,046	.3	.9	14.2	22.8	8.7	2.4	7.3	20.5	23.4
1920	20,357	.3	1.2	17.5	26.1	8.6	3.1	8.4	20.9	14.9
1921	21,450	.3	.7	18.2	25.8	9.8	3.0	8.7	10.5	23.0

APPENDIX L (Continued)

National Government Expenditure for Selected Years 1830–1975

Year	Absolute Amount[1] in 1000s	National Government Expenditure in Percentage Terms								
		Executive	Legislature	Education	Military	Public works	Welfare	Police	Public debt	Other expenditures
1922	26,568	.4	.6	14.4	22.2	8.0	2.4	7.4	19.1	25.5
1923	29,376	.3	.7	10.6	21.1	9.5	2.3	7.1	25.5	22.9
1924	35,002	.5	.7	9.6	19.2	11.4	1.9	7.4	26.2	23.1
1925	43,890	.1	.1	6.9	18.7	19.8	1.6	4.4	17.7	30.7
1926	38,892	.1	...	9.2	22.6	16.0	3.2	6.1	13.8	29.0
1927	71,646	.3	...	7.7	14.2	13.2	1.8	3.4	35.5	24.1
1928	57,414	.3	.7	8.4	15.3	18.9	3.5	5.1	12.0	35.8
1929	63,295	.3	1.1	9.3	14.7	21.9	3.9	5.0	10.4	33.4
1930	60,178	.3	.9	11.2	14.9	17.7	4.0	5.4	10.4	35.2
1931	45,177	.2	1.1	14.9	19.2	13.4	4.9	6.4	4.4	35.5
1932	42,162	.2	1.0	16.3	20.7	7.7	5.5	6.4	1.7	40.5
1933	41,842	.2	1.0	18.2	21.3	13.8	5.8	6.5	6.8	26.4
1934	48,282	.4	1.0	19.6	18.4	12.7	4.7	--c	.3	42.9
1937	103,815	.6	.7	18.9	20.6	13.9	6.8	5.4	1.7	31.4
1938	132,132	.3	.6	13.2	21.4	12.1	6.2	4.9	4.3	37.0
1939	117,201	.4	.6	13.8	21.3	10.6	6.1	--c	5.3	41.9
1943	172,462	.3	.5	14.7	24.0	9.9	6.2	5.2	8.5	30.7
1947	402,898	.3	.4	13.1	21.1	12.8	8.2	4.1	4.5	35.5
1950	425,558	.6	1.2	18.7	22.2	9.3	9.3	4.3	4.9	29.5

APPENDIX L (Continued)

National Government Expenditure for Selected Years 1830–1975

Year	Absolute Amount[1] in 1000s	National Government Expenditure in Percentage Terms								
		Executive	Legislature	Education	Military	Public works	Welfare	Police	Public debt	Other expenditures
1959	1,674,200	.3	.5	9.0	14.7	16.0	3.8	---[c]	12.5	43.2
1960	2,153,423	.3	.6	9.2	15.6	15.2	3.5	---[c]	10.3	45.3
1961	2,349,351	1.1	.7	10.4	21.2	21.2	2.9	---[c]	10.1	22.3
1962	2,132,257	.3	.7	13.3	15.4	14.2	3.2	---[c]	16.2	36.7
1973	9,179,000	.7	.1	24.9	13.8	16.1	4.7	---[c]	15.2	24.5
1974	12,581,700	.8	.1	20.9	14.9	13.9	7.3	---[c]	16.1	26.0
1975	15,456,700	.8	...	22.9	16.4	11.7	7.0	---[c]	14.2	27.0

Sources: Calculated from data in Ecuador, Ministerio de Hacienda, *Informe*, 1833, 1841, 1847, 1853, 1854, 1855, 1856, 1857, 1858, 1863, 1865, 1871, 1873, 1878, 1880, 1885, 1887, 1888, 1890, 1892, 1894, 1896–97, 1898, 1899, 1900, 1901, 1902, 1903, 1904, 1905, 1908, 1909, 1910, 1912, 1913, 1914, 1915, 1916, 1917, 1918, 1919, 1922 *Anexos*, 1925–28 1937, 1940; Ecuador, Ministerio de Hacienda, *Boletín* 4 (1928); Ecuador, Ministerio de Hacienda, *Libro de Balances* 1919/1920, 1922–1925; *El Nacional* (Quito) 224 (1866), 275 (1867), 327 (1868); Ecuador, Ministerio del Tesoro, *Informe* 1933–34; Ecuador, Contraloría, *Informe* 1933–34, 1937–38, 1938–39, 1942–44, 1947–48, 1950–51; Ecuador, Banco Central, *Memoria* 1963, 1974, 1975; Ecuador, Banco Central, *Boletín* 304–305 (1952).

[1]Current pesos 1830–1885; current sucres 1886–1975.

[a]In this year expenditures only reported as civil or military.

[b]Includes all nonmilitary expenditures.

[c]Included in other expenditures.

[d]Not a category for this year.

. . . less than .05.

APPENDIX M

Comparison of Projected and Actual Government Revenue
for Selected Years 1869–1940

Year	Budgeted[1] income	Actual[1] income	Surfeit[1]	Deficit[1]
1869[a]	1,412	1,664	252[b]	
1870[a]	1,421	2,248	827[b]	
1871[a]	1,421	2,483	1,062	
1872[a]	2,138	2,909	771[b]	
1873[a]	2,138	3,099	961	
1874[a]	2,938	3,092	154	
1875[a]	2,838	2,849		89
1876[a]	2,785	2,387		398
1877[a]	2,785	2,154		631
1878[a]	2,785	2,455		330[c]
1879	2,785	3,043	258	
1880	2,785	2,442		343
1881	3,153	2,673		480
1882	3,153	2,213		940
1883[a]	3,153	2,683		470
1884[a]	1,930	3,164	1,234[b]	
1885[a]	1,930	2,524	594[b]	
1886[a]	1,930	3,176	1,246[b]	
1887[a]	1,930	4,479	2,549[d]	
1888[a]	3,273	4,046	773[d]	
1889[a]	4,253	3,111		1,142
1890[a]	4,253	4,183		70
1891[a]	4,253	3,584		669
1892[a]	4,253	3,799		454
1893[a]	4,253	4,326	73[b]	
1894[a]	4,253	3,796		457
1895[a]	4,555	5,128	573[b]	
1896[a]	4,555	3,804		751
1897[a]	9,094	6,861		2,233
1898[a]	9,094	7,805		1,289
1899[a]	8,268	7,626		642
1900[a]	8,268	8,137		131
1901[a]	12,024	10,703		1,321
1902[a]	12,024	9,282		2,742
1903[a]	10,517	10,059		458
1904[a]	10,635	8,559		2,076

APPENDIX M (Continued)

*Comparison of Projected and Actual Government Revenue
for Selected Years 1869–1940*

Year	Budgeted[1] income	Actual[1] income	Surfeit[1]	Deficit[1]
1905[a]	11,716	11,538		178
1906[a]	12,188	12,922	734[b]	
1907[a]	12,676	12,571		105
1908[a]	12,676	12,807	131[b]	
1909[a]	15,836	15,895	59	
1910[a]	15,836	13,454		2,382[c]
1911[a]	15,836	13,536		2,300[c]
1912[a]	15,836	19,973	4,137[b]	
1913[a]	20,387	19,845		542[c]
1914	20,996	16,914		4,082
1915[a]	20,996	14,885		6,111
1916[a]	20,996	16,053		4,943
1917[a]	16,122	16,572	450[b]	
1918[a]	16,122	13,826		2,296[c]
1919[a]	16,845	15,178		1,667[c]
1920[a]	19,996	17,214		2,782[c]
1921[a]	19,996	15,654		4,342[c]
1922[a]	19,996	18,677		1,319[c]
1923[a]	19,996	18,532		1,464[c]
1924[a]	19,999	21,132	1,133[b]	
1925[a]	35,833	36,816	983[b]	
1926[a]	41,988	44,856	2,868	
1927	41,988	75,211[e]	33,223	
1928	51,588	74,866[e]	23,278	
1929	59,900	64,480	4,580[d]	
1930[a]	64,037	60,821		3,216
1931[a]	61,476	45,270		16,206
1932[a]	49,115	42,162		6,953
1933[a]	49,220	41,842		7,378
1934[a]	48,970	48,242		728
1935[a]	48,970	66,486[f]	17,516	
1936[a]	80,100	77,464		2,636
1937[a]	79,500	86,585	7,085	
1938	120,500	120,833	333	
1939	130,950	117,187		13,763
1940	113,050	108,533		4,517

APPENDIX M (Continued)

Comparison of Projected and Actual Government Revenue for Selected Years 1869–1940

Sources: Calculated from data in Appendix K; Ecuador, Ministro de Hacienda, *Informes* 1871–1931; Ecuador, Ministerio del Tesoro, *Boletín*, 5 (1946); 7 (1946).

[i]Thousands of sucres.

[a]Years in which bank loans were part of government revenue.

[b]Years in which surfeit is consumed by expenditures.

[c]Years in which the deficit is increased by unbudgeted expenditures.

[d]Years in which surfeit is reduced by expenditures.

[e]Differs from income in Appendix K since figure includes income from currency revaluation.

[f]Includes income from revaluation of gold reserves.

Notes

1: The Setting

1. For a discussion of various aspects of nation building see Karl W. Deutsch and William J. Foltz, *Nation Building* (New York: Atherton Press, 1966). Two articles in this volume are of particular interest: Joseph R. Streyer, "The Historical Experience of Nation-Building in Europe," 17–26, and Robert E. Scott, "Nation-Building in Latin America," 73–82. Also see Charles W. Anderson, *Politics and Economic Change in Latin America* (Princeton: D. Van Nostrand Company, 1967), 8–15.

2. For an analysis of the political and social institutions of the Indians of the Ecuadorian sierra which stresses their continuity and their resistance to Inca and Spanish domination see Hugo Burgos-Guevara, "El Guamán, el puma y el amarú: Structural Development of Native Government in Ecuador" (Ph.D. diss., University of Illinois, 1976), as well as Frank Salomon, "The Ethnic Lords of Quito in the Age of the Incas: the Political Economy of the North Andean Chiefdoms" (Ph.D. diss., Cornell University, 1978).

3. On the role of communications in the process of nation building and on development see Karl W. Deutsch, *Nationalism and Social Communication: An Inquiry into the Foundations of Nationality* (New York: The Technology Press of M. I. T., 1953); Lucian W. Pye, ed., *Communication and Development* (Princeton: Princeton University Press, 1963). Consult William Schramm, *Mass Media and National Development: The Role of Information in Developing Countries* (Stanford: Stanford University Press, 1964) and Wilfred Owen, "Transport Technology and Economic Development," in United Nations Conference on the Application of Science and Technology for the Benefit of the Less Developed Areas, *Science, Technology and Development*, 12 vols. (Washington, D.C.: U.S. Government Printing Office, 1963), V *Transportation*, 14–22 (hereafter cited as United Nations Conference, *Transportation*), for the effects of the technological advances that have separated communications from transportation.

4. Regionalism is not limited to the developing countries. See, for example, Organizations for Economic Co-operation and Development, *The Regional Factor in Economic Development: Policies in Fifteen Industrialized Countries* (Paris:

O.E.C.D. Publications, 1970); Robert E. Dickinson, *City Region and Regionalism: A Geographical Contribution to Human Ecology* (London: Routledge and Kegan Paul, 1960), 245–303; N. D. Glen and J. L. Simmons, "Are Regional Cultural Differences Diminishing," *Public Opinion Quarterly* 31 (Summer 1967): 176–193.

5. Theodore Wolf, *Geography and Geology of Ecuador* (Toronto: Grant and Toy Limited, 1933), 13.

6. On the Ecuadorian boundary disputes see Jorge Pérez Concha, *Ensayo histórico-crítico de las relaciones diplomáticas del Ecuador con los estados limítrofes,* 3 vols. (Quito & Guayaquil: Editorial Casa de la Cultura Ecuatoriana, 1958–1965).

7. Wolf, *Geography,* 13.

8. On the history of the Peru-Ecuador boundary dispute see Pérez Concha, *Ensayo histórico,* and David H. Zook, Jr., *Zarumilla-Marañon: The Ecuador-Peru Dispute* (New York: Bookman Associates, Inc., 1964).

9. The Oriente is currently divided into the provinces of Napo, Pastaza, Morona-Santiago, and Zamora-Chinchipe.

10. The following discussion is based on Francisco Terán, *Geografía del Ecuador* (Quito: Imprenta del Ministerio de Educación, 1952); Ulpiano Navarro Andrade, *Geografía económica del Ecuador,* 2 vols. (Quito: Editorial Santo Domingo, 1965–1966), I; Misael Acosta-Solís, *Los recursos naturales del Ecuador y su conservación,* 3 pts. (México: Instituto Panamericano de Geografía e Historia, 1965), pt. 1; American University, *Area Handbook for Ecuador* (Washington, D.C.: Government Printing Office, 1967); and Preston E. James, *Latin America* (New York: The Odyssey Press, 1959). Other sources will be cited where applicable.

11. *El Comercio* (Quito), no. 7490 (June 29, 1926), 1; no. 7498 (July 6, 1926), 3; Harold D. Clum to secretary of state, Guayaquil, January 13, 1927, United States National Archives, Record Group 84 (hereafter cited as NA, R.G. 84).

12. Clarence F. James, "Agricultural Regions of South America," *Economic Geography* 6:1 (January 1930): 30–36, discusses the problems involved in developing the Oriente. Although Ecuador's failure to occupy that territory contributed to its loss to Peru, it should be noted that the Río Protocol granted lands in the Oriente, which had formerly belonged to Peru, to Ecuador. It was in this region that Ecuador recently discovered large petroleum deposits.

13. Representatives of the major oil companies surveyed the Oriente in the 1930s and 1940s and noted the region's potential. As long as petroleum prices remained low, however, exploration and development of the Oriente involved unacceptable costs. See Michael G. Duerr, *Impact of Commodity Shortages: A World Survey* (New York: Conference Board, 1975).

14. During the last century there has been an increasing separation between the movement of information and the movement of men and goods. Some scholars refer to the first process as "communications" and to the second as "transpor-

tation." Since this distinction was almost nonexistent in Ecuador until World War II, the term "communication" will be used in this study in its broader context to mean systems of transmitting men and goods as well as information.

15. For discussions that consider transportation as a prerequisite for economic development see H. Hunter, "Transport in Soviet and Chinese Development," *Economic Development and Cultural Change* 14 (1965): 71–84; W. W. Rostow, *The Stages of Economic Growth* (Cambridge: Cambridge University Press, 1962). Works stressing the permissive role of transportation include: Albert O. Hirshman, *The Strategy of Economic Development* (New Haven: Yale University Press, 1958); Hans Heymann, Jr., "The Objectives of Transport," in Gary Fromm, ed., *Transport Investment and Economic Development* (Washington, D.C.: The Brookings Institution, 1965), 18–33; Gary Fromm, "Design of the Transport Sector," in *Transport Investment,* 89–107. For analysis of transportation policies in individual countries see Charles J. Stokes, *Transportation and Economic Development in Latin America* (New York: Praeger, 1968); Rolf Hofmeier, *Transportation and Economic Development in Tanzania* (Munich: Weltforum Verlag, 1973); B. S. Hoyle, ed., *Transport and Development* (London: Macmillan Press, 1973); John B. Lansing, *Transportation and Economic Policy* (New York: The Free Press, 1966).

16. David Ringrose, *Transportation and Economic Stagnation in Spain, 1750–1850* (Durham: Duke University Press, 1970); and Lansing, *Transportation,* discuss the limitations of some modes of transport in certain countries. Various types of transportation are evaluated by Richard B. Heflebower, "Characteristics of Transport Modes," in Fromm, *Transport Investment,* 34–68; and K. T. Healy, "General Social, Political and Economic Factors in Relation to Transport for Less Developed Areas," in United Nations Conference, *Transportation,* 1–4.

17. Wolf, *Geography,* 224–225; Dawn Ann Wiles, "Land Transportation within Ecuador" (Ph.D. diss., Louisiana State University, 1971), 29–35; Charles R. Enock, *Ecuador,* 2d ed. (London: T. Fisher Unwin Ltd., 1919), 258–262.

18. Acosta-Solís, *Los recursos,* 20–22, 25–26; Navarro Andrade, *Geografía Económica,* I, 304–313; *El Comercio,* no. 7315 (January 5, 1926), 1; no. 7526 (August 4, 1926), 2; L. F. Carbo, ed., *El Ecuador en Chicago* (New York: A. E. Chasmar y Cia., 1894), 324–325; Enock, *Ecuador,* 260–261.

19. Air transportation has developed rapidly since World War II. However, cost considerations have limited its utility for the movement of freight.

20. Richard P. Butrick to secretary of state, Guayaquil, April 15, 1926, NA, R.G. 84; Sheridan Talbott to secretary of state, Guayaquil, October 25, 1930; January 26, 1931, NA, R.G. 84.

21. Wiles, "Land Transportation," 122–124; Wolf, *Geography,* 225; Ernst B. Filsinger, *Commercial Travelers's Guide to Latin America* (Washington, D.C.: U.S. Government Printing Office, 1920), 330–331.

22. Wiles, "Land Transportation," 110–124.

23. Ibid., 160–162; Ecuador, Dirección General de Obras Públicas, *Informe,*

1926–1930, 95–97.

24. Wiles, "Land Transportation," 179–190.

25. Ibid., 124–130; Richard P. Butrick to secretary of state, Guayaquil, March 24, 1925, NA, 822.48A; November 9, 1925, NA, R.G. 84; G. A. Bading to secretary of state, Quito, March 24, 1925, NA, 822.48 A/1; March 31, 1924, NA, 822.00/579; Harold D. Clum to secretary of state, Guayaquil, January 11, 1931, NA, 822.48/6; May 3, 1931, NA, R.G. 84; El Comercio, no. 7192 (September 4, 1925); El Telégrafo (Guayaquil), no. 16825 (February 15, 1932), 2; no. 16829 (February 19, 1932), 1.

26. Wiles, "Land Transportation," 133–135; Harold D. Clum to secretary of state, Guayaquil, November 14, 1926, NA, R.G. 84; William Graham to Foreign Office, Quito, June 18, 1929, Great Britain. Public Record Office, Foreign Office Papers (hereafter cited as FO), 371/13484, A5040/5040/54; Ecuador, Misión de Consejeros Financieros. "Informe sobre el projecto Ferrocarril Quito-Esmeraldas" (Quito, March 15, 1927), 11–12, Kemmerer Papers, Princeton University (hereafter cited as KP); Harold D. Clum to secretary of state, Guayaquil, September 12, 1927, NA, R.G. 84; El Comercio, no. 7884 (July 27, 1927); no. 7905 (August 17, 1927); no. 7964 (October 15, 1927).

27. R. C. Michell to Foreign Office, Quito, April 16, 1924, FO 371/9542, A/3488/903/54; El Comercio, no. 7431 (May 1, 1926); no. 7520 (July 29, 1926); "Memorandum of a Conversation with Edwin Kemmerer," Washington, October 11, 1927, NA, 822.51 A/57; El Telégrafo, no. 15842 (June 22, 1929); Stokes, Transportation, 149–150; Lansing, Transportation, 155–157; Ringrose, Transportation and Economic Stagnation, v–vi; Heflebower, "Characteristics," 34–68.

28. Wiles, "Land Transportation," 148–160; El Comercio, no. 7648 (December 4, 1926), 2; no. 7913 (August 25, 1927), 3; El Telégrafo, no. 15387 (March 26, 1928), 1–2; no. 15410 (April 18, 1928), 1,8; no. 15831 (June 11, 1929), 1; no. 15832 (June 12, 1929), 2; no. 15842 (June 22, 1929), 2; Ecuador, Commission of Financial Advisers, "Report on the Construction of Public Works" (Quito, March 15, 1927), 6, KP; ibid., "Informe sobre el Ferrocarril Quito-Esmeraldas," KP; Ecuador, Dirección General de Obras Públicas, Informe, 1926–1930, 7–45.

29. Ecuador, Dirección General de Obras Públicas, Informe, 1926–1930, 8–12; Wiles, "Land Transportation," 190–208; Pío Jaramillo Alvarado, Historia de Loja y su provincia (Quito: Casa de la Cultura Ecuatoriana, 1955), 416–429.

30. Gerald Kraft, John R. Meyer and Jean Paul Valetti, The Role of Transportation in Regional Economic Development (Lexington: D. C. Heath and Company, 1971), 37–42; Heflebower, "Characteristics," 43–68.

31. The complex relationship between public works expenditures and national politics will be treated in subsequent chapters.

32. For a discussion of the growing commercial activity in the central highlands in the nineteenth century see Rosemary D. F. Bromley and R. J. Bromley, "The Debate on Sunday Markets in Nineteenth Century Ecuador," Journal of Latin American Studies 7:1 (May 1975), 85–108; Ralph L. Beals, Community in

Transition: Nayon—Ecuador, Latin American Studies, vol. 2 (Los Angeles: University of California, 1966), 65.

33. Compañía Guía del Ecuador, *El Ecuador: guía comercial, agrícola e industrial de la República* (Guayaquil: Talleres de Artes Gráficas de E. Rodenas, 1909), 1,115–1,118, 1,120–1,130 (hereafter cited as *El Ecuador: guía comercial*). Jaramillo Alvarado, *Historia de Loja*, 415, 434–435.

34. Bromley and Bromley, "The Debate," 94; Harold D. Clum to secretary of state, Guayaquil, December 12, 1926, NA, R.G. 84; March 26–30, 1928, NA, R.G. 84; July 25, 1929, NA, R.G. 84; April 3, 1930, NA, R.G. 84; G. A. Bading to secretary of state, Quito, March 31, 1925, NA 822.00/579; *El Comercio*, no. 7528 (August 6, 1926), 2.

35. *El Telégrafo*, no. 15845 (June 25, 1925), 1; Richard P. Butrick to secretary of state, Guayaquil, March 27, 1925, NA, R.G. 84; October 13, 1925; Harold D. Clum to secretary of state, Guayaquil, March 30, 1929, NA, R.G. 84; July 25, 1929, NA, R.G. 84; Sheridan Talbott to secretary of state, Guayaquil, January 26, 1931, NA, R.G. 84; *El Comercio*, no. 7918 (August 30, 1927), 1; no. 7151 (July 24, 1925), 5; R. M. Kohan to Foreign Office, Quito, January 18, 1930, FO 371/14224, A2502/2502/54; Ecuador, Dirección General de Estadística, *Comercio exterior de la República del Ecuador en la década 1916 a 1925* (Quito: Talleres Tipográficos Nacionales, 1927).

36. Michael T. Hamerly, *Historia social y económica de la Antigua Provincia de Guayaquil, 1763–1842* (Guayaquil: Archivo Histórico del Guayas, 1973), 99–112. On the development of the cacao trade, see Lois Weinman, "Ecuador and Cacao: Domestic Response to the Boom-Collapse Monoexport Cycle" (Ph.D. diss., University of California, Los Angeles, 1970), 199–204; Gustavo Franco and Palemón Custode, "Historia del régimen cambiario en el Ecuador," *Economía ecuatoriana* (Mexico: Instituto Panamericano de Geografía e Historia, 1960), 98; Luis A. Carbo, *Historia monetaria y cambiaria del Ecuador* (Quito: Imprenta del Banco Central del Ecuador, 1953), 104, 109–110; Charles R. Gibson, *Foreign Trade in the Economic Development of Small Nations* (New York: Praeger Publishers, 1971), 194–196; R. J. Watkins, *Expanding Ecuador's Exports: A Commodity by Commodity Study with Projections to 1973* (New York: Frederick A. Praeger, 1968), 214–216; Linda A. Rodríguez, "The Dilemma of Ecuador's Development" (unpublished paper), 1–2, 6–7, 13–14, 18–19, 22–23.

37. Robert F. Cremieux, *Geografía económica del Ecuador: economía agraria e industrial*, 2 vols. (Guayaquil: Imprenta de la Universidad de Guayaquil, 1946), I, 182–193; Rodríguez, "The Dilemma," 2–3, 6–8, 12–14, 17–18; Gibson, *Foreign Trade*, 193–194 and appendixes.

38. Appendixes A and G; James J. Parsons, "Bananas in Ecuador: A New Chapter in the History of Tropical Agriculture," *Economic Geography* 33:3 (July 1957), 201–216; Rodríguez, "Dilemma," 15–18; Gibson, *Foreign Trade*, 189–191.

39. Julio Estrada Ycaza, *Los bancos en el siglo XIX* (Guayaquil: Archivo Histórico del Guayas, 1976); Appendixes H and I; Rodríguez, "Dilemma," 22–23.

40. Rosemary D. F. Bromley, "The Demographic Background to Urban Growth and Decline in the Central Sierra of Ecuador, 1780–1900" (Paper presented at the Annual Conference of the Society for Latin American Studies, Leeds, England, March 1973); Hamerly, *Historia social*; Robson B. Tyrer, "The Demographic and Economic History of the Audiencia of Quito: Indian Population and the Textile Industry, 1600–1800" (Ph.D. diss., University of California, Berkeley, 1976), 2–93.

41. Leslie B. Rout, Jr., *The African Experience in Spanish America* (Cambridge: Cambridge University Press, 1976), 231.

42. Hamerly, *Historia social*, 16–17.

43. Ibid., 80–82.

44. See Luis T. Paz y Miño, *La Población del Ecuador* (Quito: Talleres Gráficos Nacionales, 1936), 17–19, for a critique of Villavicencio's methods and sources.

45. Manuel Villavicencio, *Geografía de la República del Ecuador* (New York: Imprenta de Robert Craighead, 1858).

46. George Earl Church, *Ecuador in 1881* (Washington D.C.: U.S. Government Printing Office, 1883), 12–15.

47. Pedro Fermín Cevallos, *Geografía de la República del Ecuador* (Lima: Imprenta del Estado, 1888), 77–78.

48. Wolf, *Geography*, 540–542.

49. Ecuador, Dirección Nacional de Estadística, *Ecuador en cifras, 1938–1942* (Quito: Imprenta de Estadística, 1944), 55.

50. American University, *Area Handbook for Ecuador*, 73.

51. John V. D. Saunders, *The People of Ecuador: A Demographic Analysis* (Gainesville: University of Florida Press, 1961), 2, 16–21.

52. Bromley, "The Demographic Background," 4–5.

53. Calculated from data in Hamerly, *Historia social*, 80, 89, 92.

54. Wolf, *Geography*, 542–552; Piedad Peñaherrera de Costales and Alfredo Costales Samaniego, "Historia Social del Ecuador," 3 vols., in *Llacta*, nos. 17–19 (Quito: Instituto Ecuatoriano de Antropología y Geografía, 1964), II, 395.

55. Paz y Miño, *La población*, 38.

56. Calculated from Hamerly, *Historia social*, 16, 80, 89, 92.

57. Wolf, *Geography*, 541–542.

58. Peñaherra de Costales and Costales, "Historia social," II, 388.

59. Migration from the highlands was an important factor in Guayaquil's growth after 1750. See Julio Estrada Ycaza, *Regionalismo y migración* (Guayaquil: Publicaciones del Archivo Histórico del Guayas, 1977), 47–84; Hamerly, *Historia social*, 65–69; Bromley, "Demographic Background," 14, 18; Bromley and Bromley, "The Debate," 85–108.

60. Appendix H.

61. Bromley, "The Demographic background," 20.

62. Appendix I; Saunders, *The People of Ecuador*, 4–7, 14–15.

63. Acosta Solís, *Los recursos,* pt. 2, tomo 1, 18–21.

64. Ecuador, Dirección General de Estadística, *Primer censo agropecuario nacional de 1954* (Quito, 1956); Peñaherrera de Costales and Costales, "Historia social," II, 518–542, 558–559; III, 740–741.

65. See Martin T. Katzman, "Ethnic Geography and Regional Economics, 1880–1960," *Economic Geography* 45:1 (January 1969), 43–53, for a discussion of the relationship between residence and economic performance of ethnic groups in the United States.

66. For a characterization of the coastal dweller see José de la Cuadra, "El Montuvio ecuatoriano," in *Obras completas* (Quito: Casa de la Cultura Ecuatoriana, 1958), 863–908.

67. Arthur P. Whitaker, *The United States and South America: the Northern Republics* (Cambridge, Mass.: Harvard University Press, 1948), 36.

68. See for example Vicente Rocafuerte's criticism of his countrymen in his private correspondence published in Jaime E. Rodríguez O., *Estudios sobre Vicente Rocafuerte* (Guayaquil: Archivo Histórico del Guayas, 1975), 130–361. Friedrich Hassaurek, the American minister to Ecuador in the 1860s, is one of many foreigners to comment on this phenomenon; see his *Four Years among Spanish Americans*, 3d. ed. (Cincinnati: Robert Clarke and Company, 1881), 121–189, 209–247.) See also Cevallos, *Geografía*, 104–162; Blair Niles, *Casual Wanderings in Ecuador* (New York: The Century Company, 1923).

69. Peñaherrera de Costales and Costales, "Historia social," II, 391; American University, *Area Handbook for Ecuador*, 75–87; Beals, *Community in Transition*, 34–46, 66. For a discussion of Indian groups in the province of Pichincha see Alfredo Costales Samaniego, *Karapungo* (Mexico: Instituto Panamericano de Geografía e Historia, 1960), 229–281.

2: Ecuadorian Politics

1. For an alternative interpretation of Ecuadorian history based on the role of the hacienda see Osvaldo Hurtado, *Political Power in Ecuador* (Albuquerque: University of New Mexico Press, 1980). Carl J. Friedrich discusses the problems of authority, tradition, and legitimacy in *Tradition and Authority* (New York: Praeger Publishers, 1972).

2. Vicente Rocafuerte believed that he could impose order in Ecuador were it not for the women "who have such influence upon the weak souls of their brothers, husbands, and relatives." He believed that "women are the ones who foment the spirit of anarchy in these countries." Quotes from Rocafuerte's correspondence in Rodríguez, *Estudios*, 228, 231. Similar views were held by Friedrich Hassaurek, the American minister to Ecuador in the 1860s who declared that "ladies take the most active part [in revolutions]. They are passionate politicians and very energetic secret agents." García Moreno banished several women

revolutionaries. According to Hassaurek: "They went, hurling defiance into his teeth. He could imprison or shoot the men, who trembled before him, but he could not break the spirit of the women," Hassaurek, *Four Years*, 215–216. The two most famous women political activists in nineteenth-century Ecuador were Manuela Sáenz and Marietta Veintimilla. See Victor von Hagen, *The Four Seasons of Manuela* (New York: Duell, Sloan, and Pierce, 1952) and Marietta Veintimilla, *Páginas del Ecuador* (Lima: Imprenta Liberal de F. Masías, 1890).

3. On the history of Indian problems see Peñaherrera de Costales and Costales, "Historia social," I. For a study of an Indian uprising in the nineteenth century see Enrique Garcés, *Daquilema Rex* (Quito: Casa de la Cultura Ecuatoriana, 1961). For reports on other Indian revolts see Ecuador, Ministerio de Guerra y Marina, *Informe, 1884*, 4–6; Julio Castillo Jacome, *Chimborazo en 1942* (Riobamba: Talleres Gráficos de la Editorial "Progreso," n.d.), 165–166; *El Telégrafo*, no. 15381 (March 20, 1928); no. 15415 (April 23, 1928); W. Allen Rhode to secretary of state, Guayaquil, February 13, 1929, NA, R.G. 84; Harold D. Clum to secretary of state, Guayaquil, October 19, 1929, NA, R.G. 84; W. C. Graham to Foreign Office, Quito, March 2, 1931, FO 371/1509, A2266/132/54.

4. For a detailed analysis of a comparable situation see Torcuato S. Di Tella, "The Dangerous Classes in Early Nineteenth Century Mexico," *Journal of Latin American Studies* 5 (May 1973), 79–105. On Ecuador see *El Cachuero* (Guayaquil), October 19, 1922; G. A. Bading to secretary of state, Quito, December 30, 1922, NA, 822.00/517; Frederic W. Goding to secretary of state, Guayaquil, November 17, 1922, NA, 822.00/511; *El Día* (Quito), no. 3649 (May 3, 1925); *El Guante* (Guayaquil), no. 5335 (May 11, 1925); no. 5340 (May 16, 1925); *El Comercio* no. 7086 (May 20, 1925); no. 7352 (February 11, 1926); no. 7784 (April 18, 1927).

5. Borrero as quoted in Georg Maier, "Presidential Succession in Ecuador, 1830–1970," *Journal of Inter-American Studies and World Affairs* 13 (July-October 1971), 475–509.

6. American University, *Area Handbook for Ecuador*, 251–252.

7. Rocafuerte's correspondence includes a scathing criticism of that tendency. Rodríguez, *Estudios*, 189–361. The author was attending the University of Houston in 1966 when the military junta then governing the country was overthrown. One Ecuadorian student reacted to the news with plans to return to his country, enter politics, and "get rich." See also R. C. Michell to Foreign Office, Quito, April 20, 1926, FO 371/11139, A 3121/285/54.

8. *El Comercio*, (June 17, 1960); Kenneth Ruddle and Philip Gillette, *Latin American Political Statistics* (Los Angeles: UCLA Latin American Center Publications, 1972), 109.

9. Peter Pyne feels that the only important structural change in the political system of Ecuador during the period from 1848 to 1960 was the growth of the electorate. Peter Pyne, "The Politics of Instability in Ecuador: The Overthrow

of the President, 1961," *Journal of Latin American Studies 7* (May 1975), 109–133.

10. Constitution of 1830, article 21, in Ramiro Borja y Borja, *Derecho constitucional*, 3 vols. (Madrid: Ediciones Cultura Hispánica, 1959), III, 109.

11. Constitution of 1835, article 3, in Borja y Borja, *Derecho Constitucional*, III, 126; Wilfrido Loor, *Manabí* (Quito: Editorial Ecuatoriana, 1969), 18–19; Pío Jaramillo Alvarado, *Historia de Loja*, 333–334.

12. These events are associated with García Moreno's rise to power. Since he is a controversial figure in Ecuadorian history, writers tend to take sides. Richard Pattee, *Gabriel García Moreno y el Ecuador de su tiempo* (Mexico: Editorial Jus, 1944), 163–205, is favorable to García Moreno. Luis Robalino Dávila, *Orígenes del Ecuador de hoy*, 7 vols. (Puebla: Editorial Cajica, 1967–1970), IV, 169–298, presents a balanced view.

13. Jaramillo Alvarado, *Historia de Loja*, 337–364.

14. Manuel E. Quintana M., *Los Ríos* (Guayaquil: Casa de la Cultura Ecuatoriana, 1957), 17–19; Castillo Jacome, *La Provincia del Chimborazo*, 143–144.

15. Interview with Julio Estrada Ycaza, Guayaquil, July 22, 1975. See also his *Regionalismo y migración*.

16. Carlos de la Torre Reyes, *La Revolución de Quito del 10 de Agosto de 1809* (Quito: Ministerio de Educación, 1962), 247–270.

17. Robalino Dávila, *Orígenes del Ecuador*, I, 244–282.

18. Quintana, *Los Ríos*, 47; Abraham Eraso, *La Provincia de Bolívar en 1934* (Quito: n.p., n.d.), 49–50.

19. Quintana, *Los Ríos*, 47–48; Castillo Jacome, *La Provincia del Chimborazo*, 147–152.

20. Quintana, *Los Ríos*, 49; Castillo Jacome, *La Provincia del Chimborazo*, 152–161.

21. Julio Troncoso, *Odio y sangre* (Quito: Editorial Fray Jodoco Ricke, 1958), 119–231; José A. Llerena, *Frustración política en veintidos años* (Quito: Casa de la Cultura Ecuatoriana, 1959), 33–43.

22. Only one strong man, General Alberto Enriquez Gallo, in 1938 convoked a constitutional convention that did not "elect" him president. The following are the conventions called by *Jefes Supremos* to write new constitutions and to ratify their power: 1830 General Juan José Flores; 1835 Vicente Rocafuerte; 1843 General Juan José Flores; 1851 Diego Noboa; 1852 General José María Urvina; 1878 General Ignacio Veintimilla; 1883 José María Plácido Caamaño; 1897 General Eloy Alfaro; 1906 General Eloy Alfaro; 1929 Isidro Ayora; 1938 General Alberto Enríquez Gallo (not elected); 1944 José María Velasco Ibarra.

Georg Maier, "Presidential Succession," 475–491 has a penetrating discussion of this phenomenon. The fifteen constitutions written between 1830 and 1946 are published in Borja y Borja, *Derecho constitucional ecuatoriano*, III, 105–699.

23. Pattee, *García Moreno*, 87–89; Jacinto Jijón y Caamaño, *Política conser-*

vadora, 2 vols. (Riobamba: La Buena Prensa de Chimborazo, 1929), I, 273–289; Vicente Rocafuerte to Juan José Flores, Quito, April 27, 1836 in Rodríguez, *Estudios*, 256–257.

24. On this point see Tulio Halpering Donghi, *The Aftermath of Revolution in Latin America* (New York: Harper and Row, 1973), 1–43. According to Rocafuerte: "our revolutions . . . have resulted from the military spirit, which contrary to all political theory, General Bolívar established." Rocafuerte to Francisco de Paula Santander, November 30, 1834 in Rodríguez, *Estudios*, 189.

25. Robalino Dávila, *Orígenes del Ecuador*, III, 480. See also David Bushnell, *The Santander Regime* (Newark: University of Delaware Press, 1954).

26. The best-known foreign military men who settled in Ecuador include: Marshal Antonio José de Sucre (Venezuelan); General Juan José Flores (Venezuelan); General Isodoro Barriga (Colombian); Colonel Francisco Tamaríz (Spanish); Colonel Bernado Daste (French); Colonel Ricardo Wright (English); Colonel Juan Illingworth (English).

27. The best study of Flores is Robalino Dávila's first volume of his *Orígenes del Ecuador* entitled *Nacimiento y primeros años de la República*.

28. Eraso, *La Provincia de Bolívar*; Robalino Dávila, *Orígenes del Ecuador*, III, 67–69.

29. Robalino Dávila, *Orígenes del Ecuador*, III, 194–218; Julio Tobar Donoso, *Monografías históricas* (Quito: Editorial *Ecuatoriana*, 1937), 99–255.

30. Robalino Dávila, *Orígenes*, III, 294–305, 355–393.

31. Ibid., III, 395–466; IV, 169–298; Eraso, *La Provincia de Bolívar*, 49–50.

32. On the antecedents of Velasquismo see: Rafael Quintero, *El Mito del populismo en el Ecuador: análisis de los fundamentos socio-económicos del surgimiento del "Velasquismo" 1895–1934* (Quito: FLASCO, 1980). On Velasco see: Georg Maier, "The Impact of Velasquismo on the Ecuadorean Political System" (Ph.D. diss., University of Southern Illinois, 1965); Robert E. Norris, "José María Velasco Ibarra: A Charismatic Figure in Ecuadorean Politics, 1934–1961" (Ph.D. diss., University of New Mexico, 1969).

33. For an alternate interpretation see Nick Dean Mills, "Liberal Opposition in Ecuadorian Politics" (Ph.D. diss., University of New Mexico, 1972). Mills argues that liberal ideologies were important in Ecuadorian politics. He maintains that the differences between liberals and conservatives centered on the issue of civil liberties.

34. Lucas Alamán of Mexico was a liberal who eventually turned conservative. On Mexican liberalism see Charles Hale, *Mexican Liberalism in the Age of Mora* (New Haven and London: Yale University Press, 1968). On Ecuador see Jijón y Caamaño, *Política conservadora*, I, 200–434; Tobar Donoso, *Monografías históricas*, 426–539. On the question of education consult Darío Guevara, *Rocafuerte y la instrucción pública* (Quito: Casa de la Cultura Ecuatoriana, 1965); Julio Tobar Donoso, *García Moreno y la instrucción pública* (Quito: Editorial Ecuatoriana, 1940); Francisco Miranda Ribadeneira, *La Primera escuela politécnica*

en el Ecuador (Quito: Editorial "La Unión," 1972); Reinaldo Murgueytio, *Bosquejo histórico de la escuela laica ecuatoriana* (Quito: Casa de la Cultura Ecuatoriana, 1972). On liberalism see, Alfonso Mora Bowen, *El Liberalismo Radical y su trayectoria histórica* (Quito: Imprenta Romero, 1940); Gabriel Cevallos García, "Las ideas liberales en el Ecuador," *Revista de historia de las ideas* 2 (October 1960), 55–72.

35. For an excellent comparison of Rocafuerte and García Moreno see Jijón y Caamaño, *Política conservadora*, I, 276–282. On the controversial nature of García Moreno see Peter Smith, "The Image of a Dictator: Gabriel García Moreno," *Hispanic American Historical Review* 45 (February, 1965), 1–24. On the question of García Moreno's relations with the Church consult William M. King, "Ecuadorian Church State Relations under García Moreno, 1859–1863" (Ph.D. diss., University of Texas, Austin, 1974); César Bustos-Videla, "Church and State in Ecuador: A History of Politico-Ecclesiastical Relations during the Age of Gabriel García Moreno, 1860–1875" (Ph.D. diss., Georgetown University, 1966).

36. For a discussion of the problems faced in analyzing regionalism see: Joseph L. Love, "An Approach to Regionalism," and Frank Safford, "Bases of Political Alignment in Early Republican Spanish America," in Richard Graham and Peter Smith, eds., *New Approaches to Latin American History* (Austin: University of Texas Press, 1974). Maier discusses the relationship that exists in Ecuador between place of birth and party affiliation in Maier, "Presidential Succession," 475–509.

37. For information on the Liberal and Conservative parties consult works cited in footnote 34. Robalino Dávila discusses the Progressives in *Orígenes del Ecuador*, VI, and Veintimilla in vol. V, pts. 1 and 2.

38. Oscar E. Reyes, *Breve historia general de Ecuador*, 2 vols. (Quito: Editorial Fray Jodoco Ricke, 1955), II, 197–260 is favorable to the liberal regimes. Luis J. Weinman is critical in, "Ecuador and Cacao."

39. Ecuador, Ministro de lo Interior, *Informe, 1885*, 25–27; *1886*, 3–6; *1887*, 3–6; *1916*, xi–xii.

40. G. A. Bading to secretary of state, Quito, April 20, 1925, NA, 822.00/582; January 15, 1924, NA, 822.00/533; Charles Hartman to secretary of state, Quito, June 1919, NA, 822.00/459; January 1, 1920, NA, 822.00/47a; January 1, 1920, NA 822.00/469; Frederic W. Goding to secretary of state, Quito, January 15, 1920, NA, 822.00/472.

41. Robalino Dávila, *Orígenes del Ecuador*, VII, pt. 1, 21–41, 63–73.

42. J. Gonzalo Orellana, *Resumen histórico del Ecuador*, 2 vols. (Quito: Editorial Fray Jodoco Ricke, 1948), I, 55–57; Robalino Dávila, *Orígenes del Ecuador*, VII, pt. 1, 77–111, 274–275; VII, pt. 2, 582; Jorge Pérez Concha, *Eloy Alfaro* (Quito: Talleres Gráficos de Educación, 1942), 129–133; *El Telégrafo*, no. 15415 (April 23, 1928); Ecuador, Ministerio de Guerra, *Informe, 1913*.

43. Pérez Concha, *Eloy Alfaro*, 201–204, 222–225, 245–255; Robalino

Dávila, *Orígenes del Ecuador*, VII, pt. 2, 659–690.

44. *El Comercio*, no. 7354 (February 13, 1926); *El Telégrafo*, no. 15415 (April 23, 1928); Robalino Dávila, *Orígenes del Ecuador*, VII, pt. 2, 619–650.

45. Luis Larrea Alba, *La Campaña de 1906* (Quito: Editorial Cyma, 1962) is the best study of the causes and consequences of the 1906 insurrection. See also Robalino Dávila, *Orígenes del Ecuador*, VIII, 18–41.

46. Larrea Alba, *La Campaña de 1906*, 123–127; Ecuador, Ministro de Guerra, *Informe, 1913*, 34–37.

47. Ecuador, Ministro de lo Interior, *Informe, 1908*, iii–iv; M. de Lambert to secretary of state, Quito, July 17, 1925, NA, 822.00/604; Larrea Alba, *La Campaña de 1906*, 128–173.

48. Francisco Güarderas, *El Viejo de Montecristi* (Puebla: Editorial Cajica, 1965), 421–450; Ecuador, Ministro de lo Interior, *Informe, 1912*, iii–iv; Robalino Dávila, *Orígenes del Ecuador*, VIII, 390–490.

49. Ecuador, Ministro de Guerra, *Informe, 1913*, 27–45; Robalino Dávila, *Orígenes del Ecuador*, VIII, 491–584, 594–611.

50. Güarderas, *El Viejo*, 421–450; Ecuador, Ministro de lo Interior, *Informe, 1912*, v–vii; Ecuador, Ministro de Guerra, *Informe, 1913*, 27; Robalino Dávila, *Orígenes del Ecuador*, VIII, 611–680; *La Prensa* (Quito), January 16, 1912; *La Constitución* (Quito), January 17, 1912; *El Grito del pueblo ecuatoriano* (Guayaquil), January 24, 1912.

51. Ecuador, Ministro de Guerra, *Informe, 1913*, 30–33; *1919*, 4; *El Comercio*, no. 7161 (August 3, 1925); Ecuador, Ministro de lo Interior, *Informe, 1915*, v–xi,xv; *1916*, v–viii; Roberto Andrade, *¡Sangre! ¿Quien la derramó? Historia de los últimos crímenes cometidos en la nación del Ecuador* (Quito: Imprenta Antigua de *El Quiteño Libre*, 1912), is an anti-Plaza attack. Segundo L. Moreno discusses the Esmeraldas campaign in *La Campaña de Esmeraldas de 1913–1916 encabezada por el Coronel Graduado Don Carlos Concha Torres* (Cuenca: Tipografía Universidad, 1939).

52. Ecuador, Ministro de lo Interior, *Informe, 1915*, v–ix, xv, xxxvi, lii, lxx; *1916*, v–x, xiv–xv. For a brief discussion of Plaza's two administrations see Troncoso, *Odio y sangre*, 63–70.

53. Ecuador, Ministro de Guerra, *Informe, 1913*, 54–70; Charles Hartman to secretary of state, January 1, 1920, NA 822.00/471; R. M. de Lambert to secretary of state, Quito, July 17, 1925, NA, 822.00/604; G. A. Bading, to secretary of state, Quito, April 20, 1925, NA, 822.00/582; *El Telégrafo*, no. 15730 (March 3, 1929); Ildefonso Mendoza, "La Revolución de Julio," *El Comercio*, no. 9033 (September 17, 1930); no. 9065 (September 19, 1930); *La Antorcha* (Quito), no. 4 (April 11, 1925).

54. R. M. de Lambert to secretary of state, Quito, July 17, 1925, NA, 822.00/604; G. A. Bading to secretary of state, Quito, April 20, 1925, NA, 822.00/582; Memorandum from Division of Latin American Affairs, Department

of State, to Dr. Rowe, Washington, D.C., May 28, 1920, NA, 822.00/485; Orellana, *Resumen histórico*, I, 84–86.

55. Charles Hartman to secretary of state, Quito, June 6, 1919, NA, 822.00/ 459; July 22, 1919, NA, 822.00/462; January 1, 1920, NA, 822.00/471; January 11, 1920, NA, 822.00/469; January 15, 1920, NA, 822.00/470; *El Telégrafo*, no. 14386 (July 9, 1925); A. M. Tweedy to J. H. Stables, Quito, May 21, 1918, NA, 822.00/453; G. A. Bading to secretary of state, Quito, June 25, 1924, NA, 822.00/549; March 31, 1925, NA, 822.00/579; April 20, 1925, NA, 822.00/ 582; February 27, 1924, NA, 822.00/536; R. C. Michell to Foreign Office, Quito, February 28, 1924, FO 371/9541, A2194/373/54.

56. *El Comercio* (August 21, 1921); Ildefonso Mendoza, "La Revolución de Julio y sus actores," *El Comercio*, no. 9066 (September 19, 1930); Ecuador, Ministro de Hacienda, *Informe, 1922*, 9–15, 31–32; *1923*, 8–10, 13–17, 28; *1921*, v; *1916*, x–xi.

57. Frederic W. Goding to secretary of state, Guayaquil, November 9, 1920, NA, R.G. 84; Harold M. Deane to secretary of state, Quito, March 31, 1922, NA, 822.00/505; Frederic W. Goding to secretary of state, Quito, November 29, 1921, NA, 822.51/340; R. C. Michell to Foreign Office, Quito, January 30, 1925, FO 371/10619, A 1229/1229/54; *El Comercio*, no. 7363 (February 22, 1926); no. 7459 (May 29, 1926); "Mensaje especial que el Señor Presidente de la República envía al Congreso Nacional," August 10, 1930, in Ecuador, Ministro de Hacienda, *Informe, 1930, Anexo*, 356–365; Ministro del Tesoro, "Informe, June 12, 1931," in Ecuador, Ministerio de Hacienda, *Boletín*, no. 38, 96–97 (hereafter cited as Ecuador, Ministro del Tesoro, "Informe, June 12, 1931").

58. Luis N. Dillon, *La crisis económico-financiera del Ecuador* (Quito: Editorial Artes Gráficas, 1927), 24–26, 36–37; *La Antorcha*, no. 1 (November 16, 1924); no. 2 (November 23, 1924); *El Abanderado* (Quito), no. 9 (January 19, 1925). The cacao crisis and the 1922 strike is discussed in Weinman, "Ecuador and Cacao." Joaquín Gallegos Lara recounts the events leading to the November 15, 1922 tragedy in his novel, *Cruces sobre el agua* (Guayaquil: Casa de la Cultura Ecuatoriana, 1946). See also Ecuador, Ministro de Hacienda, *Informe, 1921*, xxxi–xxxii.

3: Nineteenth-Century Political Economy

1. Ecuador, Director del Tesoro, "Informe, June 12, 1931"; Ecuador, Presidente, "Mensaje especial," in Ecuador, Ministro de Hacienda, *Informe, 1930*, 359.

2. Ecuador, Ministro de Estado, *Memoria 1831*.

3. Ecuador, Ministro de Hacienda, *Esposición, 1855*, Documentos; *Memoria, 1858*, 36, 5–8; *Esposición, 1865*, 1.

4. Ecuador, Ministro de Hacienda, *Informe, 1863*, 4; *1896–97*, 60–61.

244 / Notes to Pages 57–67

5. Ecuador, Ministro de Hacienda, *Esposición, 1873*, 9; *Informe, 1883*, 18; *Informe, 1896–97*, 25–26; Ecuador, Director del Tesoro, *Informe, 1930*, 21.

6. Ecuador, Ministro de Hacienda, *Informe, 1890*, 33–34; *1892*, 51–52; *1894*, 26–27; Esmeraldas, Gobernación de la Provincia, "Informe, April 11, 1894" in Ecuador, Ministerio de Hacienda, *Informe, 1894;* León, Gobernación de la Provincia, "Informe, April 18, 1894," in Ecuador, Ministerio de Hacienda, *Informe, 1896–97*, 26.

7. This same phenomenon has been noted for Gran Colombia by David Bushnell in *The Santander Regime*, 79.

8. On the obraje economy of the highlands see Robson Tyrer, "The Demographic and Economic History of the Audiencia of Quito." On the economy of the coast during the early national period see Hamerly, *Historia social y económica.*

9. Ecuador, Ministro de Hacienda, *Memoria, 1857*, 18–19.

10. Ecuador, Ministro de Estado, *Informe, 1831*, 18; "Lei de Octubre 25, 1833," in Ecuador, *Primer registro auténtico nacional* (Quito 1839), I, 427–428 (hereafter cited as *PRAN*); Ecuador, Ministro de Hacienda, *Informe, 1883*, 18.

11. Ecuador, Ministro de Hacienda, *Informe, 1885*, 18–22; *Esposición, 1867*, 12–13; *1855*, 11–12; *1857*, 18–19; *1858*, 19; *1865*, 9–10; *1873*, 18–19; *Informe, 1883*, 14–18.

12. Ecuador, Ministro de Hacienda, *Informe, 1888*, 7–11; *1896–97*, 25.

13. Ecuador, Ministro de Hacienda, *Memoria, 1857*, 12. Hamerly, in *Historia social*, seems to imply that tribute continued to be collected on the coast. Since he indicates that the demographic resurgence of the coastal Indians is largely attributable to migration from the highlands, these "sierra" immigrants may have continued to pay tribute.

14. Ecuador, Ministro de Hacienda, *Memoria, 1857*, 8–13; *Esposición*, 1858, 2–3. On the difficulty in abolishing Indian tribute consult: Mark van Aken, "The Lingering Death of Indian Tribute in Ecuador," *Hispanic American Historical Review*, 61:3 (August 1981), 429–459.

15. Ecuador, Ministro de Hacienda, *Esposición, 1858*, 2–6.

16. *El Nacional* (Quito), no. 235 (July 6, 1866); no. 225 (April 14, 1866); Ecuador, Ministro de Hacienda, *Esposición, 1867; 1873*, 10–11, 22; *Informe, 1888*, 12. For a discussion of the politics surrounding the approval of the Concordat and the subsequent amendments see Bustos-Videla, "Church and State in Ecuador," 57–97, 287–308, 326–334.

17. Ecuador, Ministro de Hacienda, *Informe, 1887*, 8; *1885*, 12; *1883*, 11; *Esposición, 1855*, 2; *Memoria, 1857*, 14, 21–22; *Esposición, 1865*, 6; *Memoria, 1880*, 14–15. For a discussion of the burden diezmos placed on the Indians see Peñaherrera de Costales and Costales, *Historia social*, I, 98–116.

18. Ecuador, Ministro de Hacienda, *Esposición, 1855, Cuadro A; 1858*, 15–16; *1873*, 10–11; Banco del Ecuador, *Historia de medio siglo, 1868–1918* (Guayaquil: Imprenta de El Independiente, 1919), 61.

19. Ecuador, Ministro de Hacienda, *Memoria, 1833,* 17; *Informe, 1885,* 12; *1890, Documentos* xiii–xv, 12–13; *1892, Cuadro E;* *1894,* 33–35. For an analysis of the role of Antonio Flores Jijón in the abolition of the diezmos see Robalino Dávila, *Orígenes del Ecuador,* VI, 219–247.

20. Ecuador, Ministro de Hacienda, *Memoria, 1857,* 2–6; Ecuador, Gobernador de la Provincia de Pichincha, "Informe, April 27, 1894," in Ministro de Hacienda, *Informe, 1894;* Ecuador, Presidente, "Mensaje, May 15, 1890," in Alejandro Noboa, *Recopilación de mensajes dirijidos por los presidentes y vicepresidentes de la república, jefes supremos y gobiernos provisorios a las convenciones y congresos nacionales desde el año de 1819 hasta nuestros días,* 5 vol. (Guayaquil: Imprenta de A. Noboa and Imprenta de El Tiempo, 1900–1908), IV, 1–13; Ecuador, Ministro de Hacienda, *Informe, 1892, Cuadro E;* Ecuador, Contaduría Mayor del Distrito del Guayas, "Informe, August 10, 1853," in Ministro de Hacienda, *Esposición, 1853.*

21. The laws regulating aguardiente in the early period are in PRAN, I, 56–57, 146–147, 185–186, 317-318, 523–534.

22. See, for example, Ecuador, Ministro de Hacienda, *Esposición, 1845,* 4–5; *1867,* 18; *Informe, 1863,* 13; *1885,* 10–12; *Esposición, 1873,* 7; *Informe, 1887,* 10; *1888,* 16–17; *1890,* 10; *1892,* 15–17.

23. The *Informes* of the ministers of hacienda contain much information on aguardiente. See especially the *Informes* from 1901 to 1904. The method of alcohol-tax collection varied throughout the country. Some areas had tax farmers while in others the government collected aguardiente levies directly. See the *Informes* of the governors of Tunguragua, Chimborazo, and Azuay, in Ecuador, Ministro de Hacienda, *Informe, 1901* for some of these different approaches.

24. For a discussion of the source of the original debt see David Bushnell, *The Santander Regime,* 112–117, and Emilio M. Terán, *Informe al Jefe Supremo General Eloy Alfaro sobre la deuda anglo-ecuatoriana* (Quito: Imprenta Nacional, 1896), 1–47.

25. Ecuador, Ministro de Hacienda, *Informe, 1912,* cxlviii–cl; Terán, *Informe,* 61–95.

26. Terán, *Informe,* 95.

27. Ibid., 222–231; Ecuador, Ministro de Hacienda, *Esposición, 1853,* 7; *1855,* 5–7; *Informe, 1912,* cxlviii–cl; *1863,* 5–7.

28. For a discussion of the criticism of the various nineteenth-century negotiations and agreements between Ecuador and the foreign bondholders see Terán, *Informe.*

29. Ibid., 417–597; Ecuador, Ministro de Hacienda, *Esposición, 1865,* 11–12; *1867,* 29–30; *1873,* 22; *Informe, 1888,* 32; *1890, Documento* xvii; Alejandro Noboa, *Recopilación de mensajes,* III, 3–14, 19, 132.

30. Terán, *Informe,* 701–735, 743, 788–793; Ecuador, Ministro de Hacienda, *Informe, 1890, Documento* xvii; *1894,* 44–50; *1912,* cl–clx; Ecuador, *Diario Ofi-*

cial, no. 245 (February 20, 1894); no. 287 (August 4, 1894); "Mensaje del Presidente al Congreso Extraordinario," May 24, 1890, in Noboa, *Recopilación de mensajes*, IV, 15–31.

31. Ecuador, Ministro de Hacienda, *Memoria, 1857*, 18, 19, 31–33; *Informe, 1863*, 1–3; "Informe del Gobernador de la Provincia del Guayas," in Ecuador, Ministro de Hacienda, *Informe, 1894*.

32. Ecuador, Ministro de Estado, *Memoria, 1831*, 16; *PRAN*, I, 35–36; Ecuador, Ministro de Hacienda, *Memoria, 1833*, 3–4; *Esposición, 1865*, 12–13; *1867*, 33–35; *1858*, 6, 10.

33. Ecuador, Ministro de Estado, *Memoria, 1831*, 15; Ecuador, Ministro de Hacienda, *Esposición, 1847*, 11–12; *1853, Cuadro* 3–4; *1867*, 33–34; *1873*, 15–21; *1875*, 20; *Memoria, 1833*, 3; "Informe de la Dirección Jeneral del Crédito Público," in Ecuador, Ministro de Hacienda, *Esposición, 1857;* Ecuador, Jeneral Jefe del Estado Mayor, *Memoria, 1833*.

34. Ecuador, Ministro de Estado, *Informe, 1831*, 17; Ecuador, Ministro de Hacienda, *Memoria, 1833*, 3, 7; *Esposición, 1853, Cuadro* 3, 71; "Informe de Contaduría Mayor del distrito del Guayas," *1853; 1847*, 11–12; *1858*, 6–10; *1865*, 12–13; *1873*, 15.

35. Ecuador, Ministro de Hacienda, *Memoria, 1833*, 1–2; *Esposición, 1853*, 13; Ecuador, Gobierno Provisorio, Secretario Jeneral, Sección de Hacienda, *Informe, 1861*, 10–11.

36. Ecuador, Presidente, "Mensaje, 1831," in Noboa, *Recopilación de mensajes*, I, 183–195; Ecuador, Ministro de Estado, *Informe, 1831*, 16; Ecuador, Ministro de Hacienda, *Esposición, 1853*, 9; *1865*, 3; *1855*, 10; *1873*, 15.

37. Julio Estrada Ycaza, *Los bancos del siglo XIX* (Guayaquil: Archivo Histórico del Guayas, 1976) 19–30, discusses the early banks.

38. *La Unión Colombiana* (Guayaquil), no. 9 (December 5, 1860).

39. Ecuador, Presidente, *Mensaje, 1863*, 4; Ecuador, Ministro de Hacienda, *Informe, 1863; 1865, Cuadro D; 1867*, 37, *Cuadro R*.

40. "Mensaje del Jefe Supremo, 1896–97," in Noboa, *Recopilación de mensajes*, IV, 222; Ecuador, Ministro de Hacienda, *Informe, 1887*, 14, *Cuadro E; 1888*, 29.

41. Estrada, *Los bancos*, 89–100; Ecuador, Ministro de Hacienda, *Informe, 1883, Documento V*.

42. Ecuador, Ministro de Hacienda, *Informe, 1894*, 41; Estrada, *Los bancos*, 59–123.

43. Estrada, *Los bancos*, 33, 48–49; Ecuador, Ministro de Hacienda, *Informe, 1867*, 37–38; Aurelio Noboa, *Colección de leyes* (Guayaquil: Imprenta de A. Noboa, 1901), 37–38.

44. Carbo, *Historia monetaria*, 33–34; *Estrella de Panamá* (Panama) June 10, 1874; Ecuador, Ministro de Hacienda, *Informe, 1892*, 29; Banco del Ecuador, *Historia de Medio Siglo*, 91–96, 135; *El Nacional*, September 1, 1886; Ecuador, Ministro de Hacienda, *Informe, 1890*, 30.

45. See Rocafuerte's letters to Flores in Rodríguez, *Estudios*, 194–341; Ecuador, Ministro del Interior, *Memoria, 1833;* Ecuador, Ministro de Estado, Esposición, 1841, 25; Noboa, *Recopilación de mensajes*, I, 259–260.

46. Ecuador, Ministro de Hacienda, *Memoria*, 1857, 18–19, 31–32; *Esposición, 1873*, 23; Ecuador, Ministro del Interior y Relaciones Exteriores, *Esposición, 1863*, 5–6, 11–15; *1865*, 12–27.

47. Fredrick B. Pike, *The United States and the Andean Republics: Peru, Bolivia, and Ecuador* (Cambridge: Harvard University Press, 1977), 114.

48. Among the studies of education, c.f., Guevara, *Rocafuerte y la educación pública* and Miranda Ribadeneira, *La Primera escuela politécnica del Ecuador.*

49. Ecuador, Ministro de Hacienda, *Informe, 1894*, 4.

4: Government Finances 1895–1925

1. For representative statements of these views see Ecuador, Ministro de Hacienda, *Informe, 1906*, 69–74; and Ecuador, Ministro de Instrucción Pública, *Informe, 1913*, 8.

2. These changes can be seen graphically by comparing commemorative publications: Carbo, *El Ecuador en Chicago* and Ecuador, Compañía *"Guía del Ecuador,"* *El Ecuador: guía comercial.*

3. Ecuador, Ministro de Hacienda, *Informe, 1896–97*, 25–26.

4. Ibid., *1901*, 6, 39–43; *1902*, 7.

5. Ibid., *1902, Cuadro N*, 7–8; *1903, Cuadro N*; *1904, Cuadro O*; *1906*, 7; *1908* 5.

6. Ibid., *1901*, 16, 40–42.

7. Ecuador, Director General de Obras Públicas, "Informe, June 30, 1908" in Ecuador, Ministro de lo Interior, *Informe, 1908*, xix, xviii; Ecuador, Ministro de Hacienda, *Informe, 1908*, 5.

8. See for example Ecuador, Ministro de Hacienda, *Informe, 1906*, 7; *1908*, 5; *1912*, xxxi; and Ecuador, Director del Tesoro, *Informe, 1933*, 20.

9. Ecuador, Ministro de Hacienda, *Informe, 1913*, xxxii–xxxiv, lxiv–lxvi; *1914*, iv; *1915*, iii, v–vii, xxxvi–xxxix.

10. Ecuador, Ministro de Hacienda, *Demostración de los servicios a que están destinadas las rentas del Estado por disposiciones de leyes y decretos especiales, y sobrante que quedaría para afrontar los gastos que demanda el sostenimiento de la Administración Pública, según las recaudaciones efectuadas en 1916* (Quito: Imprenta y Encuadernación Nacionales, 1917).

11. Ecuador, Ministro de Obras Públicas, *Informe, 1904*, xi–xiv; *1905*, vi–x.

12. Ibid., *1904*, xii–xix; *1905*, v, ix–xi; *1906*, xii, xxv, xxvi; Ecuador, Director General de Obras Públicas, "Informe, June 30, 1908," xix; Ecuador, Dirección General de Obras Públicas, *Informe, 1926–1930*, 3–4; Ecuador, Ministro de Hacienda, *Informe, 1920*, vii–viii; *1922*, 4–6; *1923*, 8–10; Ecuador, Commission

of Financial Advisers, "Report on the Construction of Public Works," 3–4, 6, KP.

13. Ecuador, Ministro de Hacienda, *Informe, 1921*.

14. Ecuador, Comisión Permanente de Legislación, *Informe, 1922; 1925;* Ecuador, Consejo de Estado, *Informe, 1924,* 9–10; Ecuador, Ministro de Hacienda, *Informe, 1921; 1922; 1923; 1924;* May 31, 1925; Ecuador, Director del Tesoro, *Informe, 1933,* 20–21; *January 12, 1931* in Ecuador, Ministerio de Hacienda, *Boletín de Hacienda,* no. 38, 96–102; *El Comercio,* no. 7162 (August 4, 1925).

15. Ecuador, Director del Tesoro, *Informe, 1933,* 20; Ecuador, Ministro de Hacienda, *Informe, 1920,* vii–viii, xiii–xiv; *1923;* William J. Rouse, "Report on the Financial Difficulties of the Government of Ecuador," in Frederic Goding to secretary of state, Guayaquil, December 12, 1921, NA, 822.51/341; Ecuador, Commission of Financial Advisers, "Report on the Construction of Public Works," 3–4; Ecuador, Comisión Permanente de Legislación, *Informe, 1922;* R. C. Michell to Foreign Office, Quito, January 30, 1925, FO 371/10619, A1229/ 1229/54.

16. Ecuador, "Contrato celebrado entre el Gobierno del Ecuador y el Señor John S. Hord" (Washington, D.C.: July 20, 1923), in KP; G. A. Bading to secretary of state, Quito, June 30, 1924, NA, 822.51/16; R. C. Michell to Foreign Office, Quito, November 11, 1924, FO 371/ 9541, A 6982/3/54; John S. Hord, "Actividades del Consultor Técnico de Hacienda desde fines de Agosto del 1923 hasta mediados de Julio del 1925" (Quito, 1925), NA, 822.51A/22; Ecuador, Ministro de Hacienda, *Informe, 1924.*

17. Weinman, "Ecuador and Cacao," 117–121, 149, 185–190, 194–197, 206–214, 260–273; Carbo, *Historia monetaria,* 83–87, 105, 113–114, 118–120; Charles Hartman to secretary of state, Quito, September 30, 1921, NA, 822.00/502; December 31, 1921, NA, 822.00/504; G. A. Bading to secretary of state, Quito, September 1924, NA, 822.00/563.

18. Ecuador, Ministro de Hacienda, *Informes 1896–1924; Informe al Ejecutivo, 1925.*

19. Ibid., *Boletín,* no. 38 (June 1931); *Informe, 1896–97,* 25–27; *1901,* 17–18; *1906,* 16–25; *1913,* xxxii–xxxiv, 142; *1915,* xxxvi–xl; Ecuador, Director del Tesoro, *Informe, 1930,* 21.

20. Ecuador, Ministro de Hacienda, *Informe, 1896–97,* 25–27; Ecuador, Director del Tesoro, "Informe, June 12, 1931."

21. For modifications of the aguardiente laws consult Ecuador, Ministro de Hacienda, *Informes, 1896–1924,* and the laws in Ecuador, Archivo del Poder Legislativo, *Anuario de Legislación Ecuatoriana: Leyes, Decretos, Acuerdos y Resoluciones del Congreso 1896–1924* (Quito: Imprenta y Encuadernación Nacionales). (Hereafter cited as Ecuador, *Anuario.*) Also see Ecuador, Gobernador de Imbabura, "Informe, June 11, 1913" in Ecuador, Ministro de Hacienda, *Informe, 1913,* 99–105, and Ecuador, Gobernador de Tunguragua, "Informe, June 7, 1901" in Ecuador, Ministro de Hacienda, *Informe, 1901; 1913,* lxvi–

lxviii; Ecuador, "Decretos Supremos," April 11, 1906; April 20, 1906; April 25, 1906 in Ecuador, Ministro de Hacienda, *Informe, 1906; 1918,* xv–xvii; *1921,* xix–xxviii; E. Morley to E. W. Kemmerer, Huigra, November 30, 1926, KP.

22. Decree (December 28, 1915), Ecuador, *Anuario, 1916,* vol. 15, tomo 2, 312–313; Ecuador, Ministro de Hacienda, *Informe, 1915,* xliv.

23. Decree (November 24, 1920), Ecuador, *Anuario, 1920,* vol. 19, tomo 2, 23–24; Decree (October 17, 1921), Ecuador, *Anuario, 1921,* vol. 20, tomo 1; Ecuador, Director del Tesoro, "Informe, June 12, 1931."

24. E. Morley to E. W. Kemmerer, Huigra, November 30, 1926, KP; Decree (March 27, 1923), Ecuador, *Anuario, 1923,* vol. 22, tomo 2, 413; Decree (September 6, 1922), Ecuador, *Anuario, 1922,* vol. 21, tomo 2, 412–418; Decree (November 4, 1922), Ecuador, *Anuario, 1922,* vol. 21, tomo 2, 453–454.

25. G. A. Bading to secretary of state, Quito, September 30, 1922, NA, 822.00/509; E. Morley to E. W. Kemmerer, Huigra, November 30, 1926, KP.

26. E. Morley to E. W. Kemmerer, Huigra, November 30, 1926, KP.

27. *El Comercio,* no. 7896 (August 8, 1927); no. 7898 (August 10, 1927); Ecuador, Ministro de Hacienda, *Informe, 1924,* 47.

28. Terán, *Informe;* Ecuador, Ministro de Hacienda, *Informe, 1896–97,* 32.

29. Corporation of Foreign Bondholders, *Annual Report of the Council of the Corporation of Foreign Bondholders 1897* (London: 1898), 100–109; *1898–1899,* 125–132; *1899–1900,* 91–94; Ecuador; Ministro de Hacienda, *Informe, 1901, Anexo L.*

30. Ecuador, Presidente, "Mensaje, 1900" in Noboa, *Recopilación de mensajes,* vol. 5, 16–17.

31. Bondholders, *Annual Report, 1900–1901,* 114–121.

32. Ibid., 101–111; Ecuador, Ministro de Hacienda, *Informe, 1901,* 59–62, *Anexo 14, Anexo L; 1904,* 15; *1906,* 59–61.

33. Ecuador, Ministro de Hacienda, *Informe, 1906,* 58; Bondholders, *Annual Report, 1907,* 164–176; *1908,* 122–139, 156–171.

34. Bondholders, *Annual Report, 1908,* 122–139, 156–171; Carbo, *Historia monetaria,* 60–62.

35. Bondholders, *Annual Reports 1910–1925;* G. A. Bading to secretary of state, Quito, March 23, 1925, NA, 822.51/406; F. W. Goding to secretary of state, Guayaquil, December 12, 1921, NA, 822.51/341; September 12, 1923, NA, 822.51/385; Ecuador, Ministro de Hacienda, *Informe, 1911,* 19; Ecuador, Consejo Central Ejecutivo a la Comisión International, "Ecuador estado financiero y económico; deuda pública," NA, 822.51/50.

36. Bondholders, *Annual Report, 1913,* 120–122; G. A. Bading to secretary of state, Quito, March 23, 1925, NA, 822/51/406; Ecuador, Presidente, *Mensaje, August 10, 1915* (Quito: Imprenta y Encuadernación Nacionales, 1915).

37. Carbo, *Historia monetaria,* 118–119, 465–489; G. A. Bading to secretary of state, Quito, September 30, 1924, NA, 822.51/563; January 14, 1926, NA, 822.00/647; Charles Hartman to secretary of state, Quito, December 31, 1921,

NA, 822.00/504; Ecuador, Ministro de Hacienda, *Informe, 1916*, cix–cxvii; 1919, lxxxvii–xciii; R. C. Michell to Foreign Office, Quito, January 30, 1925, FO 371/10619, A1229/1229/54.

38. Ecuador, Ministro de Hacienda, *Informe, 1915*, li–lii; Charles Hartman to secretary of state, Quito, July 12, 1920, NA, 822.00/481; G. A. Bading to secretary of state, Quito, September 30, 1922, NA, 822/00/509; December 31, 1923, NA, 822/00/532; March 31, 1924, NA, 822.00/544; F. W. Goding to secretary of state, Guayaquil, December 12, 1921, NA, 822.51/341; A. Moncayo Andrade, *Memorandum para servir a los estudios de la comisión permanente de legislación* (Quito: Imprenta Nacional, 1923), xxx–xxxi.

39. F. W. Goding to secretary of state, Guayaquil, November 29, 1921, NA, 822.51/340; Charles Hartman to secretary of state, Quito, December 31, 1921, NA, 822.00/504; March 31, 1922, NA, 822/00/505; Decree (October 17, 1921), Ecuador, *Anuario, 1922*, vol. 21, tomo 2, 381.

40. G. A. Bading to secretary of state, Quito, September 30, 1922, NA, 822/00/509.

41. Ibid.; July 25, 1922, NA, 822/51/361; September 4, 1922, NA, 822/51/365; September 24, NA, 822.00/563.

42. G. A. Bading to secretary of state, Quito, December 31, 1923, NA, 822.00/532; March 31, 1924, NA, 822.00/544; R. C. Michell to Foreign Office, Quito, January 30, 1925, FO 371/10619, A1229/1229/54.

43. Although most administrations, both liberal and preliberal, depended on Guayaquil banks to finance budget deficits, such loans also were granted by highland institutions. For example, in September 1884 two Quito banks, the Banco de Quito and Banco de la Unión, had unsecured note issues of 688,834 pesos. At the end of 1884 the budget deficit was 632,805 pesos. Luis Alberto Carbo, "Memorandum on Ecuador's Currency Systems," 2 pts. (Quito: December 7, 1926), KP.

44. Ecuador, Ministro de Hacienda, *Informe, 1901*, 11; *1914*, iv; *1915*, vi, cviii; *1919*, x.

45. Ecuador, Ministro de Hacienda, *Informe, 1903*, 18; *1905*, 5–6; *1908*, 4; *1914*, v; *1915*, viii–xvi; *1920*, VII–XI; Ecuador, Ministerio de Hacienda, *Boletín*, no. 10 (May 1929).

46. Ecuador, Commission of Financial Advisers, "Report in Support of a Project of Organic Budget Law" (Quito: February 28, 1927), KP; Appendix M.

47. Decree (December 30, 1922), Ecuador, *Anuario, 1922*, vol. 21, tomo 2, 492–493; Decree (December 31, 1923), Ecuador, *Anuario, 1923*, vol. 22, tomo 2, 495; Decree (January 1, 1921); Decree (December 31, 1921), Ecuador, *Anuario, 1921*, vol. 20, tomo 2, 261, 310; Ecuador, Ministro de Hacienda, *Informe, 1924*, 26–27, 30.

48. Bondholders. *Annual Report, 1897*, 127; Ecuador, Ministro de Hacienda, *Informe, 1896–97*.

49. Ecuador, Ministro de Hacienda, *Informe, 1901*, 9–10.

50. Ibid., *1908*, 4–5; *1918*, ix–xiv; *1920*, vii–viii, xiii–xiv; Ecuador, Director de Tesoro, *Informe, 1933*, 20; Ecuador, Presidente, "Mensaje especial" in Ecuador, Ministro de Hacienda, *Informe, 1930, Anexo*, 356–365.

51. Carbo, "Memorandum," pt. 1, 6; pt. 2, KP. Ecuador, Ministro de Hacienda, *Informe, 1915*, xx; For a discussion of the continuing rivalry between Guayaquil's two major banks see Estrada, *Los bancos*.

52. R. M. de Lambert to secretary of state, Quito, June 30, 1925, NA, 822.00/598; *El Comercio*, no. 7083 (May 17, 1925).

53. Melchior Palyi, *The Twilight of Gold 1914–1936: Myths and Realities* (Chicago: Henry Regnery Company, 1972), chaps. 2 and 3; René Sedillot, *Histoire du Franc* (Paris: Recueil Sirey, 1939), 277–340; Edwin Walter Kemmerer, *Kemmerer on Money* (Chicago: John Winston Company, 1934); Eleanor Lansing Dulles, *The Dollar, the Franc and Inflation* (New York: The Macmillan Company, 1933); League of Nations, *Memorandum sur les Monnales et Les Banques Centrales 1913–1924*, 2 vols. (Geneva, 1925), II.

54. The banking law passed June 11, 1897, effective from January 1, 1898, required that banks of issue have gold reserves equal to 50% of their note issues. Prior to 1898 the metallic reserve requirement was 33.3% as required by the banking laws of November 5, 1871 and June 4, 1878. Decree (August 29, 1914), Ecuador, *Anuario, 1914*, vol. 13, tomo 1, 24–25; Decree (September 25, 1915), Ecuador, *Anuario, 1915*, vol. 14, tomo 1, 52–53; Carbo, *Historia monetaria*, 449.

55. For a discussion of economic turmoil in this period, particularly its impact on the developed western countries, see Palyi, *The Twilight of Gold*. For a general discussion of Ecuador's monetary and exchange problems in this period see Carbo, *Historia monetaria;* Decree (November 30, 1917), Ecuador, *Anuario, 1917*, vol. 16, tomo 2, 319–320; Decree (March 6, 1919); Decree (March 26, 1919); Decree (May 9, 1919); Decree (June 10, 1919); Decree (June 23, 1919), Ecuador, *Anuario, 1919*, vol. 18, tomo 2, 156–160, 168, 173–174, 176–177; Decree (November 23, 1922), Ecuador, *Anuario, 1922*, vol. 21, tomo 2, 472–478; Ecuador, Ministro de Hacienda, *Informe, 1923*, 70; *1924*, 20, 24; G. A. Bading to secretary of state, Quito, September 30, 1923, NA 822.00/526; June 30, 1924, NA, 822.00/551; September 30, 1924, NA, 822.00/563; December 31, 1924, NA, 822.00/572; R. M. de Lambert to secretary of state, Quito, July 17, 1925, NA, 822.00/605; July 31, 1925, NA, 822.00/605; July 31, 1925, NA, 822.5151/93; R. C. Michell to Foreign Office, Quito, June 20, 1924, FO 371/9541, A4685/3/541; October 18, 1924, FO 371/9541, A6576/3/54; Ecuador, Ministerio de Hacienda, *Codificación de los decretos ejecutivos sobre incautación de giros, 31 Agosto de 1923* (Quito: Talleres Tipográficos de la Sección de Especias, 1923).

56. For a history of banking in Ecuador see Estrada, *Los bancos*.

57. Víctor Emilio Estrada, *El momento económico en el Ecuador* (Guayaquil: Litografía e Imprenta la Reforma Jacinto Jouvin Arce e Hijos, 1950), 37; *El Guante*, no. 5353 (May 29, 1925); *El Comercio*, no. 7095; R. M. de Lambert to secretary of state, Quito, July 17, 1925, NA, 822.00/604.

58. *La Antorcha,* año 1, no. 1 (November 16, 1924); año 1, no. 2 (November 23, 1924); Leonardo N. Muñoz, "Interview" (Quito: December 3, 1971); *El Abanderado* año 1, no. 4 (December 15, 1924); año 1, no. 3 (December 8, 1924); año 10 (January 26, 1925); año 1, no. 9 (January 19, 1925); Luis A. Rodríguez, "Interview" (Quito; March 26, 1972); Luis A. Rodríguez, "Mis recuerdos," 25; *El Comercio,* no. 7095 (May 29, 1925).

59. *La Antorcha,* año 1, no. 6 (November 16, 1924); año 1, no. 8 (December 31, 1924); año 1, no. 12 (January 31, 1925); año 1, no. 13 (February 7, 1925); año 1, no. 16 (February 28, 1925); año 2, no. 2 (March 30, 1925); *El Abanderado,* año 1, no. 15 (March 2, 1925); año 1, no. 15 (March 2, 1925); Rodríguez, "Mis recuerdos," 30.

60. For a detailed discussion of the formation of the Liga Militar and the coup of July 9, 1925 see Linda A. Rodríguez, "The Liberal Crisis and the Revolution of 1925 in Ecuador" (Master's Thesis, University of Texas, Austin, 1972). *El Telégrafo,* no. 14391 (July 12, 1925); no. 14399 (July 19, 1925); no. 14389 (July 11, 1925); no. 14394 (July 14, 1925); *El Ejército Nacional,* año 4, no. 26 (1925).

5: The Politics of Reform

1. For traditional interpretations see Reyes, *Breve historia,* II, 782–787; Gabriel Cevallos García, *Historia del Ecuador* (Cuenca: Editorial "Don Bosco," 1964), 439–442; Leopoldo Benítes, *Ecuador: drama y paradoja* (Mexico: Fondo de Cultura Económica, 1950), 249–252. The traditional view is even enshrined in a work by the Guayaquil novelist Alfredo Pareja Diezcanseco, *Los Nuevos años: la advertencia* (Buenos Aires: Editorial Losada, 1956). It was recently reaffirmed in the highly regarded study by the president of Ecuador, Oswaldo Hurtado, *Political Power in Ecuador,* 80, 117, 129–130, 135. Pike, who relied on the best secondary sources, also accepts the traditional view in his, *The United States and the Andean Republics,* 190–192.

2. *El Telégrafo,* no. 14418 (August 7, 1925); no. 15258 (November 19, 1927); *El Comercio,* no. 7197 (September 9, 1925); no. 7227 (October 9, 1925); no. 7228 (October 10, 1925); no. 7313 (January 3, 1926); no. 7333 (January 23, 1926); no. 7334 (January 24, 1926); no. 7463 (June 2, 1926); no. 7464 (June 3, 1926); no. 7510 (July 19, 1926); no. 7566 (September 13, 1926); no. 7569 (September 16, 1926); no. 7570 (September 17, 1926); no. 8000 (November 20, 1927); no. 8001 (November 21, 1927); no. 8007 (November 27, 1927); G. A. Bading to secretary of state, Quito, October 12, 1925, NA, 822.00/ 630; R. C. Michell to Foreign Office, Quito, May 1, 1926, FO 371/11139, A3122/160/54; Richard P. Butrick to secretary of state, Guayaquil, July 16, 1926, NA, R.G. 84; Harold D. Clum to secretary of state, Guayaquil, September 11,

1926, NA, R.G. 84; W. Allen Rhode to secretary of state, Guayaquil, December 14, 1927, NA, R.G. 84; March 14, 1928, NA, R.G. 84.

3. Rodríguez, "The Liberal Crisis," 106–114.

4. Decree, no. 11 (July 17, 1925), Ecuador, *Anuario, 1925,* vol. 24, tomo 1, 13–14; Ecuador, Ministro de lo Interior, *Informe, 1926–1928,* 7–17; *El Telégrafo,* no. 14226 (August 15, 1925); no. 15815 (May 26, 1929); *El Guante* (September 15, 1925); *El Día,* no. 3705 (July 8, 1925); *El Comercio,* no. 7143 (July 16, 1925); no. 7163 (August 5, 1925); no. 7197 (September 9, 1925); no. 7198 (September 10, 1925); no. 7201 (September 13, 1925); no. 7459 (May 29, 1926); no. 7652 (December 8, 1926); no. 7730 (February 24, 1927); R. M. de Lambert to secretary of state, Quito, July 17, 1925, NA, 822.00/604; July 31, 1925, NA, 822.516/13; Richard P. Butrick to secretary of state, Guayaquil, July 20, 1925, NA, 822.00/602; G. A. Bading to secretary of state, June 12, 1926, NA, 822.516/12.

5. Ecuador, Ministerio de Hacienda, *Las instituciones de crédito del Ecuador en 1925: Banco Comercial y Agrícola (Guayaquil)* (Quito: Talleres Tipográficos del Ministerio de Hacienda, 1926).

6. Ibid.; table 33; Decree, no. 355 (November 13, 1925), Ecuador, *Anuario, 1925,* vol. 24, tomo 1, 437–438.

7. *El Comercio,* no. 7122 (June 26, 1925); no. 7134 (July 8, 1925); *El Guante,* no. 5379 (June 24, 1925).

8. Decree, no. 253 (October 14, 1925), Ecuador, *Anuario, 1925,* vol. 24, tomo 1, 306–330; Decree, no. 298 (October 26, 1925), Ecuador, *Anuario, 1925,* vol 24, tomo 1, 368–369; Decree, no. 320 (October 31, 1925), Ecuador, *Anuario, 1925,* vol. 24, tomo 1, 393–394; Decree, no. 163 (September 15, 1925), Ecuador, *Anuario, 1925,* vol, 24, tomo 1, 210; R. M. de Lambert to secretary of state, Quito, July 31, 1925, NA, 822.516/13; Richard P. Butrick to secretary of state, Guayaquil, October 23, 1925, NA, 822.516/18; November 5, 1925, NA, 822.00/634; G. A. Bading to secretary of state, Quito, October 30, 1925, NA, 822.516/19; November 30, 1925, NA, 822.516/22; January 12, 1926, NA, 822.00/645; February 11, 1926, NA, 822.516/26; February 27, 1926, NA, 822.51/420; March 31, 1926, NA, 822.00/664; June 28, 1926, NA, 822.516/37; July 30, 1926, NA, 822.516/41; July 31, 1926, NA, 822.516/43; August 12, 1926, NA, 822.516/44; Richard P. Butrick to secretary of state, Guayaquil, April 15, 1926, NA, R.G. 84; August 12, 1926, NA, R.G. 84; R. C. Michell to Foreign Office, Quito, January 30, 1926, FO 371/11139, A1465/285/54; April 5, 1926, FO 371/11139, A2595/285/54; *El Ejército Nacional,* vol. 5, no. 29, 22–231; *El Comercio,* no. 7206 (September 18, 1925); nos. 7211–7214 (September 23–26, 1925); no. 7217 (September 29, 1925); no. 7218 (September 30, 1925); no. 7234 (October 16, 1925); no. 7235 (October 17, 1925); no. 7245 (October 26, 1925); no. 7248 (October 30, 1925); nos. 7250–7252 (November 1–3, 1925); no. 7254 (November 5, 1925); no. 7256 (November 7, 1925); no. 7262 (November 13, 1925); no. 7264 (November 15, 1925); no. 7287 (December 8, 1925); no. 7314 (Janu-

ary 4, 1926); no. 7318 (January 8, 1926); no. 7321 (January 11, 1926); no. 7322 (January 12, 1926); no. 7327 (January 17, 1926); no. 7329 (January 19, 1926); no. 7332 (January 22, 1926); no. 7344 (February 3, 1926); no. 7348 (February 7, 1926); *El Guante,* (September 15, 1925); *El Telégrafo,* no. 14416 (August 5, 1925); no. 15492 (July 9, 1928); William Graham to Foreign Office, Quito, November 12, 1925, FO 371/10619, A6448/1/54.

9. *El Comercio,* no. 7197 (September 9, 1925); no. 7202 (September 14, 1925); no. 7340 (January 30, 1926); no. 7346–7348 (February 5–7, 1926); no. 7355 (February 14, 1926); no. 7360 (February 19, 1926); no. 7361 (February 20, 1926); no. 7363 (February 22, 1926); no. 7365 (February 24, 1926); no. 7367 (February 26, 1926); no. 7369 (February 28, 1926); *El Telégrafo,* no. 14223 (August 12, 1925); no. 14226 (August 15, 1926); G. A. Bading to secretary of state, Quito, February 13, 1926, NA, 822.00/654; March 13, 1926, NA, 822.00/622; April 16, 1926, NA, 822.00/666; William W. Morse to secretary of state, Guayaquil, March 20, 1926, NA, R.G. 84; R. C. Michell to Foreign Office, Quito, March 9, 1926, FO 371/11139, A2121/160/54; Ecuador, Economic Conference, "Transfer of Gold Held by Banks," KP; R. M. de Lambert to secretary of state, Quito, July 17, 1925, NA, 822.00/604.

10. R. C. Michell to Foreign Office, Quito, December 31, 1923, FO 371/9542, A895/895/54; Ecuador, Ministro de lo Interior, *Informe, 1926–1928,* 5–6.

11. Decree, no. 58 (April 30, 1926), Ecuador, *Anuario, 1926,* vol. 24, tomo 2, 95–99; *El Comercio,* no 7461 (May 30, 1926); no. 7472 (June 11, 1926); G. A. Bading to secretary of state, Quito, April 16, 1926, NA, 822.00/666; June 12, 1926, NA, 822.516/12; June 28, 1926, NA, 822.516/16; Richard P. Butrick to secretary of state, Guayaquil, June 5, 1926, NA, R.G. 84; Harold D. Clum to secretary of state, Guayaquil, September 11, 1926, NA, R.G. 84; March 14, 1927, NA, R.G. 84; A. Moncayo Andrade to Edwin Kemmerer, Quito, October 27, 1926, KP.

12. Decree, no. 166 (June 16, 1926), Ecuador, *Anuario, 1926,* vol. 24, tomo 2, 361–362; no. 192 (June 25, 1926), Ecuador, *Anuario, 1926,* vol. 24, tomo 2, 392–395; no. 476 (October 18, 1926), Ecuador, *Anuario, 1926,* vol. 24, tomo 2, 962–964; Decree, no. 1 (April 1, 1926), Ecuador, *Anuario, 1926,* vol. 24, tomo 2, 2; G. A. Bading to secretary of state, Quito, June 28, 1926, NA, 822.516/37; June 30, 1926, NA, 822.00/675; July 30, 1926, NA, 822.516/41; July 31, 1926, NA, 822.516/43; July 31, 1926, NA, 822.00/678; Richard P. Butrick to secretary of state, Guayaquil, July 16, 1926, NA, R.G. 84; August 11, 1926, NA, R.G. 84; Harold D. Clum to secretary of state, Guayaquil, September 11, 1926, NA, R.G. 84; October 13, 1926, NA, R.G. 84; November 14, 1926, NA, R.G. 84; January 13, 1927, NA, R.G. 84; February 11, 1927, NA, R.G. 84; *El Comercio,* no. 7480 (June 19, 1926); no. 7485–7487 (June 24–26, 1926); no. 7490 (June 29, 1926); nos. 7493–7495 (July 2–4, 1926); no 7508 (July 17, 1926); no. 7511 (July 20, 1926); no. 7520 (July 29, 1926); no. 7526 (August 4, 1926); no. 7536

(August 14, 1926); no. 7603 (October 20, 1926); no. 7652 (December 2, 1926); no. 7700 (January 25, 1927); *El Telégrafo,* no 14,391 (July 12, 1925); (October 21, 1926).

13. E. W. Kemmerer to V. Estrada, Quito, November 13, 1926, KP; *El Comercio,* no. 7648 (December 4, 1926); no. 7700 (January 25, 1927); Harold D. Clum to secretary to state, Guayaquil, December 12, 1926, NA, R.G. 84; January 13, 1927, NA, R.G. 84; February 11, 1927, NA, R.G. 84.

14. For an example of the accomplishments of one of these foreign experts, see Wolf, *Geography.*

15. Since this study is concerned with Ecuador, it does not analyze the motivations of the developed nations. For a discussion of the Kemmerer Missions from the viewpoint of the United States see Robert N. Seidel, "American Reformers Abroad: The Kemmerer Missions in South America, 1923–1931," *The Journal of Economic History* 32:2 (June 1972), 520–545.

16. Memorandum from the Division of Latin American Affairs of the Department of State to Dr. Rowe, Washington, D.C., May 28, 1920, NA, 822.00/485; Sumner Welles to General Crowder, Washington, D.C., November 26, 1921, NA, 822.51/337a; John Hord to Charles E. Hughes, Havanna, December 6, 1921, NA, 822.51/338; Francis White to secretary of state, Washington, D.C., June 1, 1923, NA, 822.51A/2; secretary of state to General Russell, Washington, D.C., June 9, 1923, NA, 822.51A/a; General Russell to secretary of state, Port au Prince, June 13, 1923, NA, 822.51a/a; Ecuador, "Contrato celebrado entre el Gobierno del Ecuador y el Señor John S. Hord," Washington, D.C., July 20, 1923, NA, 822.51A/9.

17. G. A. Bading to secretary of state, Quito, July 2, 1923, NA, 822.51/6; *El Telégrafo* (August 21, 1923); *El Guante* (August 21, 1923); *El Universo* (August 21, 1923); *La Prensa* (August 22, 1923); Frederic W. Goding to secretary of state, Guayaquil, August 25, 1923, NA, 822.51A/10; William Phillips to Wallace Thompson, Washington, D.C., August 28, 1923, NA, 822.51A/7; G. A. Bading to secretary of state, Quito, August 29, 1923, NA, 822.51A/9; September 27, 1923, NA, 822.51A/11.

18. G. A. Bading to secretary of state, Quito, December 31, 1923, NA, 822.00/532; April 30, 1924, NA, 822.51A/15; May 28, 1924, NA, 822.51A/16; June 30, 1924, NA, 822.00/551; Ecuador, Ministro de Hacienda, *Informe, 1924,* 14–18; John S. Hord, "Actividades del Consultor Técnico de Hacienda desde fines de agosto del 1923 hasta mediados de julio de 1925," NA, 822.51A/22; R. C. Michell to Foreign Office, Quito, August 4, 1924, FO 371/9542, A5355/4386/54; November 11, 1924, FO 371/9541, A6982/3/54; November 15, 1924, FO 371/9541, A6982/3/54; R. M. de Lambert to secretary of state, Quito, June 30, 1925, NA, 822.00/598; July 18, 1925, NA, 822.00/595; July 28, 1925, NA, 822.51A/21; *El Comercio,* no. 7149 (July 22, 1925); no. 7152 (July 25, 1925); no. 7209 (September 21, 1925); no. 7458 (May 28, 1926); no. 7465

(June 4, 1926); no. 7535 (August 13, 1926); no. 7860 (July 3, 1927); Waldemar J. Callman to secretary of state, Quito, July 16, 1927, NA, 822.51A/55.

19. G. A. Bading to secretary of state, Quito, June 30, 1924, NA, 822.51A/ 16; September 30, 1924, NA, 822.00/563; R. C. Michell to Foreign Office, Quito, November 11, 1924, FO 371/9541, A6982/3/54; John S. Hord, "Actividades," NA, 822.51A/22.

20. G. A. Bading to secretary of state, Quito, July 15, 1927, NA, 822.00/718; Waldemar J. Callman to secretary of state, Quito, July 16, 1927, NA, 822.51a/55; El Comercio, no. 7860 (July 3, 1927).

21. G. A. Bading to secretary of state, Quito, March 6, 1926, NA, 822.51A/ 26; April 12, 1926, NA, 822.00/665; Richard P. Butrick to secretary of state, Guayaquil, April 15, 1926, NA, R.G. 84; V. E. Estrada to E. W. Kemmerer, Guayaquil, April 5, 1925, KP; El Comercio, no. 7602 (October 19, 1926); R. C. Michell to Foreign Office, Quito, FO 371/11139, A2595/285/54.

22. American Economic Review, 39:6 (December 1949), n. p.; Edwin W. Kemmerer, Modern Currency Reform (New York: The MacMillan Co., 1916); El Comercio, no. 7603 (October 20, 1926); E. W. Kemmerer to J. Barberis, Princeton, April 9, 1926, KP.

23. For examples of letters of recommendation see: Frank McIntyre to E. W. Kemmerer, Washington, D.C., April 23, 1926, KP; Louis A. Riart to E. W. Kemmerer, Asunción, May 30, 1926, KP: Thomas H. Healy to E. W. Kemmerer, Washington, D.C., April 16, 1926, KP; E. W. Kemmerer to Harward M. Jefferson, Princeton, May 21, 1926, KP; E. W. Kemmerer to O. C. Lockhart, Princeton, May 21, 1926, KP; E. W. Kemmerer to Henry West, Princeton, May 14, 1926, KP; E. Feely to E. W. Kemmerer, New York, May 26, 1926, KP; E. W. Kemmerer to William W. Renwick, Princeton, June 5, 1926, KP; E. W. Kemmerer to E. Feely, Warsaw, August 16, 1926, KP; September 9, 1926, KP; E. Feely to E. W. Kemmerer, Princeton, September 9, 1926, KP.

24. J. Barberis to E. W. Kemmerer, Washington, D.C., April 30, 1926, KP; Francisco Banda to E. W. Kemmerer, Washington, May 1, 1926, KP; May 10, 1926, KP. See KP, Box I, folder 4–2, "Ecuador Currency," for examples of opinions of groups: chambers of commerce, agricultural societies, newspapers, businessmen, industrialists, etc.; El Comercio, no. 7450 (May 19, 1926); E. W. Kemmerer to E. Feely, Princeton, May 11, 1926, KP; E. W. Kemmerer to Howard M. Jefferson, May 21, 1926, KP; El Comercio, no. 7458 (May 28, 1926); no. 7536 (August 14, 1926); no. 7542 (August 19, 1926); no. 7587 (October 4, 1926); G. A. Bading to secretary of state, Quito, May 31, 1926, NA, 822.00/673; V. E. Estrada to E. W. Kemmerer, Turin, July 2, 1926, KP; E. Feely to E. W. Kemmerer, Princeton, August 16, 1926, KP; J. Cueva to E. Feely, New York, August 20, 1926, KP; G. A. Bading to secretary of state, Quito, October 16, 1926, NA, 822.00/686; October 30, 1926, NA, 822.00/687; N. Clemente Ponce, "Economic Recovery: Regeneration or Tragedy," KP.

25. G. A. Bading to secretary of state, Quito, October 30, 1926, NA, 822.00/687; December 14, 1926, NA, 822.00/693; *El Comercio*, no. 7599 (October 16, 1926), no. 7600 (October 17, 1926); no. 7603 (October 20, 1926), no. 7604 (October 21, 1926); no. 7606 (October 24, 1926); *El Telégrafo* (October 13, 1926). For examples of advice to Kemmerer Mission see *El Día, El Universo, Los Andes* (Riobamba), from October 1926 through February 1927; Cámara de Comercio y Agricultura to E. W. Kemmerer, Bahía, October 25, 1926, KP; Emiliano Donoso to E. W. Kemmerer, Cuenca, October 28, 1926, KP; Sociedad Obrera de Nuestra Señora del Quinche to E. W. Kemmerer, Quito, November 6, 1926, KP; V. E. Illingworth to E. W. Kemmerer, Guayaquil, November 7, 1926, KP.

26. *El Comercio*, no. 7606 (October 22, 1926); G. A. Bading to secretary of state, Quito, March 14, 1927, NA, 822.51A/45; E. W. Kemmerer to Arthur N. Young, Guayaquil, March 21, 1927; G. A. Bading to secretary of state, Quito, October 23, 1926, NA, 822.51A/36; January 27, 1927, NA, 822.51A/39; *El Porvenir* (October 22, 1926); *El Universo* (October 22, 1926), KP; Edwin W. Kemmerer, "Diary," October 22, 1926–December 9, 1926; January 9, 1927–March 15, 1927, KP; Ecuador, Commission of Financial Advisers, "Memorandum on Proposed Revision of Tax on Rural Property," KP; *El Comercio*, no. 7620 (November 6, 1926); "Memorandum on the Conferences with the Kemmerer Commission held with the Central Committee and Sub-Committees appointed by the Governor of Guayas Province," December 9, 1926, KP; A. Moncayo Andrade to E. Feely, Quito, December 17, 1926, KP; December 20, 1926, KP.

27. Edwin W. Kemmerer, "Economic Advisory Work for Governments," *American Economic Review*, 17:1 (1927), 1–12; *El Comercio*, no. 7716 (February 10, 1927); no. 7718 (February 12, 1927); E. W. Kemmerer to W. W. Cumberland, La Paz, April 29, 1927, KP; G. A. Bading to secretary of state, Quito, February 15, 1927, NA, 822.51A/42; Ecuador, Ministro de Hacienda, *Informe, July 10, 1926*, 40; Ecuador, Comisión de Consejeros Financieros, *Proyectos de Ley y exposiciones de motivos presentados por la Misión de Consejeros Financieros de Gobierno del Ecuador* (Quito 1927), KP.

28. Ecuador, Commission of Financial Advisers, "Report on the Construction of Public Works," March 15, 1927, KP; Ecuador, Misión de Consejeros Financieros, "Informe sobre el Projecto Ferrocarril Quito-Esmeraldas," March 15, 1927, KP; Ecuador, Commission of Financial Advisers, "Report on Public Credit," March 15, 1927, KP; Ecuador, Commission of Financial Advisers, "Project of an Organic Budget Law," February 28, 1927, KP; Ecuador, Commission of Financial Advisers, "Report in Support of a Project of an Organic Budget Law," February 28, 1927, KP.

29. *El Comercio*, no. 7716 (February 10, 1927); no. 7727 (February 21, 1927); no. 7860 (July 3, 1927); G. A. Bading to secretary of state, Quito, February 15, 1927, NA, 822.51A/42; March 31, 1927, NA, 822.00/706; E. W.

Kemmerer to Walter Van Deusen, Quito, February 23, 1927, KP.

30. *El Comercio*, no. 7683 (January 8, 1927); no. 7741 (March 6, 1927); no. 7743 (March 8, 1927); no. 7932 (September 13, 1927); no. 7793 (September 14, 1927); no. 7943 (September 24, 1927); G. A. Bading to secretary of state, Quito, November 26, 1926, NA, 822.00/692; February 11, 1927, NA, 822.00/698; March 11, 1927, NA, 822.00/702; Walter Gallman to secretary of state, Quito, August 30, 1927, NA, 822.00/722; September 15, 1927, NA, 822.00/725; September 30, 1927, NA, 822.00/735; June 25, 1928, NA, 822.00/755; *El Telégrafo*, no. 15365 (March 5, 1928); no. 15396 (April 4, 1928); no. 15585 (October 10, 1928); G. A. Bading to secretary of state, Quito, May 29, 1928, NA, 822.00/756; R. M. Kohan to Foreign Office, Quito, October 30, 1928, FO 371/12762, A8379/657/54; Ecuador, Ministro de lo Interior, *Informe, 1926–1928*, 5; A. Moncayo Andrade to E. W. Kemmerer, Quito, August 2, 1930, KP; Decree (March 19, 1927), Ecuador, *Registro Oficial*, año 1, no. 289, 2533–2551; Decree (March 12, 1927), Ecuador, *Registro Oficial*, año 1, no. 283, 2437–2491; Decree (April 30, 1927), Ecuador, *Registro Oficial*, año 2, no. 323, 2821–2915; Decree (June 10, 1927), Ecuador, *Registro Oficial*, año 2, no. 357, 3200–3393.

31. "Los Trabajos de la Misión Kemmerer," *El Ejército Nacional*, año 6, no. 33 (1927), 133–138; *El Comercio*, no. 7743 (March 8, 1927), no. 7776 (March 31, 1927); no. 7768 (April 2, 1927); no. 7783 (April 17, 1927); E. W. Kemmerer to Harry L. Tompkins, Quito, January 24, 1927, KP; G. A. Bading to secretary of state, Quito, March 31, 1927, NA, 822.51A/48; April 15, 1927, NA, 822.00/708; April 30, 1927, NA, 822.00/710; M. A. Navarro to B. B. Milner, Quito, June 7, 1927, KP; Walter Gallman to secretary of state, Quito, July 31, 1927, NA, 822.00/720.

32. Ecuador, Commission of Financial Advisers, "Project of a Monetary Law," February 11, 1927, KP; Ecuador, Commission of Financial Advisers, "Report in Support of a Monetary Law," February 4, 1927, KP; Decree (March 19, 1927), Ecuador, *Registro Oficial*, año 1, no. 289, 2533–2551; Ecuador, Commission of Financial Advisers, "Report in Support of the Project for the Creation of the Central Bank of Ecuador," KP; Ecuador, Commission of Financial Advisers, "Project of Law for the Creation of the Central Bank of Ecuador," 1927, typed copy in the Library of the Banco Central del Ecuador; Decree (March 12, 1927), Ecuador, *Registro Oficial*, año 1, no. 283, 2437–2491; Ecuador, Misión de Consejeros Financieros, "Suplemento a la exposición de motivos de la Ley de Monedas," March 3, 1927, KP.

33. E. B. Schwulst to E. W. Kemmerer, Quito, September 9, 1927; September 20, 1927, KP; G. A. Bading to secretary of state, Quito, January 30, 1928, NA, 822.51A/63; April 15, 1927, NA, 822.00/708; May 15, 1927, NA, 822.00/711; *El Comercio*, no. 7766 (March 31, 1927); no. 7775 (April 9, 1927); no. 7805 (May 9, 1927); no. 7807 (May 11, 1927); no. 7809 (May 13, 1927); Harold D. Clum to secretary of state, Guayaquil, May 14, 1927, NA, R.G. 84.

34. E. B. Schwulst to E. W. Kemmerer, Quito, September 20, 1927, KP; G. A. Bading to secretary of state, Quito, January 30, 1928, NA, 822.51A.63; June 30, 1927, NA, 822.00/717; July 15, 1927, NA, 822.00/718; Harold D. Clum to secretary of state, Guayaquil, June 10, 1927, NA, R.G. 84: September 12, 1927, NA, R.G. 84; Walter Gallman to secretary of state, Quito, July 31, 1927, NA, 822.00/720; August 15, 1927, NA, 822.00/721; August 30, 1927, NA, 822.00/722.

35. E. B. Schwulst to E. W. Kemmerer, Quito, September 20, 1927; September 29, 1927, KP; Walter Gallman to secretary of state, Quito, September 30, 1927, NA, 822.00/735.

36. E. W. Schwulst to E. W. Kemmerer, Quito, September 29, 1927, KP; *El Comercio*, no. 8010 (November 30, 1927); G. A. Bading to E. B. Schwulst, Quito, January 28, 1928, NA, 822.51A/63; E. B. Schwulst to G. A. Bading, Quito, November 15, 1927, NA, 822.00/743; November 30, 1927, NA, 822.00/745; January 30, 1928, NA, 822.51A/63; W. Allen Rhode to secretary of state, Guayaquil, December 14, 1927, NA, R.G. 84; January 14, 1928, NA, R.G. 84; March 14, 1928, NA, R.G. 84; G. A. Bading to secretary of state, Quito, February 2, 1928, NA, 822.51A/64; February 14, 1928, NA, 822.51A/65; Harold D. Clum to secretary of state, Guayaquil, February 10, 1928, NA, R.G. 84; *El Día*, (February 10–12, 1928); *El Telégrafo*, no. 15348 (February 16, 1928); W. Allen Rhode to secretary of state, Guayaquil, August 16, 1928, NA, R.G. 84.

37. Ecuador, Commission of Financial Advisers, "Report in Support of a General Banking Law," February 25, 1927, KP; Ecuador, Commission of Financial Advisers, "Project of a General Banking Law," February 25, 1927, KP; Ecuador, Economic Conferences, "Report on the Committee on the Establishment of a Superintendency of Banks," March 7, 1926, KP.

38. W. J. Gallman to secretary of state, Quito, August 11, 1927, NA, 822.516/73; August 15, 1927, NA, 822.00/721; August 15, 1927, NA, 822.00//21; *El Comercio*, no. 7997 (November 17, 1927); no. 7999 (November 19, 1927); E. B. Schwulst to E. W. Kemmerer, Quito, September 9, 1927, KP; September 29, 1928, KP; G. A. Bading to secretary of state, Quito, January 30, 1928, NA, 822.51A/63; February 14, 1928, NA, 822.51A/65; Harold D. Clum to secretary of state, Guayaquil, September 12, 1927, NA, R.G. 84; February 10, 1928, NA, R.G. 84; *El Telégrafo*, no. 15348 (February 16, 1928).

39. G. A. Bading to secretary of state, Quito, October 30, 1928, NA, 822.51A/66; November 15, 1928, NA, 822.51A/67; W. Allen Rhode to secretary of state, Guayaquil, November 15, 1928, NA, R.G. 84; February 15, 1929, NA, R.G. 84; January 16, 1929, NA, R.G. 84; February 13, 1929, NA. R.G. 84; *El Telégrafo*, no. 15829 (June 9, 1929); R. M. Kohan to Foreign Office, Quito, January 18, 1930, FO 371/14224, A2502/2502/54; W. J. Gallman to secretary of state, Quito, June 13, 1928, NA, 822.516/110; May 22, 1929, NA, 822.51A/73; October 18, 1930, NA, 822.51A/102; William Dawson to secretary of state,

Quito, September 12, 1930, NA, 822.51A/102; May 8, 1931, NA, 822.51A/112; June 11, 1932, NA, 822.51A/121; August 1, 1932, NA, 822.51A/123; Dayle C. McDonough to secretary of state, Guayaquil, April 27, 1937, NA, 822.51A-Tompkins, H.L./13; March 12, 1937, NA, 822.51A-Tompkins, H.L./18; Herbert C. Hengstler to secretary of state, Quito, February 17, 1933, NA, 822.51A/133.

40. Ecuador, Commission of Financial Advisers, "Project of a Law for the Reorganization of the Government Accounting and Auditing, and the Creation of an Office of Accounting and Fiscal Control Known as the Contraloría," March 8, 1927, KP; Ecuador, Commission of Financial Advisers, "Report in Support of a Project of Law for the Reorganization of Government Accounting and Auditing, and the Creation of an Office of Accounting and Fiscal Control Known as the Contraloría," Quito, March 8, 1927, KP; *El Comercio*, no. 7743 (March 8, 1927); James H. Edwards to E. W. Kemmerer, Quito, June 10, 1927, KP; G. A. Bading to secretary of state, Quito, June 29, 1927, NA, 822.51A/54; E. W. Kemmerer to James H. Edwards, La Paz, July 8, 1927, KP; W. J. Gallman to secretary of state, Quito, August 15, 1927, NA, 822.00/721; September 15, 1927, NA, 822.00/725; September 30, 1927, NA, 822.00/735; October 15, 1927, NA, 822.00/741; W. Allen Rhode to secretary of state, Guayaquil, December 14, 1927, NA, R.G. 84; November 14, 1927, NA, R.G. 84; Harold D. Clum to secretary of state, Guayaquil, March 26–30, 1928, NA, R.G. 84; A. Moncayo Andrade to E. W. Kemmerer, Quito, August 2, 1930, KP; W. Allen Rhode to secretary of state, Guayaquil, December 15, 1928, NA, R.G. 84; Ecuador, Ministro de Hacienda, *Informe, 1930*, 6–8, 35–36; W. Allen Rhode to secretary of state, Guayaquil, February 13, 1929, NA, R.G. 84; G. A. Bading to secretary of state, Quito, May 13, 1929, NA, 822.51A/75; *El Telégrafo*, no. 15762 (April 3, 1929); Harold D. Clum to secretary of state, Guayaquil, October 19, 1929, NA, R.G. 84; Ecuador, Ministerio de Hacienda, *Boletín*, no. 1 (June 1928), 18–28.

41. Ecuador, Commission of Foreign Advisers, "Project of a Law for the Revision of the Present Export Duties on Ivory Nuts," December, 1926; "Proposed Decree Governing Customs Documents Originating Abroad," December 1926; "Project of Organic Law of Customs Administration," March 1927; "Report in Support of the Project of Law Governing Customs Administration," March 1927; "Project of a Customs Import Tariff," March 1, 1927; "Memorandum for the Minister of Finance in Reference to a Project of Customs Import Tariff," March 1927; *El Comercio*, no. 7759 (March 24, 1927); no. 7859 (July 21, 1927); no. 7862 (July 4, 1927); no. 7863 (July 5, 1927); Ecuador, Ministerio de Hacienda, *Boletín*, no. 1 (June 1928), 25–26; no. 5 (October 1928), 14–16; *Registro Oficial*, no. 323 (April 30, 1927); no. 367 (June 22, 1927); no. 388 (July 18, 1927); no. 48 (June 1, 1926); no. 357 (June 10, 1927); W. J. Gallman to secretary of state, Quito, August 30, 1927, NA, 822.00/722; September 30, 1927, NA, 822.00/735; *El Telégrafo*, no. 15326 (June 25, 1928); Harold D. Clum to secretary of

state, Guayaquil, March 20–30, NA, R.G. 84; July 13, 1927, NA, R.G. 84; W. Allen Rhode to secretary of state, Guayaquil, June 9, 1929, NA, R.G. 84; July 16, 1929, NA, R.G. 84; Ecuador, Comisión Permanente de Legislación, *Informe, 1925*, 146; R. M. Kohan to Foreign Office, Quito, January 18, 1930, FO 371/14224, A2502/2502.54; *El Telégrafo*, no. 16001 (November 28, 1929); no. 16003 (November 30, 1929); no. 16018 (December 15, 1929); no. 16019 (December 16, 1929); Ecuador, Dirección General de Aduanas, "Informe," February 22, 1930, in Ecuador, Ministro de Hacienda, *Informe, 1930;* W. J. Gallman to secretary of state, Quito, January 4, 1930, NA, 822.51A.88; Harold D. Clum to secretary of state, Guayaquil, February 5, 1930, NA, R.G. 84; G. A. Bading to secretary of state, Quito, January 11, 1928, NA, 822.51/450; W. J. Gallman to secretary of state, Quito, February 26, 1930, NA, 822.51A/91; William Dawson to secretary of state, Quito, September 2, 1930, NA, 822.51A.101; November 26, 1930, NA, 822.51A/103; Sheridan Talbott to secretary of state, Guayaquil, December 5, 1930, NA, 822.51A.105; William Dawson to secretary of state, Quito, December, 18, 1930, NA, 822.51A/106; January 10, 1931, NA, 822.51A/107.

6: The Aftermath of Reform

1. Edwin Kemmerer realized that his reform proposals would have to be modified to meet changing conditions and as implementation brought problems into focus. See Edwin W. Kemmerer, "Economic Advisory Work for Governments," *American Economic Review* 17:1 (1927), 1–12.

2. For a history of the Comptroller's Office see Ecuador, Contraloría General, *Contraloria General de la Nación: 25 años* (Quito: Editorial "La Unión Católica, C.A.," 1952).

3. W. J. Gallman to secretary of state, Quito, November 20, 1929, NA, 822.51/526; W.C. Graham to Foreign Office, Quito, September 3, 1931, FO 371/15091, A6237/306/54; *El Telégrafo*, no. 16780 (January 2, 1932); G. A. Bading to secretary of state, Quito, March 14, 1928, NA, 822.516/89; William Dawson to secretary of state, Quito, March 13, 1928, NA, 822.516/142; June 1, 1931, NA, 822.404/5; November 16, 1931, NA, 822.516/171; January 27, 1932, NA, 822.51/609; Ecuador, Banco Central, *Boletín*, no. 52 (November 1931), 5–10; Ecuador, Ministro de Hacienda, *Informe, July 10, 1931*, 137–178; G. A. Bading to secretary of state, Quito, 822.51/498; December 20, 1927, NA, 822.51/444.

4. Harold D. Clum to secretary of state, Guayaquil, October 27, 1931, NA, R.G. 84; W. C. Graham to Foreign Office, Quito, September 3, 1931, FO 371/15091, A6237/306/54; *El Telégrafo*, no. 16780 (January 2, 1932); W. C.

Graham to Foreign Office, Quito, October 15–16, 1931, FO 371/15091, A6149/306/54; March 2, 1931, FO 371/15091, A2266/132/54.

5. *El Telégrafo* no. 16780, January 2, 1832; A. Moncayo Andrade to E. W. Kemmerer, Quito, March 17, 1934, KP; Harold B. Quarton to secretary of state, Guayaquil, August 18, 1933, NA, R.G. 84; *Registro Oficial*, año 1, no. 138 (March 26, 1929); see particularly article 95 which prevents ministers removed from office by a vote of no confidence from holding office for a two-year period; "Constitución Política de la República del Ecuador de 1928–29" in *Anuario*, vol. 27, pt. 1 (1931), Section III, article 97.

6. W. C. Graham to Foreign Office, Quito, October 31, 1931, FO 371/15091, A6502/306/54; October 24, 1931, FO 371/15091, A6629/306/54; November 15, 1931, FO 371/15091, A7494/306/54; *El Telégrafo*, no. 16780 (January 2, 1932); no. 16781 (January 3, 1932); no. 16785 (January 7, 1932); no. 16787 (January 9, 1932); no. 16788 (January 10, 1932); no. 16810 (February 1, 1932); no. 16812 (February 2, 1932); no. 16813 (February 3, 1932); no. 16814 (February 4, 1932); no. 16817 (February 7, 1932); no. 16819 (February 9, 1932); Decree no. 162 (September 5, 1932), Ecuador, *Registro Oficial*, no. 3 (1932); A. Moncayo Andrade to E. W. Kemmerer, Quito, January 6, 1933, KP; Taylor W. Gannett to secretary of state, Guayaquil, November 25, 1933, NA, R.G. 84; December 14, 1933, NA, R.G. 84; Appendix J.

7. Frank W. Fetter, "Ecuadorian Report," NA, 822.51A/160; United States, Department of Commerce, *Foreign Commerce Yearbook 1938*, 423; Ecuador, Director del Tesoro, *Informe, 1933*, 87–92; E. W. Kemmerer to A. Moncayo Andrade, Princeton, January 18, 1932, KP; Taylor W. Gannett to secretary of state, Guayaquil, March 23, 1924, NA, R.G. 84; April 20, 1934, N:A, R.G. 84.

8. R. M. Kohan to Foreign Office, Quito, October 17, 1929, FO 371/13483, A8591/2807/54; W. C. Graham, "Memorandum for Council of Foreign Bondholders," March 2, 1931, FO 371/15091, A2266/132/54; Ecuador, Ministro de Hacienda, *Informe, 1931*, 48–51.

9. Great Britain, Department of Overseas Trade, *Report on the Economic and Commercial Conditions in Ecuador, 1932*, 13–15; *1934*, 13–22; *1936*, 3–16; *1938*, 2–23; Ecuador, Ministro de Hacienda, *Informe 1931–1932*, xcviii–cxviii. For the laws on exchange, tariff modifications, and trade agreements see Ecuador, *Anuario, 1930–1934* and Ecuador, *Registro Oficial, 1931–1940*. A. Moncayo Andrade to E. W. Kemmerer, Quito, December 12, 1934, KP; Ecuador, Ministerio del Tesoro, *Boletín*, no. 25–28 (1951), vii–xx.

10. Taylor W. Gannett to secretary of state, Guayaquil, NA, R.G. 84; Harold D. Clum to secretary of state, Guayaquil, October 20, 1933, NA, R.G. 84. A few local industries did benefit from import substitution, for example, textiles, lard, and flour, but the Ecuadorian market was too small to efficiently support large-scale industrialization. Also, trade barriers restricted the possibilities

for external sales. On this see Harold D. Clum to secretary of state, Guayaquil, June 6, 1934, NA, R.G. 84.

11. José Alfredo Llerena, *Frustración politica en veintidos años* (Quito: Casa de la Cultura Ecuatoriana, 1959), discusses the political turmoil during these years. Carbo, *Historia monetaria*, 169–252, examines the economic policy changes during this period. See also Great Britain, Department of Overseas Trade, *Report on the Economic and Commercial Conditions in Ecuador 1936*, 3; *1938*, 28–29; Taylor W. Gannett to secretary of state, Guayaquil, August 20, 1932, NA, R.G. 84; Harold D. Clum to secretary of state, Guayaquil, January 27, 1933, NA, R.G. 84.

12. Ecuador, Banco Central, *Boletín*, año 12, no. 137–138 (December 1938–January 1939), n.p.; William Dawson to secretary of state, Quito, January 27, 1932, NA, 822.51/609; A. Moncayo Andrade to E. W. Kemmerer, Quito, August 2, 1930, KP; Harold D. Clum to secretary of state, Guayaquil, April 15, 1931, NA, R.G. 84; May 3, 1931, NA, R.G. 84; January 27, 1933, NA, R.G. 84; Ecuador, Banco Central, *Boletín*, no. 47 (June, 1931), 5–10.

13. *El Telégrafo* (May 4, 1930); no. 16780 (January 2, 1932); no. 16805 (January 27, 1932); A. Moncayo Andrade to E. W. Kemmerer, Quito, August 2, 1930; January 2, 1931, KP; Ecuador, Ministro de Hacienda, *Informe, 1930*, 66; Enrique Cueva to E. W. Kemmerer, Guayaquil, February 6, 1931, KP; William Dawson to secretary of state, Quito, March 18, 1931, NA, 822.51G/143.

14. Harold D. Clum to secretary of state, Guayaquil, January 20, 1932, NA, R.G. 84; *El Telégrafo*, no. 16791 (January 13, 1932); no. 16805 (January 27, 1932); no. 16819 (February 9, 1932); Decree, February 7, 1933, Ecuador, *Registro Oficial*, 67; William Dawson to secretary of state, Quito, January 20, 1932, NA, 822.51/614; *El Telégrafo*, no. 16821 (February 11, 1932); no. 16834 (February 24, 1932); no. 16835 (February 25, 1932); no. 16841 (March 2, 1932); no. 16844 (March 5, 1932); no. 16851 (March 12, 1932); Enrique Cueva to E. W. Kemmerer, Quito, April 15, 1932, KP.

15. Ecuador, Banco Central, *Boletín*, año 11, no. 122 (September, 1937), 5–13; E. Carbo to E. W. Kemmerer, Ambato, May 22, 1933, KP; E. Carbo to E. W. Kemmerer, Guayaquil, November 24, 1934, KP; Ecuador, Banco Central, *Boletín*, año 13, no. 150–151 (January-February 1940), 20–27.

16. M. Gómez Morín, "Esposición al Sr. Ministro de Hacienda, sobre sus labores en el Ecuador," Ecuador, Banco Central, *Boletín*, año 11, no. 125 (December 1937), 10–23; Ecuador, Comisión Financiera, "Exposición de motivos para la Ley del Banco Central del Ecuador," Ecuador, Banco Central, *Boletín*, año 11, no. 125 (December 1937), 28–59; Decree, no. 120–121 (December 30, 1937), Ecuador, Banco Central, *Boletín*, año 11, no. 125 (December 1937), 72–115; Ecuador, Ministro de Hacienda, "Exposición que hace el gobierno a la Nación respecto a las nuevas Leyes de Banco Central y de Monedas," Ecuador, Banco Central, *Boletín*, año 11, no. 125 (December 1937), 3–9; Antonio Manero,

"Projecto de Reorganización Bancaria," Ecuador, Banco Central, *Boletín*, año 14, no. 166 (May 1941), 14–25.

Conclusion

1. Albert O. Hirschman discusses economic policy making in Colombia, Chile, and Brazil in the context of what he has called "reformmongering," a concept that has applicability in Ecuador. *Journeys Toward Progress: Studies of Economic Policy-Making in Latin America* (New York: The Twentieth Century Fund, 1963). John D. Martz has an excellent discussion of Ecuador since 1950 that demonstrates the difficulty of reform and the continuity of traditional patterns. *Ecuador: Conflicting Political Cultures and the Quest for Progress* (Boston: Allyn and Bacon, Inc., 1972).

Bibliography

I. Manuscript Collections

Ecuador

Archivo Nacional de Historia (Quito)
    Fondo del Ministerio de Finanzas
Biblioteca del Banco Central (Quito)
    Misión de Consejeros Financieros

Great Britain

Public Record Office (London)
    Foreign Office Papers: FO 371

United States

National Archives (Washington, D.C.)
    Department of State: Record Group 59
    Department of State: Record Group 84
Princeton University (Princeton)
    Harvey S. Firestone Memorial Library: Edwin W. Kemmerer Papers
    Seely G. Mudd Manuscript Library: Edwin W. Kemmerer Papers
Luis A. Rodríguez S. Papers in the possession of Jaime E. Rodríguez (Los Angeles)

II. Other Sources

El Abanderado (Quito), 1924–1925.
Acosta Solís, Misael. *Los Recursos naturales del Ecuador y su conservación.* 3 parts. México: Instituto Panamericano de Geografía e Historia, 1965.

American University. Foreign Area Studies. *Area Handbook for Ecuador.* Washington, D.C.: Government Printing Office, 1967, 1973.

Anderson, Charles W. *Politics and Economic Change in Latin America.* Princeton: D. Van Nostrand Company, Inc., 1967.

Los Andes (Riobamba), 1926–1927.

Andrade, Roberto. *¿Sangre. Quién la derramo? Historia de los últimos crimenes cometidos en la nación del Ecuador.* Quito: Imprenta Antigua de El Quiteño Libre, 1912.

Banco del Ecuador. *Historia de medio siglo 1868–1918.* Guayaquil: Imprenta de El Independiente, 1919.

Beals, Ralph L. *Community in Transition: Nayon-Ecuador.* Los Angeles: UCLA Latin American Center Publications, University of California, 1966.

Benites, Leopoldo. *Ecuador: drama y paradoja.* Mexico: Fondo de Cultura Económica, 1950.

Borja y Borja, Ramiro. *Derecho constitucional ecuatoriano.* 3 vols. Madrid: Ediciones Cultura Hispánica, 1950.

Bromley, Rosemary D. F. "The Demographic Background to Urban Growth and Decline in the Central Sierra of Ecuador 1780–1900." Paper read at the Annual Conference of the Society for Latin American Studies, Leeds, March 1973.

Bromley, Rosemary D. F., and R. J. Bromley, "The Debate on Sunday Markets in Nineteenth Century Ecuador." *Journal of Latin American Studies* 7:1 (1975).

Burgos-Guevara, Hugo. "El Guamán, el puma y el amarú: Structural Development of the Native Government in Ecuador." Ph.D. dissertation, University of Illinois, 1975.

Bushnell, David. *The Santander Regime in Gran Colombia.* Newark: University of Delaware Press, 1954.

Bustos-Videla, César. "Church and State in Ecuador: A History of Politico-Ecclesiastical Relations During the Age of Gabriel García Moreno, 1860–1875." Ph.D. dissertation, Georgetown University, 1966.

El Cachuero (Guayaquil), 1922.

Carbo, Luis Alberto. *Historia monetaria y cambiaria del Ecuador.* Quito: Imprenta del Banco Central del Ecuador, 1953.

Carbo, L. F. *El Ecuador en Chicago.* New York: Imprenta de A. E. Chasmar y Cía., 1894.

Castillo Jacome, Julio. *La Provincia del Chimborazo en 1942.* Riobamba: Talleres Gráficos de la Editorial "Progreso," n.d.

Cevallos, Pedro Fermín. *Geografía de la República del Ecuador*. Lima: Imprenta del Estado, 1888.

Cevallos García, Gabriel. "Las ideas liberales en el Ecuador: breve esquema para su historia," *Revista de historia de las ideas* 2 (1960).

Church, George Earl. *Ecuador in 1881*. Washington, D.C.: Government Printing Office, 1883.

Compañía Guía del Ecuador. *El Ecuador: guía comercial, agrícola e industrial de la República*. Guayaquil: Talleres de Artes Gráficas de E. Rodenas, 1909.

De la Cuadra, José. *Obras completas*. Quito: Casa de la Cultura Ecuatoriana, 1958.

De la Torre Reyes, Carlos. *La Revolución de Quito del 10 de agosto de 1809*. Quito: Ministerio de Educación, 1962.

Deutsch, Karl W. *Nationalism and Social Communication: An Inquiry into the Foundations of Nationality*. New York: The Technology Press of M.I.T., 1953.

Deutsch, Karl and William J. Foltz, eds. *Nation Building*. New York: Atherton Press, 1966.

El Día (Quito), 1924–1926.

Dickinson, Robert E. *City, Region and Regionalism: A Geographical Contribution to Human Ecology*. London: Routledge and Kegan Paul Ltd., 1960.

Dillon, Luis N. *La Crisis económico-financiera del Ecuador*. Quito: Editorial Artes Gráficas, 1927.

Di Tella, Torcuato S. "The Dangerous Classes in Nineteenth Century Mexico." *Journal of Latin American Studies* 5 (1973).

Duerr, Michael G. *Impact of Commodity Shortages: A World Survey*. New York: Conference Board, 1975.

Dulles, Eleanor Lansing. *The Dollar, the Franc and Inflation*. New York: The Macmillan Company, 1933.

Ecuador. Archivo del Poder Legislativo. *Anuario de legislación ecuatoriana: leyes, decretos, acuerdos y resoluciones del congreso*. Quito: Imprenta y Encuadernación Nacionales, 1896–1924.

——. Asamblea nacional. *Registro Oficial*. Quito: Imprenta Nacional, 1927–1940.

——. Banco Central. *Boletín*. Quito: Imprenta del Banco Central, 1927–1945.

——. Comisión Coordinadora y Supervisora del Censo Agropecuario Nacional. *Primer censo agropecuario nacional, 1954*. Quito: Talleres Gráficos de la Dirección General de Estadística y Censos, Ministerio de Economía, 1956.

———. Comisión Permanente de Legislación. *Informe.* Quito: Talleres Tipográficos del Ministerio de Hacienda, 1922, 1925.

———. Consejo de Estado. *Informe.* Quito: n.p., 1924.

———. Contaduría Mayor del Distrito del Guayas. "Informe 1853," Ecuador, Ministro de Hacienda. *Memoria 1853.* Quito: Imprenta del Gobierno, 1853.

———. Contraloría General. *Contraloría General de la Nación: 25 años.* Quito: Editorial "La Unión Católica, C.A.," 1952.

———. *Informe.* Quito: Talleres Tipográficos del Ministerio de Hacienda, 1938–1939.

———. Departamento Central de Estadística. *Estadística comercial de aduana, 1913–1915.* Quito: n.p., n.d.

———. *Diario Oficial,* 1894.

———. Dirección Jeneral del Crédito Público. "Informe 1857," Ecuador, Ministro de Hacienda. *Informe 1857.* Quito: Imprenta de V. Valencia, 1857.

———. Dirección General de Aduanas. "Informe 1930," Ecuador, Ministro de Hacienda. *Informe 1930.* Quito: Talleres Tipográficos del Ministerio de Hacienda, 1930.

———. Dirección General de Estadística. *Comercio exterior de la República del Ecuador en la decada 1916 a 1925.* Quito: Talleres Tipográficos Nacionales, 1927.

———. Dirección General de Obras Públicas. *Informe 1926–1930.*

———. Dirección de Ingresos. *Informe al señor Ministro de Hacienda.* Quito: Talleres Tipográficos del Ministerio de Hacienda, 1939.

———. Dirección Nacional de Estadística. *Ecuador en cifras, 1938–1942.* Quito: Imprenta del Ministerio de Hacienda, 1944.

———. Director del Tesoro. *Informe 1930–1933.*

———. Director General de Obras Públicas. "Informe June 30, 1908." Ecuador, Ministro de lo Interior. *Informe 1908.*

———. Gobernador de Imbabura. "Informe June 11, 1913." Ecuador, Ministro de Hacienda, *Informe 1913.*

———. Gobernador de la Provincia de Esmeraldas. "Informe April 11, 1984." Ecuador, Ministro de Hacienda, *Informe 1894.*

———. Gobernador de la Provincia del Guayas. "Informe." Ecuador, Ministro de Hacienda, *Informe 1894.*

———. Gobernador de la Provincia de León. "Informe April 18, 1894." Ecuador, Ministro de Hacienda, *Informe 1896–1897.*

———. Gobernador de la Provincia de Pichincha. "Informe April 27, 1984." Ecuador, Ministro de Hacienda, *Informe 1894.*

———. Gobernador de Tunguragua. "Informe, June 7, 1901." Ecuador, Ministro de Hacienda, *Informe 1901.*

———. Gobierno Provisorio. Secretario Jeneral, Sección de Hacienda. *Informe 1861.*

———. Jeneral Jefe del Estado Mayor. *Memoria 1833.*

———. Ministerio de Hacienda. *Balance general y sus anexos 1919–1920, 1920, 1922–1925.*

———. *Boletín 1929–1933* (monthly).

———. *Boletín de estadística fiscal y comercial 1910–1914* (yearly or irregularly).

———. *Codificación de los decretos ejecutivos sobre incautación de giros, 31 agosto de 1923.* Quito: Talleres Tipográficos de la Sección de Especies, 1923.

———. *Demostración de los servicios a que están destinadas las rentas del Estado por disposiciones de leyes y decretos especiales, y sobrante que daría para afrontar los gastos que demanda el sostenimientos en la Administración Pública, según las recaudaciones efectuadas en 1916.* Quito: Imprenta y Encuadernación Nacionales, 1917.

———. *Las Instituciones de crédito del Ecuador en 1925: Banco Comercial y Agrícola (Guayaquil).* Quito: Talleres Tipográficos del Ministerio de Hacienda, 1926.

———. Ministro de Estado. *Memoria 1831, 1841* (yearly; title varies).

———. Ministro de Guerra y Marina. *Informe 1913–1919* (yearly; title varies).

———. Ministro de Hacienda. *Informe 1833–1940* (yearly; title varies).

———. Ministro de lo Interior. *Informe 1833–1916* (yearly; title varies).

———. Ministro de Instrucción Pública. *Informe. 1894–1928* (yearly; title varies).

———. Ministro de Obras Públicas. *Informe 1904–1906* (yearly).

———. Ministro del Tesoro. *Informe 1933–1946* (yearly).

El Ejército Nacional 1925–1927. (Quito).

Eraso, Abraham. *La Provincia de Bolívar en 1934.* Quito: n.p., n.d.

Estrada, Victor Emilio. *Ensayo sobre la balanza económica del Ecuador.* Guayaquil: Tipografía y Papelería de Julio T. Foyain, 1922.

———. *El Momento económico en el Ecuador.* Guayaquil: Litografía e Imprenta la Reforma Jacinto Jouvin Arce e Hijos, 1950.

Estrada Ycaza, Julio. *Los Bancos del siglo XIX.* Guayaquil: Publicaciones del Archivo Histórico del Guayas, 1976.

———. *Regionalismo y migración.* Guayaquil: Publicaciones del Archivo Histórico del Guayas, 1977.

Estrada Ycaza, Julio. Entrevistas Oral. See Linda Alexander Rodríguez and Jaime E. Rodríguez.

Estrella de Panamá (Panama), 1872.

Filsinger, Ernst B. *Commercial Travelers' Guide to Latin America.* Washington, D.C.: Government Printing Office, 1920.

Franco, Gustavo, and Palemón Custode. "Historia del régimen cambiario en el Ecuador." *Economia Ecuatoriana.* Mexico: Instituto Panamericano de Geografía e Historia, 1960.

Friedrich, Carl J. *Tradition and Authority.* New York: Praeger Publishers, 1972.

Fromm, Gary. "Design of the Transport Sector," in Gary Fromm, ed. *Transport Investment and Economic Development.* Washington, D.C.: The Brookings Institution, 1965, 89–107.

Gallegos Lara, Joaquín. *Cruses sobre el agua.* Guayaquil: Ediciones de la Casa de la Cultura Ecuatoriana, 1946.

Garces, Enrique. *Daquilema Rex.* Quito: Casa de la Cultura Ecuatoriana, 1961.

Gibson, Charles R. *Foreign Trade in the Economic Development of Small Nations: The Case of Ecuador.* New York: Praeger Publishers, 1971.

Glen, N. D., and J. L. Simmons, "Are Regional Cultural Differences Diminishing?" *Public Opinion Quarterly* 31 (Summer 1967): 176–193.

Graham, Richard, and Peter Smith, eds. *New Approaches to Latin American History.* Austin: University of Texas Press, 1974.

Great Britain. Department of Overseas Trade. *Report on Economic and Commercial Conditions in Ecuador 1920–1938.* London: His Majesty's Stationery Office, 1920–1938 (biyearly; title varies).

El Grito del Pueblo Ecuatoriano (Guayaquil), 1922.

El Guante (Guayaquil), 1923–1929.

Guarderas, Francisco. *El Viejo de Montecriste.* Puebla: Editorial Cajica, 1965.

Guevara, Dario. *Rocafuerte y la instrucción pública.* Quito: Casa de la Cultura Ecuatoriana, 1965.

Hale, Charles. *Mexican Liberalism in the Age of Mora.* New Haven and London: Yale University Press, 1968.

Halpering-Donghi, Tulio. *The Aftermath of Revolution in Latin America.* New York: Harper and Row, 1973.

El Hambriento (Guayaquil), 1922.

Hamerly, Michael T. *Historia social y económica de la antigua provincia de Guayaquil 1763–1842.* Guayaquil: Archivo Histórico del Guayas, 1973.

Hassaurek, Friedrich. *Four Years Among Spanish Americans.* Cincinnati: Robert Clarke and Company, 1881.

Healy, K. T. "General Social, Political and Economic Factors in Relations to Transport for Less Developed Areas." In United Nations Conference on the Application of Science and Technology for the Benefit of the Less Developed Areas. *Science, Technology, and Development.* 12 vols. Washington, D.C.: U.S. Government Printing Office, 1963, V, 1–4.

Heflebower, Richard B. "Characteristics of Transport Modes." In Gary Fromm, ed. *Transport Investment and Economic Development.* Washington, D.C.: The Brookings Institution, 1965, 34–68.

Heymann, Hans Jr., "The Objectives of Transport." In Gary Fromm, ed. *Transport Investment and Economic Development.* Washington, D.C.: The Brookings Institution, 1965, 18–33.

Hirschman, Albert O. *Journey Toward Progress: Studies of Economic Policy-Making in Latin America.* New York: The Twentieth Century Fund, 1963.

———. *The Strategy of Economic Development.* New Haven: Yale University Press, 1958.

Hofmeier, Rolf. *Transportation and Economic Development in Tanzania.* Munich: Weltforum Verlag, 1973.

Hoyle, B. S., ed. *Transport and Development.* London: MacMillan Press, 1973.

Hunter, H. "Transport in Soviet and Chinese Development." *Economic Development and Cultural Change* 14 (1965): 71–84.

Hurtado, Osvaldo. *Political Power in Ecuador.* Albuquerque: University of New Mexico Press, 1980.

James, Clarence F. "Agricultural Regions of South America." *Economic Geography.* 6:1 (January 1930): 30–36.

James, Preston E. *Latin America.* 3d ed. New York: The Odyssey Press, 1960.

Jaramillo Alvarado, Pío. *Historia de Loja y su provincia.* Quito: Casa de la Cultura Ecuatoriana, 1955.

Jijón y Caamaño, *Política conservadora.* 2 vols. Riobamba: La Buena Prensa del Chimborazo, 1929.

Katzman, Martin T. "Ethnic Geography and Regional Economics, 1880–1960." *Economic Geography* 45:1 (January 1969): 43–53.

Kemmerer, Edwin W. "Economic Advisory Work for Governments."

American Economic Review 17:1 (1927).

―――. *Kemmerer on Money.* Chicago: John Winston Company, 1934.

―――. *Modern Currency Reform.* New York: The MacMillan Co., 1916.

King, William M. "Ecuadorian Church and State Relations under García Moreno, 1859–1863." Ph.D. dissertation, University of Texas, Austin, 1974.

Kraft, Gerald, John R. Meyer, and Jean-Paul Valetti, *The Role of Transportation in Regional Economic Development.* Lexington: D.C. Heath and Company, 1971.

Lansing, John B. *Transportation and Economic Policy.* New York: The Free Press, 1966.

Laso, Luis Eduardo. "Contribución al estudio de la economía política ecuatoriana." *Revista jurídica y de ciencias sociales* 4 (1930): 1–82.

Larrea Alba, Luis. *La Compaña de 1906.* Quito: Cima, 1962.

League of Nations. *Memorandum sur les Monnales et les Banques Centrales 1913–1924,* 2 vols. Geneva, 1925.

Llerena, José A. *Frustración política en veintidos años.* Quito: Casa de la Cultura Ecuatoriana, 1959.

Loor, Wilfredo. *Manabí.* Quito: Editorial Ecuatoriana, 1969.

Love, Joseph L., "An Approach to Regionalism," in Richard Graham and Peter Smith, eds. *New Approaches to Latin American History.* Austin: University of Texas Press, 1974.

Maier, Georg. "Impact of Velasquismo on the Ecuadorian Political System." Ph.D. dissertation, University of Southern Illinois, 1965.

―――. "Presidential Succession in Ecuador, 1830–1970." *Journal of Inter-American Studies and World Affairs* 13:3–4 (July-October 1971): 475–509.

Martz, John D. *Ecuador: Conflicting Political Culture and the Quest for Progress.* Boston: Allyn and Bacon, Inc., 1972.

Mills, Nick Dean, Jr. "Liberal Opposition in Ecuadorian Politics: 1830–1845." Ph.D. dissertation, University of New Mexico, 1972.

Miranda Ribadeneira, Francisco. *La Primera escuela politécnica del Ecuador.* Quito: Editorial "La Unión," 1972.

Moncayo Andrade, A. *Memorandum para servir a los estudios de la comisión permanente de legislación.* Quito: Imprenta Nacional, 1923.

Mora Bowen, Alfonso. *El Liberalismo radical y su trayectoria histórica.* Quito: Imprenta Romero, 1940.

Morales y Eloy, Juan. *Ecuador: Atlas histórico-geográfico.* Quito: Ministerio de Relaciones Exteriores, 1942.

Moreno, Segundo Luis. *La Campaña de Esmeraldas de 1913–1916 en-*

cabezada por el Coronel Graduado Don Carlos Concha Torres. Cuenca: Tipográfica Universidad, 1939.

Murgueytio, Reinaldo. *Bosquejo histórico de la escuela laica ecuatoriana.* Quito: Casa de la Cultura Ecuatoriana, 1972.

Noboa, Alejandro. *Recopilación de mensajes dirijidos por los Presidentes y Vicepresidentes de la República, jefes Supremos y Gobiernos Provisorios a las convenciones y congresos nacionales desde el año de 1819 hasta nuestros dias.* 5 vols. Guayaquil: Imprenta de A. Noboa and Imprenta de El Tiempo,1900–1910.

Noboa, Aurelio. *Colección de leyes.* Guayaquil: Imprenta de A. Noboa, 1901.

El Nacional (Quito), 1866, 1886.

Navarro Andrade, Ulpiano. *Geografía económica del Ecuador.* 2 vols. Quito: Editorial Santo Domingo, 1965–1966.

Niles, Blair. *Casual Wanderings in Ecuador.* New York: The Century Company, 1923.

Norris, Robert E. "José María Velasco Ibarra: A Charismatic Figure in Ecuadorean Politics, 1934–1961." Ph.D. dissertation, University of New Mexico, 1969.

Orellana, J. Gonzalo. *Guía geográfica comercial.* 2 vols. Quito: Tipografía de la Escuela de Artes y Oficios, 1928.

———. *Resumen histórico del Ecuador 1830–1930, 1947.* Quito: Editorial "Fr. Jodoco Ricke," 1948.

Organization for Economic Co-operation and Development. *The Regional Factor in Economic Development: Policies in Fifteen Industrialized Countries.* Paris: O.E.C.D. Publications, 1970.

Owen, Wilfred. "Transport Technology and Economic Development." United Nations Conference on the Application of Science and Technology for the Benefit of the Less Developed Areas. *Science Technology and Development.* 12 vols. Washington, D.C.: U.S. Government Printing Office, 1963.

Palyi, Melchior. *The Twilight of Gold 1914–1936.* Chicago: Henry Regnery Company, 1972.

Pareja Diescanseco, Alfredo. *Los Nuevos años: la advertencia.* Buenos Aires: Editorial Losada, S.A., 1956.

Parsons, James J. "Bananas in Ecuador: A New Chapter in the History of Tropical Agriculture." *Economic Geography* 33:3 (July 1957): 201–216.

Pattee, Richard. *Gabriel García Moreno y el Ecuador de su tiempo.* Mexico: Editorial Jus, 1944.

Paz y Mino, Luis T. *La Población del Ecuador*. Quito: Talleres Gráficos Nacionales, 1936.

Peñaherrera G., A. *Informe de la Dirección General de Estadística, Registro Civil y Censo*. Quito: Tipografía Fernandez, 1934.

Peñaherrera de Costales, Piedad, and Alfredo Costales Samaniego, "Historia social del Ecuador." 3 vols. *Llacta* 17–19 (1964).

Pérez Concha, Jorge. *Ensayo histórico-crítico de las relaciones diplomáticas del Ecuador con los estados limítrofes*. 3 vols. Quito and Guayaquil: Editorial Casa de la Cultura Ecuatoriana, 1958–1965.

Pike, Frederick B. *The United States and the Andean Republics: Peru, Bolivia, and Ecuador*. Cambridge: Harvard University Press, 1977.

La Prensa (Quito), 1925.

Primer registro auténtico nacional (Quito), 1839.

El Porvenir (Guayaquil), 1922.

Pye, Lucian W., ed. *Communication and Development*. Princeton: Princeton University Press. 1963.

Pyne, Peter. "The Politics of Instability in Ecuador: The Overthrow of the President, 1961," *Journal of Latin American Studies* 7:1 (May 1975): 109–133.

Quintana M., Manuel E. *Los Ríos*. Guayaquil: Casa de la Cultura Ecuatoriana, 1957.

Quintero, Rafael, *El Mito del populismo en el Ecuador: análisis de los fundamentos socio-económicos del surgimiento del "Velasquismo," 1895–1934*. Quito: FLASCO, 1980.

Reyes, Oscar Efren. *Breve historia general del Ecuador*. 2 vols. Quito: Editorial "Fray Jodoco Ricke," 1955.

Ringrose, David. *Transportation and Economic Stagnation in Spain 1750–1850*. Durham: Duke University Press, 1970.

Robalino Dávila, Luis. *Orígenes del Ecuador de hoy*. 7 vols. Puebla: Editorial Cajica, 1967–1970.

Rodríguez, Linda Alexander. "The Dilemma of Ecuador's Development," Los Angeles, 1975.

———. "The Liberal Crisis and the Revolution of 1925 in Ecuador." Master's thesis, University of Texas, Austin, 1972.

Rodríguez, Linda Alexander, and Jaime E. Rodríguez O. Entrevistas Orales con Julio Estrada Ycaza. Guayaquil, 1975.

———. Entrevistas Orales con Leonardo Muñoz. Quito, 1975.

———. Entrevistas Orales con Luis A. Rodríguez, S., Quito, 1972, 1975.

Rodríguez O., Jaime E. *Estudios sobre Vicente Rocafuerte*. Guayaquil: Archivo Histórico del Guayas, 1975.

Rodríguez S., Luis A. "Mis recuerdos," Quito: 1970.

Rostow, W. W. *The Stages of Economic Growth.* Cambridge: Cambridge University Press, 1962.

Rout, Leslie, Jr. *The African Experience in Spanish America.* Cambridge: Cambridge University Press, 1976.

Ruddle, Kenneth, and Philip Gillette, *Latin American Political Statistics.* Los Angeles: UCLA Latin American Center Publications, 1972.

Safford, Frank. "Bases of Political Alignment in Early Republican Spanish America." In Richard Graham and Peter Smith, eds. *New Approaches to Latin America History.* Austin: University of Texas Press, 1974.

Salomon, Frank. "The Ethnic Lords of Quito in the Age of the Incas: the Political Economy of the North-Andean Chiefdoms." Ph.D. dissertation, Cornell University, 1978.

Saunders, John V. D. *The People of Ecuador: A Demographic Analysis.* Gainesville: University of Florida Press, 1961.

Schramn, William. *Mass Media and National Development: The Role of Information in Developing Countries.* Stanford: Stanford University Press, 1964.

Scott, Robert E. "Nation-Building in Latin America." In Karl W. Deutsch and William J. Foltz, eds. *Nation Building.* New York: Atherton Press, 1966, 73–82.

Sedillot, Rene. *Histoire du Franc.* Paris: Recueil Sirey, 1939.

Seidel, Robert N. "American Reformers Abroad: The Kemmerer Missions in South America, 1923–1931." *Journal of Economic History* 32:2 (June 1972): 520–545.

Smith, Peter. "The Image of a Dictator: Gabriel García Moreno." *Hispanic American Historical Review* 45:1 (February 1965): 1–24.

Stokes, Charles J. *Transportation and Economic Development in Latin America.* New York: Praeger, 1968.

Strayer, Joseph R. "The Historical Experience of Nation-Building in Europe." In Karl W. Deutsch and William J. Foltz, eds. *Nation Building.* New York: Atherton Press, 1966, 17–26.

El Telégrafo (Guayaquil), 1922–1940.

Terán, Emilio M. *Informe al Jefe Supremo General Eloy Alfaro sobre la deuda anglo-ecuatoriana.* Quito: Imprenta Nacional, 1896.

Terán, Francisco. *Geografía del Ecuador.* Quito: Imprenta del Ministerio de Educación, 1952.

Tobar Donoso, Julio. *García Moreno y la instrucción pública.* Quito: Editorial Ecuatoriana, 1940.

———. *Monografías históricas.* Quito: Editorial Ecuatoriana, 1937.

Troncoso, Julio C. *Odio y Sangre*. Quito: Editorial "Fray Jodoco Ricke," 1958.

Tyrer, Robson B. "The Demographic and Economic History of the Audiencia of Quito: Indian Population and the Textile Industry, 1600–1800." Ph.D. dissertation, University of California, Berkeley, 1976.

La Unión Colombiana (Guayaquil), 1860.

United Nations Conference on the Application of Science and Technology for the Benefit of the Less Developed Areas, *Science, Technology and Development*. 12 vols. Washington D.C.: U.S. Government Printing Office, 1963.

United States Department of Commerce. *Trade Information Bulletin* no. 517. Washington: U.S. Government Printing Office, 1927.

United States Senate, Bureau of the American Republics. *Handbook of Ecuador*. 2d ed. Washington D.C.: U.S. Government Printing Office, 1894.

El Universo (Guayaquil), 1925–1927.

Van Aken, Mark, "The Lingering Death of Indian Tribute in Ecuador." *Hispanic American Historical Review* 61:3 (August 1981): 429–459.

Vazconez E., Eduardo. *Resumen estadístico comercial del Ecuador*. Quito: Talleres Tipográficos Nacionales, 1923.

Vientimilla, Marietta. *Páginas del Ecuador*. Lima: Imprenta Liberal de R. Masías, 1890.

Villavicencio, Manuel. *Geografía de la República del Ecuador*. New York: Imprenta de Robert Craighead, 1858.

Von Hagen, Victor. *The Four Seasons of Manuela*. New York: Duell, Sloan, and Pierce, 1952.

Watkins, R. J. *Expanding Ecuador's Exports: A Commodity by Commodity Study with Projections to 1973*. New York: Frederick A. Praeger, 1967.

Weinman, Lois. "Ecuador and Cacao: Domestic Response to the Boom-Collapse Monoexport Cycle." Ph.D. dissertation, University of California, Los Angeles, 1970.

Whitaker, Arthur P. *The United States and the Northern Republics*. Cambridge: Harvard University Press, 1948.

Wiles, Dawn Ann. "Land Transportation within Ecuador 1822–1954." Ph.D. dissertation, Louisiana State University, 1971.

Wolf, Theodore. *Geography and Geology of Ecuador*. Toronto: Grant and Toy Limited, 1933.

Zook, David H., Jr. *Zarumilla-Marañon: The Ecuador-Peru Dispute*. New York: Bookman Associates, Inc., 1964.

Index

Designer:	UC Press Staff
Compositor:	Prestige Typography
Printer:	Thomson-Shore, Inc.
Binder:	John H. Dekker and Sons
Text:	10/13 Stempel Garamond
Display:	Folkwang Expanded